Embodied Love

EMBODIED LOVE

SENSUALITY AND RELATIONSHIP AS FEMINIST VALUES

Edited by Paula M. Cooey,
Sharon A. Farmer,
& Mary Ellen Ross

1817

Harper & Row, Publishers, San Francisco

Cambridge, Hagerstown, New York, Philadelphia, Washington
London, Mexico City, São Paulo, Singapore, Sydney

Grateful acknowledgment is given for the use of the following: poem "What's in a Quilt?," author unknown, from *Women, Work and Worship in the United Church of Canada,* by S. Davy (editor). Copyright © 1983 by the United Church of Canada. Reprinted by permission of the United Church of Canada; "Reverence for Life: The Need for a Sense of Finitude" from *Laughter of Aphrodite* by Carol Christ. Copyright © 1987 by Carol P. Christ. Reprinted by permission of Harper & Row, Publishers, Inc.

FIRST EDITION

Library of Congress Cataloging-in-Publication Data

Embodied love.

   1. Feminism—Religious aspects. 2. Women—Religious life. I. Cooey, Paula M., 1945–   II. Farmer, Sharon A. III. Ross, Mary Ellen, 1950–
HQ1393.E43   1988   305.4'2   87-27093
ISBN 0-06-254837-9

87 88 89 90 91 HC 10 9 8 7 6 5 4 3 2 1

With gratitude to
Lois Boyd

Contents

Acknowledgments

We the coeditors appreciate the efforts of all who made this anthology possible. We thank the contributors for their cooperation and patience and Trinity University for providing funding for research, travel, and copyediting. Judi Lipsett edited the final copy, and Justus George Lawler, our editor with Harper & Row, and Lois Boyd, our teacher and friend, believed in this project even when we weren't so sure it was really going to happen. Bill Walker, chair of the Trinity University Department of Religion, allocated additional necessary funding, and, more importantly, provided sustained emotional and intellectual support. And most of all we thank each other for surviving storms we never dreamed we'd encounter.

Introduction

SHARON A. FARMER

The title of this work reflects a startling thematic unity among its essays. Startling for two reasons. First, the editors did not attempt to elicit from the contributors a single feminist approach to religion. And second, the women whose visions, voices, and experiences fit together here into a single patchwork design (to borrow Elisabeth Schüssler Fiorenza's metaphor) represent considerable chronological, religious, social, and geographical range. Among the authors are Catholic, Jew, nature mystic, agnostic, and biblical Protestant; among the women we study, ancient Hebrews, early Christians, modern Africans, Europeans, and Americans. Yet despite these diverse backgrounds and orientations, our essays return again and again to two intimately connected themes: the embodied side of human nature and the relational side of community, divinity, and ethics.

Embodiment and relationality. Both have been devalued in the dominant, patriarchal strains of Western religion. Both have been used to characterize women and hence to exclude or subordinate us. Both are affirmed and valued by the women whose voices resound in this volume.

Embodiment, Identity, and Value

The assumption that women are more embodied, more tied to our bodies, than are men, begins with the fact that we are physically different from men: that we menstruate, lactate, and bear children. These physical differences have served as primary reasons, in the Jewish and Christian traditions, for women's exclusion from the priesthood and from ritual functions.[1] Theologians and philosophers, moreover, have cited these differences to support a gender dichotomy that associates women with the more physical side of human nature and men with the more spiritual or rational. Underlying this gender dichotomy is a dualism in Western thought that places mind and body, or the spiritual and material realm, in opposition to each other and values mind and the spiritual realm over body and the material realm.[2]

What are the consequences of women's association with the material realm and of the devaluing of that realm? In general, the essays in this anthology tend to address the ways in which the devaluing of embodiment and the material realm impoverishes, for both men and women, our ethical values, our ability to relate, and our ability to communicate. Clearly, however, the association of women with the devalued material realm also contributes to our oppression, and it is appropriate to begin with a discussion of this issue.

Although the assumption that women have a close affiliation with the material realm begins with the fact of physical difference, the conditions of our existence are not the inevitable result of biology. Rather, social and cultural forces contribute to women's association with embodiment, and they mediate the ways in which that association is experienced and interpreted. To be sure, women are more closely involved than are men with the bearing and rearing of children, largely because we are the ones who physically give birth and lactate. But the degree to which these childbearing and nurturing activities constrain women depends, in part, on the degree to which the private and public—the reproductive and productive—spheres are separated. Feminist scholars, including Elisabeth Schüssler Fiorenza and Rosemary Radford Ruether in this volume, have suggested that the relationship between the two spheres is the result of social and political forces and that modern capitalism has exacerbated the separation.[3]

The social separation of the private and public spheres produces a set of physical circumstances that limits women's activities. The symbolic ordering of those two spheres further augments women's oppression. Patriarchal societies value the public realm, the realm of production for exchange and political interaction, more than they do the private realm of reproduction, nurturing, and sustenance.[4] One can even argue that this hierarchical valuing of public over private contributes as much to the spiritual/physical gender dichotomy as do the biological realities of men's and women's bodies: perceptions of the activities of the private, domestic realm (for instance, cooking, nurturing) as "concrete" and "natural" rather than "abstract" and "cultural" can lead to the conclusion that women are more physical, or at least more physically oriented, than are men.[5]

Our sex is biologically determined, but our "gender" is a cultural construction. Whatever its relationship to the physical and tangible circumstances of bodies and of the domestic realm, this cultural construction—the way in which we perceive and define masculinity and femininity—constitutes part of the symbolic order. Our bodies and physical activities provide the foundation for the circumstances of our existence, but those material foundations are mediated by cultural sources of meaning and value. Menstruation may be a biologically determined condition of women's existence, but there is not an inevitable relationship between female biology and the cultural assumption that women are less rational or spiritual than are men. Women's sexual impulses may be different from men's, but sexuality and sexual desire are mediated by language, value systems, and our general cultural heritage. Women lactate and give birth, and for that reason they predominate, almost universally, in the domestic sphere, but cultural values, not the innate qualities of physical activities, lead to perceptions of domestic activities as natural or physical. Those perceptions, moreover, are distorted: cooking, after all, is an art, which distinguishes us from animals, as does language, which we learn first in the home, generally from the women who nurture us.[6]

Because they are culturally constructed, gender dichotomies and material/spiritual hierarchies have the potential for change. Nevertheless, they are powerful cultural forces, and the combination of the two has resulted in pervasive religious themes that are detrimental to women. Western theologians, for instance, have associated women, the body, and sin with the devalued material realm, and for this reason some have argued that women represent not only the body but also sin, or the temptation to sin.[7] Women's identities, moreover, are "gendered"—we cannot help but interiorize to some extent the messages that our cultures and our religions send us about our bodies and our femaleness.

The first section of this volume focuses explicitly on strategies that women can take in confronting the symbolic, social, and cultural sources of our oppression, particularly insofar as they affect our individual and collective identities. The authors whose essays comprise this section suggest that our identities are relational and embodied—that we, as individual women, need to be connected to our sisters, our foresisters, and our physicality in order to come to know ourselves and our potentials.

In a discussion that appropriately introduces the central themes of this anthology, Paula Cooey poses the question, "How do body, language, and value interact to form an individual woman's sense of self?" She suggests that existing theories that have attempted to answer this question are problematic for two reasons: they emphasize either biology or culture (language and symbols) too exclusively, and they tend to be deterministic, not allowing for the possibility of change. As an alternative she proposes a new theoretical emphasis on touch, which brings together both body and symbolic communication. She then analyzes a number of novels by women in which touch has worked either coercively, as a source of identity imposed by men on women, or persuasively, as a means of communication between women that helps them to form affirming relationships and to transform their own identities.

Schüssler Fiorenza considers historical memory an essential source of identity, and she analyzes the partiarchal silence that has prevented women from knowing their past. Drawing on the New Testament example of Phoebe of Cenchreae, she analyzes the linguistic and cultural prejudices that contribute to this silence. Schüssler Fiorenza proposes that we must account for these sources of silence and attempt to recover the muffled voices of women of the past. Breaking silence is an essential task for us if we are to forge new identities.

Ruether and Carol Christ build on the assumption that embodiment and embodied activity are important components of women's identities. Christ portrays a special relationship between women and nature, which gives us a reverence for life. And Ruether argues that the conditions of women's work both define and limit their status and identity. Reverence for life and the status of women have been constrained, both authors suggest, because the dualism that values the mind over the body and the spiritual realm over the physical realm has dominated Western thought since the time of Plato. Both authors then argue that this dualism cripples our ethical responses to some of the most painful problems of our modern world. Christ suggests that it has contributed to the numb acceptance, on the part of our dominant contemporary culture, of the possibility that we may annihilate the earth with nuclear weapons. Ruether argues that it inclines conventional Christians to ignore the redemption of the world through social and political change. To this general position of liberation theology Ruether then adds a feminist's observation that women are confronted not only with the dualism separating the material and spiritual realms but also with that separating the private and the public. This second dualism, as I have already explained, is closely related to the first.

Like several other authors in this volume Ruether compels us to consider the inextricable links connecting embodiment and relationality. As a liberation theologian she suggests that embodied Christians—those who do not ignore the material realm—are relational Christians, who perceive sin and redemption in social as well as personal terms. As a feminist Christian she envisions a world in which the private, concrete, and relational realm of nurturing and mutually sustaining activity is organically linked to the public realm.

The essays of Cooey, Schüssler Fiorenza, Christ, and Ruether serve to introduce the various strategies that the contributors to this anthology have taken in confronting the sources of women's oppression. Schüssler Fiorenza and Cooey explicitly examine ways in which women can overcome cultural sources of oppression. Similarly, Ruether and Christ attempt to unveil some of the cultural constructions that enter into gender definitions, and Cooey discusses some of the strengths and weaknesses of gender analyses. Finally, Ruether, Christ, and Cooey present an alternative to the cultural system that devalues both embodiment and women. They move women and embodiment from positions of subordination or marginality to more central locations, where they can play a role in defining the human norm, or at least part of it.[8] Insofar as our essays affirm both embodiment and women's relational visions, this entire anthology represents the more inclusive version of this strategy: women's perspectives, we maintain, must be incorporated into our definitions of humanity. Some of our essays, however (that of Christ, for instance, and perhaps those of Linell Cady and Mary Ellen Ross), move in the direction of a more radical stance, which presents women's perspective as the desirable norm.

Embodiment, Communication, and Ethics

While the essays in the first section of this volume share a common thread in their implication that an experiential affirmation of physicality and relationships can enhance women's sense of identity and assist them in overcoming oppression, those of the second section focus on links between self and other and on the need for theoretical and theological stances that would strengthen such links.

Sheila Davaney, Sharon Farmer, and Claudia Camp begin with discussions of communication, the most essential means of connecting conscious beings. All three authors suggest that embodiment is a necessary component of communication, and that the disembodiment and decontextualization of words and ideas can both obscure communication and lead to dangerous dogma.

Davaney argues that a number of contemporary feminist theologians run the risk of turning contextualized, lived perspectives into decontextualized, disembodied dogma. Despite theological differences, she maintains, feminists such as Ruether, Schüssler Fiorenza, and Mary Daly employ similar methods, with similar internal contradictions. In their critique of patriarchal religion, they begin with a perspectival point of view, implicitly accepting the assertions of Nietzsche and Foucault who maintained that there is no absolute truth. Rather, there are only the perspectives of individuals and groups who seek to impose their versions of reality on others. When, however, these feminists develop their own visions of reality, they abandon their perspectival assumptions, suggesting instead that their visions are grounded in ontological reality. They implicitly assume that their own normative representations transcend the limitations of distorted perspectives but that the normative representations of others do not. Davaney suggests as a solution to this contradiction that feminist theologians should seek to validate their visions not with claims to ultimate reality, but with the pragmatic stance that such visions open the way to preferable (more just, relational, egalitarian) forms of existence.

Feminist theologians who continue to ground their social and ethical visions in a belief system may not find Davaney's pragmatic relativism completely satisfying. Nevertheless, she offers a serious critique of some of the assumptions and apparent contradictions that lie behind their theoretical and theological stances. Her argument is particularly relevant to this anthology, moreover, because she is suggesting to feminist theologians that they recognize the "embodied" nature of their representations of reality—that they acknowledge the specific contexts and communities from which their visions are born.

The essays of Farmer and Camp implicitly support Davaney's assertion that communication and theory need to arise from embodied contexts, and they suggest that in the past women especially have been associated with embodied communication.

Farmer builds on theories of orality and literacy, which have suggested that the spoken word is a more embodied form of communication than is the written word because both hearer and speaker must be in close physical contact in order for communication to take place. This "embodied" nature of the spoken word, she suggests, helps explain why women were associated with the power of oral persuasion in ancient and medieval literature. Early medieval writers gave a negative interpretation to women's association with oral persuasion, but thirteenth-century theologians interpreted that association positively because they were in the process of revaluing both oral persuasion and the physical realm. Farmer's discussion of these thirteenth-century theologians leads her to the conclusion that embodiment is not an issue for feminists alone, since communication, and hence our ability to understand one another, must be grounded in concrete and sensual experience. The thirteenth-century reevaluation of the physical realm also suggests that feminists need to provide a more nuanced analysis of the role that physical/ spiritual dualism has played in Western thought.

Drawing on examples from Hebrew scripture, Camp also demonstrates that women of the past have been associated with embodied and oral communication. She argues that written text needs the human voice to interpret it, authorize it, and give it meaning in the present, and she points out that wherever Hebrew scripture describes such an authorization of a text it is a woman who provides the actualizing and authorizing voice.

In her discussion of Proverbs, Camp analyzes the transformation that takes place in the transition from oral to written communication: pithy sayings, originally spoken in specific lived contexts, lose their vitality and attain the appearance of general moral principles. For this reason, they have the danger of becoming decontextualized, disembodied dogma. Wisdom, personified in the book of Proverbs as a woman, represents the practical knowledge that prevents us from decontextualizing and disembodying the written message. She gives us the capacity to reincorporate the written text into the appropriate living context.

The essays of Cady and Ross move us from a discussion of the basic communicative links between self and other to a broader consideration of philosophical and theological approaches to affectivity. Post-Kantian rationalist philosophers have often placed affection and relationship in positions of hierarchal subordination. Not only have they venerated and taken as a given the autonomous individual, but they have also asserted that the virtues governing the public realm—law and reason—are superior to the feelings of love and caring governing the private realm.[9] The assumptions of these rationalist philosophers arise in part from their tendency to categorize emotions—the feelings that bind us to other human beings—as "natural" phenomena, and to place them in opposition to reason, culture, and ethics. This dualistic approach has serious flaws. Historians have argued that both romantic and maternal love, for instance, are cultural, rather than natural, products and that they vary from society to society.[10] Some philosophers, moreover, have suggested that even the most "irrational" of emotions, such as falling in love, involves a complex series of rational choices.[11] And feminist ethicists, including Christ in this volume, have argued that a failure to give priority to feeling, to that which connects us to others, can have dire ethical consequences.[12]

One might argue that modern rationalist philosophers who devalue relationality and feelings represent a break with Western religious traditions, which, after all, have placed considerable importance on community, mutuality, and love. Cady's essay suggests, however, that even in Christianity, which has given the highest ethical priority to love, we find a tendency to devalue relationality. According to the dominant interpretation, Cady argues, Christian agapeic love entails self-sacrifice as an end in itself, and it thus centers on the solitary individual. She proposes as an alternative to this vision an interpretation of love as a means of building relationships between the self and the other.

Like Cady, Ross confronts the idea of the solitary, autonomous individual, whom she calls, following Philip Rieff, "psychological man." Psychological man, the predominant character type of modern Western society, has detached himself from traditional sources of authority and hence from coherent worldviews. He lives in a "negative community"; his highest goods are the pursuit of personal pleasure and the avoidance of personal pain; he is incapable of an appropriate response to pressing ethical issues such as world hunger. Ross perceives in the harmonious, preoedipal character formation of girls both an alternative to the character type of psychological man, and the potential for new, more responsible and connected ethical visions.

Explaining Difference

An emphasis on the differences between women's values and means of relating and those of men arises not only in Ross's essay, but also in those of Christ, Cooey, Patricia Hill, Ellen Umansky, and Gregor Goethals. On the surface, it might appear that the authors of these essays are traveling down a dangerous path that could lead back to traditional patriarchal characterizations of women.[13] They offer, however, several causal explanations for the distinctive aspects of women's values and identities, and some of these explanations can serve to undermine patriarchal assumptions about sexual difference.

Ross, for instance, roots her interpretation in psychological formation. Building upon the work of Nancy Chodorow, she assumes that women's characters differ from men's because mothers, at least those in postindustrial Western society, treat preoedipal infant girls differently from preoedipal infant boys: with girls they prolong harmony and minimize differentiation; with boys they emphasize difference and separation. The distinctive way in which girls are nurtured serves to explain why women develop, on the positive side, strong relational characteristics and, on the negative side, weak self-esteem. Chodorow indicates, and Ross implies, that this kind of character formation is a cultural, not a biological, product: both male and female personalities would and could change if social and political arrangements allowed mothers and fathers to share the roles of primary nurturers.[14]

While Ross offers a psychological explanation for women's affective orientations, Umansky and Hill point to historically specific circumstances. Umansky suggests that women's role in traditional European Jewish communities inclined them to think of religion in personal rather than communal terms. She also observes that a linguistic split between women's Yiddish devotional texts and men's Hebrew training enhanced and helped perpetuate the differences between men's and women's religious values and expressions. Both Umansky and Hill, moreover, take into account the fact that nineteenth- and early twentieth-century women—Jewish and Protestant—developed affective religious visions within the context of broader cultural developments, such as romanticism, pietism, and the veneration of motherhood.

Hill, Umansky, and Ross affirm the value of women's distinctive perspective, but their analyses indicate that this perspective is "gendered"—it is culturally formed, and, hence, there is potential for both men and women to change. Feminist essentialists, by contrast, both affirm women's difference and root it in biology. As Cooey explains in her essay, such essentialism characterizes the position of French feminists. It also characterizes, in this volume, the essay of Christ, who implies that women's ethical visions grow out of our special relationship to our bodies and to nature.

Embodiment, Relationship, and Religious Experience

The essays of Umansky and Hill, along with those of Goethals and Terri Castaneda, analyze specific historical examples of women whose values, visions, and actions have been, either explicitly or implicitly, distinctively relational and embodied. Insofar as they focus on the historical contexts that gave rise to women's roles and women's visions, these analyses, as I have already indicated, provide compelling support for the argument that gender and gendered identities are culturally constructed. The focus on historical specificity also represents the kind of "embodied" knowledge that Davaney advocates.

Castaneda's essay demonstrates that twentieth-century feminists and liberation theologians were not the first to discover in Christianity possibilities for social and economic change. Castaneda portrays native African women who actively ameliorated their own circumstances by weaving their way between the patriarchal institutions and ideologies of Christian missionaries and the patriarchal institutions of their own culture. Women employed Christianity to mold alternatives to the oppressive material and social conditions of their existence, and they turned the message of Christianity (in the historically specific forms in which the missionaries had presented it to them) back on the colonialists, in cogent criticisms of apartheid.

Castaneda's discussion of African women reminds us that religions have never been collections of disembodied spiritual messages. They consist as well of tangible institutions and codes of behavior that affect actual lives. When people—men and women—interact with religious institutions, ethical codes, and spiritual messages, they transform both the religious traditions and the material circumstances of their own existence.

Hill, Umansky, and Goethals depict specific women of the past whose religious and ethical visions resemble those of Cady and Ross. Hill argues that Harriet Beecher Stowe developed a new vision of Christianity that emphasized love, sorrow, suffering, and self-sacrifice. Stowe gave women a central place in this model of Christianity because she believed that women have a special capacity for both love and sorrow.

Umansky analyzes the many sermons of Lily Montagu and Tehilla Lichtenstein, Jewish leaders of the late nineteenth and early twentieth centuries, and she highlights their distinctive relational visions by contrasting the writings of each woman with those of a male rabbi with whom she closely associated. Umansky finds that unlike the men, Montagu and Lichtenstein emphasized a personal and emotional rather than an intellectual Judaism, and they tended, in their religious language, to draw on daily experience.

Goethals also analyzes the relational visions of two creative women. She argues that while Dorothea Lange and Kaethe Kollwitz—artists of the early twentieth century—shared with male artists of their time a concern for social justice, the pictorial representations of the two women (the one American, the other German) reveal a distinctive intimacy, an emphasis on human—especially parent-child—relationships, and a blurring of boundaries, the effect of which is to minimize the separateness of individual figures and to mold them instead into organic groupings. Goethals implies that the distinctive style of Kollwitz and Lange is a matter not only of form but also of content: the aesthetic vision of these two artists is also their prophetic message. Their powerful images confront us with the primacy and unity of love and justice, and they evoke the "inescapable bonding" of human beings.

The essence of Kollwitz's and Lange's images—their emphatic linking of form to content and self to other—epitomizes the central themes of this anthology. In revaluing embodiment, our essays, like the images of Kollwitz and Lange, point to the inextricable connections between body and mind, form and content, the material and spiritual realms. In revaluing relationality, we emphasize, as do Kollwitz and Lange, the inescapable bonds uniting self and other.

Like the images of these two artists, moreover, our essays are both descriptive and prescriptive. We describe qualities that are intrinsic to human existence; but we also prescribe new attitudes towards those qualities. The valorization and recognition of embodiment relationality, we maintain, has the revolutionary potential of transforming not only our religious and ethical visions, but also our individual and collective identities.

NOTES

1. Leviticus 12, 15; Ida Raming, *The Exclusion of Women from the Priesthood: Divine Law or Sex Discrimination?* trans. Norman R. Adams (Metuchen, NJ: Scarecrow, 1976), 48, 49, 53, 142; Shulamith Shahar, *The Fourth Estate: A History of Women in the Middle Ages,* trans. Chaya Galai (London: Methuen, 1983), 73.
2. On the physical/rational gender dichotomy see Sharon Farmer's essay in this volume, n. 12; and Carol Christ, "Why Women Need the Goddess: Phenomenological, Psychological, and Political Reflections," in *Womanspirit Rising: A Feminist Reader in Religion,* ed. Carol P. Christ and Judith Plaskow (San Francisco: Harper & Row, 1979), 279. On the relationship between the gender dichotomy and mind/body dualism see Rosemary Radford Ruether, "Motherearth and the Megamachine: A Theology of Liberation in a Feminist, Somatic, and Ecological Perspective," in *Womanspirit Rising,* ed. Christ and Plaskow, 43–52.
3. Karen Sacks, "Engels Revisited: Women, the Organization of Production, and Private Property," in *Woman, Culture, and Society,* ed. Michelle Zimbalist Rosaldo and Louise Lamphere (Stanford: Stanford University Press, 1974), 207–22; Joan Kelly, "The Social Relations of the Sexes: Methodological Implications of Women's History," *Signs: Journal of Women in Culture and Society* 1 (1976): 809–23; Jean Quataert, "The Shaping of Women's Work in Manufacturing: Guilds, Households, and the State in Central Europe, 1648–1870," *American Historical Review* 90 (1985): 1122–48.
4. Michelle Zimbalist Rosaldo, "Woman, Culture, and Society: A Theoretical Overview," in *Woman, Culture, and Society,* ed. Rosaldo and Lamphere, 17–42.
5. Sherry B. Ortner, "Is Female to Male as Nature Is to Culture?" in *Women, Culture, and Society,* ed. Rosaldo and Lamphere, 77–78.

6. Ortner, "Is Female to Male," 79–80. Carol McMillan also provides an insightful critique of the tendency to view domestic activities as natural, but she misunderstands and misrepresents feminist thought, and she draws fallacious conclusions in the second half of her book: *Women, Reason, and Nature: Some Philosophical Problems with Feminism* (Princeton: Princeton University Press, 1982), 1–15, 30–56. On language and imagination as mediators of sexual experience, see Jane Gallop, "Snatches of Conversation," in *Women and Language in Literature and Society*, ed. Sally McConnell-Ginet, Ruth Borker, Nelly Furman (New York: Praeger, 1980), 274–83.

7. Ruether, "Motherearth."

8. For a broader discussion of the emergence of a "women-centered" analysis, see Hester Eisenstein, *Contemporary Feminist Thought* (Boston: G. K. Hall, 1983), 45–101.

9. Naomi Scheman, Jane Flax, and Nancy Hartsock offer feminist critiques of philosophical individualism in *Discovering Reality: Feminist Perspectives on Epistemology, Metaphysics, Methodology, and Philosophy of Science*, ed. Sandra Harding and Merrill Hintikka (Dordrecht, Holland: Kluwer Academic, 1983). On the hierarchical view of the state and family, which are considered, respectively, the realm of reason and the realm of feeling, see McMillan, *Women, Reason, and Nature*, 16–29.

10. Stephen Wilson provides a thorough, albeit critical, review of the most recent historical literature on maternal love: "The Myth of Motherhood a Myth: The Historical View of European Child-rearing," *Social History* 9 (1984): 181–98. On romantic love, see C. S. Lewis, *The Allegory of Love* (London: Oxford University Press, 1951).

11. R. C. Solomon, *The Passions: The Myth and Nature of Human Emotion* (Garden City: Doubleday, 1976).

12. For a similar argument, see B. Harrison, "Human Sexuality and Mutuality," in *Christian Feminism: Visions of a New Humanity*, ed. Judith L. Weidman (San Francisco: Harper & Row, 1984), 141–57.

13. L. Kerber argues along these lines in her critical analysis of C. Gilligan's work: "Some Cautionary Words for Historians," in "On *In a Different Voice:* An Interdisciplinary Forum," *Signs: Journal of Women in Culture and Society* 11 (1986): 309.

14. N. Chodorow, *The Reproduction of Mothering: Psychoanalysis and the Sociology of Gender* (Berkeley: University of California Press, 1978).

Part One

EMBODIMENT, IDENTITY, AND VALUE

CHAPTER 1

The Word Become Flesh: Woman's Body, Language, and Value

PAULA M. COOEY

What does it mean to be a woman? What role does sexual identification as female play in shaping woman's identity? Both queries presuppose a prior question: how do body, language, and value interact to form an individual woman's identity as "woman"? I propose that an analysis of touch as symbol for communicating power provides a starting point for exploring women's identity in a way that avoids the inadequacies of our more usual accounts of sexual identity.

The Dilemna Posed By Essentialism and Cultural Determinism

Understanding "woman" is existentially crucial for women. Unlike men who are oppressed for being poor, of color, losers in a war, or on the "wrong" side of an ideology, women are oppressed simply for being women. *Patriarchy* does not mean the rule over all women by all men. Rather it signifies that males of the ruling classes of patriarchal culture define the identity of "woman" according to the race, class, and creed of the men with whom such women are affiliated and to whom they are subordinated. The significance of the ostensible sexual differences between men and women thus becomes central for a woman's self-understanding.

Feminist and nonfeminist theorists account for sexual difference and its role in forming identity in a variety of ways that, nevertheless, share a concern with how body, language, and value interact. To discern the character of this interaction assumes added urgency because of a long-standing tradition in Western culture of identifying "woman" with "body" and "nature," an identification that distinguishes "feminine" in contrast to "masculine" attributes. This contrast emerges from the perception, interpreted accurately or not, of biological differences. The premise is that woman's identity *necessarily* stands more directly related to her embodiment as female, compared to man's identity, which arises apart from direct consideration of male biology. Hence, the feminine/masculine polarity: femininity involves passivity, receptiveness, irrationality, and carnality in contrast to masculine activity, aggressiveness, rationality, and spirituality.[1]

This identification, in a patriarchal context, whether the identification occurs in the form of explicit misogyny or as a romanticizing and mystifying of woman, nature, and body, has historically devalued women and buttressed arguments for female subordination to males. Removed in theory from its patriarchal context in current debates among feminists, the question remains: What is the significance of this identification *for women?* Is there an essentially feminine character, essential and feminine because it is in some sense related to female biology? Or conversely: Is the feminine/masculine polarity strictly a cultural construct, in no way grounded in biological differences, one that serves male interests in sustaining domination over women?

At one extreme, feminists, most notably the French, have taken what has come to be known as an "essentialist" position. At the other extreme, feminists, usually American, have attributed the significance of sexual difference to cultural determinism, particularly as that is manifested by language.[2] Neither position is tenable. Essentialism fails to account for the extent to which body and nature are culturally constructed. Cultural determinism fails to take seriously material existence at its most fundamental level, the human body itself. Most problematic of all, because both positions are deterministic, neither provides sufficient account for individual and social transformation.

Kaja Silverman, in *"Histoire d'O:* The Construction of a Female Subject," illustrates the problem involved. She argues cogently that the meaning and value of embodiment itself, especially the significance of sexual difference, is formed by culture rather than derived from actual biological differences between males and females.[3] She analyzes *The Story of O* as pornographic allegory for patriarchal definition of female identity, as this is anchored in female embodiment. She emphasizes that the significance of female embodiment is defined by men to the extent that O's identity is totally passive; even her words are not her own. While Silverman argues that the construction of identity leans heavily upon the reality of embodiment, she nevertheless refutes French feminist claims that, because of a female's relation to her body, her sexuality and her identity as feminine escape symbolic structuring, associated with maleness. French theorists argue that because of differences between male and female relations to embodiment—differences that prefigure gender-defined characteristics—there exists a feminine essence that precedes and transcends cultural definition. This precedence yields potential for a female identity as sexuality freed from and untamed by culture. Arguing that no such essence, and therefore no such identity, exists, Silverman concludes:

Histoire d'O is more than O's story. It is the history of the female subject—of the territorialization and inscription of a body whose involuntary internalization of a corresponding set of desires facilitates its complex exploitation. That history will never read otherwise until the female subject alters her relation to discourse—until she succeeds not only in exercising discursive power, but in exercising it differently (HO, 346).

For Silverman, actual biological differences notwithstanding, human beings as language users make meaning and create value through interpretation. It follows that meaning and value reflect human interest and need. He or she who has the power of the word has the power to coparticipate in a reciprocity of shaping and being shaped by language, or discourse, as this generates value. This complex interaction yields identity.

Silverman's argument is hardly novel; Mary Daly raised the issue of power and language in *Beyond God the Father: Toward a Philosophy of Women's Liberation.* [4] Even earlier, Virginia Woolf discussed the significance of women's writing in terms of a feminine/masculine polarity in *A Room of One's Own.* [5] If we take Silverman's final challenge seriously, then the question becomes: How? How do we as women alter our relation to discourse? Are we so autonomous in spite of culture that we simply wake up one morning and decide to alter our relation to language? Hardly. If not, then where do we begin?

Touch as Symbol For Communicating Power

We begin by examining the role played by touch as symbolic of a power to confer identity. Silverman's analysis of the development of O's identity by implication extends language to include touch along with voice and written word. Touch as communication thus becomes a symbol for tracing the strengthening or weakening of identity. Touch, understood as a form of communication in addition to being one of the five senses, avoids certain problems to which both positions of extreme essentialism and extreme denial of any significance to embodiment are subject. Most importantly, touch provides the possibility for freedom and change, both personal and social.

Why touch? Though the contexts for permission and restriction of touch are culturally defined, the exercise of one's sense of touch is the exercise of one's nature to communicate. Touch also communicates in a way that exceeds or transcends reduction to verbalization. Touch, then, never occurs uninterpreted (and therefore unmediated by language), but it escapes total translation into words. Right when words fail, touch becomes a major expression of extreme feelings ranging from aggression to intimacy. A discussion of the significance of touch in women's lives hence serves as an excellent starting point, for touch presupposes the inseparability of word and flesh as touch communicates value by signaling danger or pleasure. Because touch exceeds the limitations of language, it can exceed culturally defined norms of permission and restriction. Touch, therefore, potentially facilitates and symbolizes cultural and social change in values whether positive or negative; as such it represents tremendous power to create and to destroy. In the extreme, touch can symbolize either domination and brutality or an abiding intimacy that presupposes equality.

Touch is ambiguous and complex. As a symbol for power it signals a range of intentions from coercion to persuasion, any one of which may further elicit a complex range of responses involving pain and pleasure. Touch as coercion may take the form of brutality or seduction. Whether brutality or seduction, the point is to exert control over others. By contrast, touch that signals an attempt to persuade presupposes recognition of respect for another, symbolized by a release of power.[6] Such power reflects shared energy, usually responsibility, rather than control. Ironically, coercive touch exercised as seduction may elicit pleasure as a response in the seduced, whereas persuasive touch may elicit resistance due to a recipient's anticipation of pain.

Intentions are often not self-evident, nor are responses necessarily unmixed. Coercion manifested as brute force or seduction, and persuasion arising out of respect provide nevertheless limiting cases that illustrate various roles played by touch in the interaction of body, language, and value that yields personal and social identity.

Coercive Touch

The necessity for women to exert power of language differently from its patriarchal expression derives from the negative ways in which men and women have touched to exert control over others. Coercive touch reveals the socioeconomic character of brutality exercised by individual human beings upon one another. Whether manifested overtly as sexual violence or in some other form, brutality transcends class and race and ties directly to political violence. Coercive touch also occurs masked as the pleasure of romantic love. The commemoration of coercive touch as narrative, because it unites word and flesh through the act of remembering, marks a first step toward employing the power of discourse or language differently. Such acts of commemoration constitute a revolution in value.

For example, in Agnes Smedley's fictionalized autobiography, *Daughter of Earth,* touch connects economics and politics with sexuality as forms of unrelenting brutality.[7] The main character, Marie, representing Smedley, grows up in Colorado mining towns at the turn of the century in extreme poverty. Her father beats her mother; her mother in turn beats Marie. Marie's Aunt Helen is forced by economic need into prostitution and subsequently suffers the ongoing effects of poor physical health due to venereal disease. (She, of all the women who people Marie's early life, appeals most to Marie for having retained her economic independence.) Marie herself aborts two unwanted pregnancies. She is later raped by a political radical with whom she works closely for the liberation of India from the British—a rape made all the more appalling because of her willingness to internalize responsibility for her own victimization.

What all of these events (with one exception) share is an attempt to control another through touch. Marie's assuming responsibility for her rape presupposes a sexist psychology that defines rape as a man's uncontrollable response to a woman's seduction. This psychology, when accepted by the victim, involves an ironic attempt, often unconscious, to seize back power as control. If a person is only getting what she deserves, then she at least retains some kind of power, albeit negative and self-destructive. In its attempt to deny the ultimacy of the power of touch to abuse in a definitive way this denial is still defined, however negatively, by touch itself.

Willingness to take questionable responsibility for her victimization characterizes Marie's negative view of her embodiment and sexuality throughout the book. Early in the narrative, Marie states, "My mind watched my body as if the two were separate units. My mind was I. . . . [M]y body was a foreign thing" (DE, 126). This conscious splitting of mind and body becomes her frequent and most positive defense against the physical brutality she suffers. The mind/body dualism generates a further dichotomy—love for a man versus freedom as a woman. Forced to decide between them she chooses freedom and ends her second marriage, leaving her conflicts regarding sexuality unresolved.

Lest we suffer the delusion that brutality restricts itself to the context of poverty, Joan Didion's *A Book of Common Prayer* testifies to the contrary.[8] A scathing critique of the involvement of wealthy California men and not-so-wealthy male intellectuals in leftist revolution, *A Book of Common Prayer* ostensibly focuses upon the character Charlotte as revealed through the eyes of Grace.[9] Charlotte, the well-to-do, all-American girl next door, becomes unknowingly a center of political intrigue in a fictional Central American country pointedly called Boca Grande ("Big Mouth"). Just as Boca Grande symbolizes the geographical territory for revolutionary penetration and combat, so Charlotte's body symbolizes territory for sexual conflict among the various men in her life.

Through Didion's skillful interplay of imagery, land and female body become identified as static, passive, enigmatic, ill-defined, and blank entities awaiting male formation in order to come to life in male-defined terms. Furthermore, the power to create, sustain, and destroy existence is contingent upon competition among men for whom such conflicts are serious and deadly games.

Whereas *Daughter of Earth* and *A Book of Common Prayer* connect female embodiment and powerlessness with overt male brutality, Rona Jaffe's "Rima the Bird Girl" portrays the more subtle psychological quality of the definition of female subjectivity by internalizing male need and desire.[10] Middle-class Rima, bright, talented, lively, and physically appealing, undergoes a succession of metamorphoses corresponding to a succession of unsatisfactory romantic liaisons with men, each of whom ultimately rejects her. Rima's energy focuses exclusively upon getting and keeping a man, but each man with whom Rima involves herself has an existing commitment to another woman. Once involved, she devotes herself to acquiring all the visible characteristics of the woman to whom her lover is already committed. Rima alters her looks, her wardrobe, her furnishings, her tastes—in short, her entire life—in an effort to accommodate each new lover. As Rima becomes more and more the visual embodiment of her "competitor," Rima's lover ironically becomes more and more confused and dissatisfied. As a consequence, once any given metamorphosis is complete, the relationship necessarily falls apart. Rima is left, abandoned, until the next man arrives.

The greatest irony lies in the source of Rima's physical attraction. What draws each new man to Rima is an identity she creates under false pretenses to accommodate his predecessor. The narrator concludes:

Had there ever been a real Rima? Born and reborn to a splendid image, she had never looked for herself, nor had anyone else. Being each man's dream of love, she had eventually failed him, and so he had failed her, and so finally she had failed herself (RB, 294).

Rima intends to seduce. She views herself as agent rather than victim. Yet she never gets what she wants, a lasting relationship with a man. She remains powerless to break out of the syndrome in which she is caught up because she attempts to control another by shaping herself to fit what she perceives to be his expectations. In striking contrast to Marie, who in *Daughter of Earth* is far too willing to assume unwarranted responsibility, Rima takes none whatsoever.

Objectified female embodiment, defined by men, characterizes the lives of Marie, Charlotte, and Rima alike. All three women incorporate this to some degree as part of their respective identities. Marie differs from Charlotte and Rima, whose identities become submerged by male construction of their sexuality. Through denying her sexuality and rejecting erotic love, Marie by contrast achieves agency, though at great cost to her sensuality. That she might insist upon both freedom and love, both agency and sexuality, is no alternative because she is not in a position to challenge these culturally imposed dualisms as they shape her identity.

The content of these three narratives not only explores the negative significance of female identity as this depends upon meaning and value attributed to female embodiment by men. It also offers the relationship between the central character and the "narrator" or author as an alternative. Both *A Book of Common Prayer* and "Rima the Bird Girl" include ostensible narrators as fictional characters. We know Charlotte's story because Grace tells us; we know Rima's plight because her unnamed roommate describes it. Both narrators bear witness, and the question is, why? One inference common to both stories is the act of bearing witness as the narrator's responsibility for valuing the life and the suffering of the ostensibly central character. Grace and the unnamed roommate remember Charlotte and Rima, respectively. Marie, who bears her own witness (and Agnes Smedley's), remembers her past for the purposes of healing her present and simultaneously bearing witness to the people of the earth. Memory verbalized symbolically puts the body back together in a manner that preserves the identity of both witnessed and witness.

Taking the responsibility for bearing witness through memory synthesizes verbal imagery as an act of revaluation. While words cannot erase what flesh and blood experience, they can commemorate people and events. As commemoration, the narrative at once reveals and conceals the character of the event witnessed, the character of the witness herself, and the witness of character. What the subject reveals and conceals regarding the identity of character and the character of identity depends largely upon who is literally and metaphorically touching whom.

Persuasive Touch

Focus upon relations between women, whether author and character, ostensible narrator and narrated character, or simply one woman character and another, registers not only a change in content and perspective in narrative, but more importantly a shift in the power to shape identity. As Virginia Woolf wrote, "It was strange to think that all the great women of fiction were, until Jane Austen's day, not only seen by the other sex, but seen only in relation to the other sex. And how small a part of a woman's life is that; and how little can a man know even of that when he observes it through the black or rosy spectacles which sex puts upon his nose" (RO, 86). For discourse to be exercised differently from patriarchally defined forms, the nature of power itself must change—from coercion to persuasion. The female body, touched in this instance by another woman, plays a major role in such a change.

Transformation of particular women, effected by women persuasively touching one another, alters how we imagine and conceive women's identity at a more abstract level. A change in the kind of power exercised, as well as how and by whom it is exercised, modifies the interaction of body, language, and value that generates identity. This requires creating new discourse by using language differently, discovering value through sensual pleasure, and recognizing one's own transformation through ritual. Touch, exercised persuasively, provides a symbol for recognizing such change.

Transformation of language entails wrestling with its inherent tension to alienate as well as liberate the speaker's or writer's sense of identity and worth. This means creating new discourse or language. Maxine Hong Kingston's autobiographical work, *The Woman Warrior: Memoirs of a Girlhood Among Ghosts,* provides an illustration.[11]

The Woman Warrior presents Kingston's struggle toward maturity in relation to her parents' conflict between their Chinese culture and that of their new home in the United States. This struggle, articulated in a series of memories, involves primarily the sexist, and often contradictory, Confucian myths and Chinese history that her mother passes on as an oral legacy or "talk-story." In the book two events relating touch to language mark Kingston's escape from male-determined identity: her appropriation of the myth of the woman warrior early in her girlhood and her "confession" to her parents as she approaches adulthood.

Kingston's mother tells her the story of Fa Mu Lan, the woman warrior with superhuman powers who saves her people. Fantasizing herself as a woman warrior, Kingston volunteers to take her father's place in the military draft. In preparation her parents ritualistically carve revenge upon her back so that "[w]herever you go, whatever happens to you, people will know our sacrifice, . . . [a]nd you'll never forget either" (WW, 41). Kingston points out that Kuan Kung, the god of war, is also the god of literature (WW, 46). She interprets the significance of her fantasy by stating, "The swords-woman and I are not so dissimilar. . . . What we have in common are the words at our back. The idioms for *revenge* are 'report a crime' and 'report to five families.' The reporting is the vengeance—not the beheading, not the gutting, but the words. And I have so many words—'chink' words and 'gook' words too—that they do not fit on my skin" (WW, 262–63).

Later we discover that Kingston's mother has clipped the frenum of her daughter's tongue early in her childhood—an act that remains enigmatic to Kingston and the reader until the end of the book. Is it to keep her quiet or to allow her to speak? Kingston associates sex, silence, and femininity with a long list of troubling acts, thoughts, and questions that she regards as her secret "sins." When she can no longer keep quiet, she frees herself as she defiantly tells her mother, "You can't stop me from talking. You tried to cut off my tongue but it didn't work." Her mother replies, "I cut it to make you talk more, not less, you dummy" (WW, 235).

Fantasized carving, identified with actual cutting, shapes King-ston's identity. She becomes a woman warrior, a singer of both Chinese and barbarian songs, as modified by her own imagination and experience. She writes the stories that began with her mother; however, "the endings are her own" (WW, 240). As an author she becomes a creative person, responsible to her people as ethnic Chinese, responsible to herself as a woman. Her mother passes this power to her by cutting her frenum so that she might speak more freely, and in their struggle with one another, Kingston appropriates this strength as uniquely her own.

To become a coauthor of discourse, that is, to pick up where the story left off and contribute one's own ending, is to coparticipate in the creation and sustenance of value as well as meaning. One's identity is simultaneously transformed from victim of the words of others to author of one's own moral character and agency as a woman. This strength, conferred symbolically through touch, has its source in several other female relationships as well as that of mother and daughter. Sisters, friends, lovers, and strangers often play midwife to this strength.

The Color Purple, an epistolary novel by Alice Walker, traces a movement from strangers to friends to lovers and again to friends in the relationship between two black women, Shug Avery and Celie.[12] This pairing redeems all of Celie's other broken or lost relationships, including her relationship with divine power and being. Touch plays a major role in this transformation. Shug and Celie's husband, Mister, were lovers, and clearly he still loves Shug. Celie and Shug first meet when Mister brings the sick Shug to their home. In spite of Shug's verbal abuse, Celie lovingly nurses Shug back to health. She bathes Shug; she feeds her; she sews her clothes; she fetches for her; she combs her hair. Celie gradually tames Shug's hostility:

Shug Avery sit up in bed a little today. I wash and comb out her hair. She got the nottiest, shortest, kinkiest hair I ever saw, and I loves every strand of it. . . .

I work on her like she a doll . . . or like she mama. I comb and pat, comb and pat. First she say, hurry up and git finish. Then she melt down a little and lean back gainst my knees. That feel just right, she say. That feel like Mama used to do. . . . Start to hum a little tune.

What that song? I ask. Sound low down dirty to me. . . .

She hum a little more. Something come to me, she say. Something I made up. Something you help scratch out of my head (CP, 57).

Through patience and endurance Celie works her magic upon Shug and wins her over from "bitch" to friend. To a rhythm of "comb and pat, comb and pat" Shug's health strengthens and her own creativity again soars. As Shug, unlike Celie, has distinctive character prior to their encounter, the magic Celie works upon Shug actually marks the beginning of Celie's own transformation, characterized by her refusal to remain passive in the face of Shug's abuse. Though Celie is not confrontive, she pursues friendship with Shug by insisting on loving her. As her first act of engaging in relationship with another, it is Celie's first conscious act of valuing and, not accidentally, her first experience of pleasure.

Pleasure as abiding joy characterizes Celie's new life. Celie awakens to sexual orgasm, to beauty in nature, to delight in another's joy. Like Jeremiah, she talks back to God, the addressee of her letters for most of the book. Indeed, God at the hands of Shug undergoes transformation for Celie from white male patriarch to source, expression, and comprehension of all that is. Not without its own pain, this love provides the context in which Celie's experience of pleasure, delight in herself and another, sanctifies her life by transforming her vision of reality from the color purple to the nature of deity.

Positive value, both received and bestowed in the experience of pleasure, is generated in relation to sensuality. Celie's transformation and her transformed vision of God reflect an integrity of flesh and soul in which body and value are inextricably and positively linked. Unlike Charlotte and Rima, Celie escapes immersion in embodiment as primary source of her identity. Unlike Marie, Celie finds freedom through sensuality, rather than through denial. As in the cases of both Marie and Kingston, Celie's liberation includes coauthorship for new language or discourse. Whereas the unity of body and value is inseparable, an integrity of flesh and soul is not a given, but the effect of a transformation of suffering that entails revaluation of the significance of embodiment itself.

Celie's and Shug's discussions of sex illustrate this revaluation. Stunned that Celie has never experienced physical pleasure in sexual intercourse, Shug explains female anatomy to Celie, and Celie discovers her own clitoris for the first time. When Shug asks Celie to tell her what sex was like with Celie's stepfather who fathered Celie's two children, Celie recounts the repeated acts of rape, the first of which occurred on the occasion of her cutting his hair. Celie sums up her litany of misery by saying:

My mama die. . . . My sister Nettie run away.

Mr. _____ come git me to take care his rotten children. He never ast me nothing bout myself. He clam on top of me and fuck and fuck, even when my head bandaged. Nobody ever love me, I say.

She say, I love you, Miss Celie. And then she haul off and kiss me on the mouth.

Um, she say, like she surprise. I kiss her back, say, um, too. Us kiss and kiss till us can't hardly kiss no more. Then us touch each other.

I don't know nothing bout it, I say to Shug.

I don't know much, she say.

Then I feels something real soft and wet on my breast, feel like one of my little lost babies mouth.

Way after while, I act like a little lost baby too (CP, 109).

The cutting of her stepfather's hair conjures up the image of Celie's "comb and pat, comb and pat" with Shug by way of violent contrast. Lovemaking between Shug and Celie, while it cannot erase the experiences of incest and rape, nevertheless inscribes Celie with new identity as one who, as a woman, is genuinely loved and loving and not simply a victim of male brutality. Celie and Shug literally nurse one another to new life. Because of Shug, Celie's life, characterized by brutal incest, the loss of her babies and her sister, and a miserable marriage, takes on dignity, meaning, sensuality, merriment, and the grace to survive and transcend pain.

Transformation from a negative to a positive relationship between body and value needs formal recognition as the birth of a new identity. Ritual allows this recognition to occur. As symbolic activity involving language, touch, and movement, it sustains, through affirmation, the new interaction of body, discourse, and value. Ritual integrates a person's bodily sense, intellect, and emotion, on the one hand, and binds the individual subject to a wider historical community, on the other hand. Because of its power to reinforce identity, ritual serves potentially as both an obstacle and a catalyst to change.

Praisesong for the Widow by Paule Marshall examines ritual's capacity for validating creative change in a dramatic manner.[13] Marshall's novel, in contrast to *The Color Purple,* involves women who have never met before and may never meet again. The book studies the transformation of Avey Johnson, sixty-two years old, a black woman who has, with her now deceased, once upwardly mobile husband, assimilated almost totally into white, middle-class culture. While on a Caribbean cruise, Avey jumps ship in Granada for reasons unclear to her at the time. Sidetracked from her intention to return home to New York by a series of apparently random events, she makes a pilgrimage to the mysterious island of Carriacou during the yearly celebration of holy days venerating ancestors and tribe. She emerges as Avatara Johnson, at once incarnation and divinization of black femaleness.[14]

Avey in no way seeks this transformation; on the contrary, she diligently resists it. Nevertheless, a different, more positive identity befalls her like grace ultimately irresistible, and her only recourse is to consent. The turning point occurs after a violent passage by boat from Granada to Carriacou. Wrenched by vomiting and loss of bowel control, Avey finds herself in the hands of Rosalie Parvey, a stranger who bathes Avey in preparation for the most important event of the celebration, the "Beg Pardon."[15]

The bathing, performed as if it were "an office performed every day for some stranger passing through" (PW, 220), not only cleanses Avey of the vestiges of her illness, but also provides an experience of long-forgotten pleasure. Her body, discreetly and impersonally washed, rinsed, oiled with limes, and kneaded until it tingles with a bittersweet pleasure, awakens to new life under the touch of previously unknown women.

This cleansing prefigures the awakening of Avatara's spirit in the midst of the dance of the nations during the "Beg Pardon" that evening. Her physical bath foreshadows the later metaphorical anointing during which Avey acknowledges her identity as Avatara and assumes her calling, long ago discarded, as seer and teller of her people's story, including her own. The bathing is, in short, a baptism.

The convergence of the ritual structure, the impersonality of the bathing, and the unexpectedness of the sensual pleasure forms an altogether unusual image for the alteration of identity. Sensual pleasure not dependent upon genital contact, intimacy not reliant upon preexisting familiarity, and transformation not sought but resisted call into question assumptions regarding human sexuality in general and female identity in particular. Avatara emerges responsible and committed, her individual identity bound to that of a wider community. Pleasure from a stranger is the gift that frees her to assume her identity as visionary and prophet—a seer and a teller of tales.

Touch and Woman's Identity

Tracing the role played by touch in women's narrative allows an alternative to tendencies toward reductionism and dualistic thinking characteristic of both essentialist and cultural determinist positions. Reducible neither to nature nor to culture, woman's identity as woman emerges from how, whom, and what women actually value. Touch as an act of valuing that exemplifies the unity in reciprocity of language and body, culture and nature, communicates the complexity and diversity of women's values, women's worth in different contexts, and therefore an individual woman's identity as "woman."

Chief among the values characteristic of woman's identity in the narratives examined is a propensity to love and be loved that is at once women's greatest strength and greatest source of conflict. Exhibited as strength in the transformations of Maxine Hong Kingston, Celie, and Avatara Johnson, this love generates individual integrity in a way that simultaneously creates and sustains community. Such love is at once sensual and moral, particular and universal.

This kind of integrity is difficult to sustain in a patriarchal society, however. Dualistic thinking, a major characteristic of such societies, more often forces women to make wrenching choices between self and other, between love for an individual person and love for a community, between sexuality and freedom. Socialized to emotional and economic dependence on particular men, women are made especially vulnerable by the very propensity to love that is otherwise a strength. In different ways Charlotte and Rima represent the self-destructiveness of this propensity to love that degenerates into sensuality without morality and other-directedness without integrity. Marie, forced into what is for her an agonizing choice between love for a man and love for the people of the earth, chooses the latter, knowing it means a great cost to her own integrity.

Charlotte, Rima, and Marie (to the extent that she continues to regard herself to be defective as a woman) remain victims of patriarchy and, in so doing, unwittingly participate in its perpetuation by internalizing and acting out its values.

The toughest choice women face today is the extent to which we willingly assume responsibility for the how, whom, and what we value, for our acts of valuing ultimately define our identities. Choosing requires becoming aware of the ambiguity of our propensity to love and be loved. To love universally in and through particular people and communities is not the same thing as loving indiscriminately. Whereas to love indiscriminately perpetuates women's subordination to men as definitive of woman's identity as "woman" in a negative sense, to love with integrity is to participate in a revolution in value that transforms identity in ways yet to be imagined.

NOTES

1. The extent to which this polarity dominates the entire history of Western culture is debatable; however, it plays a major role in twentieth-century thought. See S. Ortner, "Is Female to Male as Nature Is to Culture?" in *Woman, Culture, and Society,* ed. M. Z. Rosaldo and L. Lamphere (Stanford: Stanford University Press, 1974), 17–42. See also J. Plaskow, *Sex, Sin, and Grace* (Washington, DC: University Press of America, 1980), 1–51.
2. See H. Eisenstein and A. Jardine, eds., *The Future of Difference* (Boston: G. K. Hale, 1980); E. Marks and Ida Courtivrou, eds., *New French Feminisms* (Amherst: University of Massachusetts Press, 1980); C. Vance, ed., *Pleasure and Danger* (Boston: Routledge & Kegan Paul, 1984); and A. R. Jones, "Writing the Body: Toward an Understanding of *l'Ecriture Feminine,"* in *Feminist Criticism,* ed. E. Showalter (New York: Pantheon Books, 1985), 361–77.
3. In *Pleasure and Danger,* ed. Vance, hereafter cited as HO in text.
4. M. Daly, *Beyond God the Father: Toward a Philosophy of Women's Liberation* (Boston: Beacon Press, 1973), 8, 9, 33, 37, 47–49, 100, 105–6, 120, 121, 159, 167, 175, 189.
5. V. Woolf, *A Room of One's Own* (1929; reprint, New York: Harcourt Brace Jovanovich, 1957). Hereafter cited as RO in text.
6. By this definition, commercial advertisements coerce rather than persuade one to purchase goods. Coercion is more accurate, because consumption, not meeting need or furthering enjoyment, is the end sought.
7. A. Smedley, *Daughter of Earth* (New York: The Feminist Press, 1976). Hereafter cited as DE in text.
8. J. Didion, *A Book of Common Prayer* (New York: Paperback Books, 1977).
9. It becomes clear by the end of the novel that Grace figures at least as centrally to the narrative as Charlotte.
10. Rona Jaffe, "Rima the Bird Girl," in *Images of Women in Literature,* ed. M. A. Ferguson (Boston: Houghton Mifflin Co., 1973). Hereafter cited as RB in text.
11. M. H. Kingston, *The Woman Warrior: Memoirs of a Girlhood Among Ghosts* (New York: Random House, 1976). Hereafter cited as WW in text.
12. A. Walker, *The Color Purple* (New York: Harcourt, Brace, Jovanovich, 1982). Hereafter cited as CP in text.
13. P. Marshall, *Praisesong for the Widow* (New York: Obelisk, E. T. Dutton, 1984). Hereafter cited as PW in text.
14. *Avatar* is a Hindu term for the appearance or incarnation of a deity.

Marshall's use of the term as a name for a black woman reflects the historical interaction of Hindus with blacks in the Caribbean.

15. For the meaning of the "Beg Pardon" and the significance of ritual in the novel see B. Christian, "Ritualistic Process and the Structure of Paule Marshall's *Praisesong for the Widow,"* in *Black Feminist Criticism: Perspectives on Black Women Writers* (New York: Pergamon Press, 1985).

CHAPTER 2

The "Quilting" of Women's History: Phoebe of Cenchreae

ELISABETH SCHÜSSLER FIORENZA

I would like to address the question of women's early Christian history, how it is written, produced, and transmitted in historical consciousness. I will illustrate my methodological proposals by looking at the scant information we have about a leading woman in early Christianity: Phoebe of Cenchreae. In doing so it will become obvious that we can learn at least one lesson from women's life and history: one significant element of our oppression is the fact that our history was stolen from us, that our leaders and foremothers have been forgotten, and that our language and education have alienated us from ourselves and from each other.

The predominant popular understanding of how history is written holds that historians are scientists who give us an objective and unbiased account of the past. To know our history means to memorize the dates of significant events and the names of important historical figures who "made" history, almost all of whom seem to be men. Historians supposedly assemble historical facts drawn from sources to tell us with scientific objectivity what has actually happened. If it is true that historiography objectively mirrors historical reality, then women have had almost no historical significance.

I would like to suggest therefore that we replace this popular understanding of historiography[1] with another one derived from women's experience and work. The image of the historian as objective reporter needs to be replaced with that of the historian as a quilt maker fitting together the surviving scraps of historical information into an overall design that gives meaning to the individual pieces.

An unknown Canadian woman has described her quilt making in the following way:

WHAT'S IN A QUILT?

You look at my quilt with a quizzical eye,
Remark on its beauty and ask—
If it's worth all the time and work that it took
To complete such a painstaking task.
"Twas a labour of love," I try to explain—
A means to express what I feel
And preserve for the future some small part of me
That everyday life may conceal.
Into its patches I've stitched all the thoughts,
The dreams, the struggles, the fights,
The gladness, the sadness, the joy and the pain,
And the search for beauty and rights.
It's a simple quilt, really, just pieced out of scraps
In a pattern I worked out one day.
I sorted and pondered before I began,
And finally arranged it this way. . . .[2]

Just as a quilt brings together patchwork pieces into an artistic overall design, so also the writing of history does not provide a ready-made mirror of past events but a stitching together of historical information into a coherent overall design or interpretative model. In order to write a historical account scholars have to make inferences based in part upon their sources and in part upon their general understanding of human behavior and society. We not only interpret our historical sources in order to present a coherent historical story, but also ascribe historical significance to so-called "data" in accordance with a theoretical model or perspective that orders our information and evidence.[3]

Reconstructive inferences, selection of evidence, and ascription of historical significance depend not only on the choice of explanatory models but also on the rhetorical aims and interests of the work. History is not written for people of past times but for people of today and tomorrow. Far from recording with utmost objectivity "what actually happened," historians have written history for the dominant groups in society. History has often been conceived as a history of wars and empires, or of political or cultural heroes, to instill national pride or cultural hegemony.

Social historians have pointed out that we know little about the everyday lives of most societal groups and ordinary people. Our sources speak only rarely about the experiences and deeds of slaves, working-class people, native peoples, and women of lower classes. Historians of oppressed groups have made us conscious that in the past, history was written by and for the historical winners. The oppressed and vanquished of the past do not have a written history. The oppression and devaluation of people becomes total when they are deprived of their history and prevented from remembering their own past.

Although women have participated in the production and teaching of history for quite a while, feminist scholars have only recently challenged the overall intellectual and scientific frameworks that generate and perpetuate androcentric (male-centered) scholarship, making women invisible or peripheral in what we know about the world, human life, and cultural or religious history. In all areas of intellectual inquiry feminist studies are in the process of inaugurating a scientific revolution or paradigm shift from an androcentric worldview and intellectual framework of discourse to a feminist comprehension of the world, human culture, and history. Placing women's experience and subjectivity at the center of intellectual inquiry has challenged the theoretical frameworks of all academic disciplines. While androcentric scholarship defines women as the "other" or as the "object" of male scholarship, feminist studies insist on the reconceptualization of our language as well as of our intellectual framework in such a way that women as well as men become the subjects of human culture and scholarly discourse. A feminist critique of the ideological functions of androcentric language not only particularizes male scholarship but also highlights its male bias. Far from being objective or descriptive, androcentric texts and knowledge perpetuate the silence and invisibility of women.

If a feminist reconstruction of history can no longer take androcentric texts at face value it must develop a "hermeneutics of suspicion" in order to read what the texts say and what they do not say about historical events and reality. Although women are neglected in traditional historical texts, the effects of our lives and actions are a reality in history. In the past decade feminist historians have therefore tried to articulate the theoretical problem of how to move from androcentric text to historical context, or of how to write women back into history. Joan Kelly has succinctly stated the dual goal of women's history as both "to restore women to history and to restore our history to women. . . . In seeking to add women to the fund of historical knowledge, women's history has revitalized theory, for it has shaken the conceptual foundations of historical study."[4]

Like historians of other oppressed groups, feminist historians seek to break the silences, inconsistencies, incoherence, and ideological mechanisms of androcentric records in order to reappropriate the patriarchal past of women who not only have suffered the pain and dehumanization of oppression but also participated in social transformation and human development.

Although feminist historians agree that we need to search for theoretical models that could make women's agency and experience central to the writing of history as the history of women *and* men, they differ widely in their definition of "woman" and in their understanding of women's oppression. While some feminists seek the incorporation of women into androcentric intellectual and social frameworks, others posit a special uncorrupted nature of women grounded in our biology. Marxist feminists understand women as an oppressed class, while cultural feminists see women as a minority group or caste. White middle-class feminists often understand women as the social opposite of a sex, namely men, whereas Third World feminists insist that they have greater allegiance to their men than to the women of the dominant group. While some (for example, Simone de Beauvoir) have stressed that women were powerless in history, others (for instance, Mary Beard) have emphasized women's historical agency and influence. Although such a diversity in feminist perspective enhances our overall analysis, a particular feminist historical reconstruction must develop a specific model or pattern for the quilting of its historical narrative.

In writing my book *In Memory of Her: A Feminist Reconstruction of Early Christian Origins,* I have sought to develop a model that could do justice to most of these alternatives and highlight the interconnections among race, class, and gender.[5] Such a model, I submit, must distinguish between on the one hand the androcentric language and mindset that produce gender dualism, and on the other hand patriarchy as a social male system of graded dominations and subordinations rather than social relationships of equality.

First: A feminist interpretation cannot take masculine language at face value. A historically adequate translation and reading must take into account the implications of androcentric language that functions as inclusive language in a patriarchal culture. Such masculine inclusive language mentions women only when we are explicitly addressed, when our presence has become in any way a problem, or when we are exceptional. It does not mention women explicitly in so-called normal situations but subsumes us under *man* and *he*. Before the ramifications of such androcentric inclusive language had become conscious even women writers referred to themselves with masculine pronouns and expressions. Such so-called masculine inclusive language functions in the same way in biblical texts as in modern Western languages.

Historians and theologians of early Christianity interpret such androcentric language in a twofold way: as generic and as gender-specific language. They presuppose that women as well as men were members of the early Christian communities and do not assume that the early Christian movement was a male cult like the Mithras-cult. Therefore they understand masculine terms (in the original Greek) such as elect, saints, brothers, and sons as generic language including both women and men. These terms do not apply only to male Christians, designating them over and against female Christians, but they apply to all Christians characterizing them over and against non-Christians. While masculine language with respect to the community is understood in an inclusive way, the same masculine language is understood in a gender-specific way when referring to leadership functions, such as apostles, missionaries, ministers, overseers, or elders. Although we find in the New Testament masculine leadership titles that refer to women, New Testament scholars often presuppose that only men had leadership functions in early Christianity.

While the books and essays on women in the Bible take androcentric language at face value, I would submit that a historically adequate analysis must take into account that androcentric language functions as generic language until proven otherwise. The passages of the New Testament that directly mention women are not descriptive or comprehensive but indicative of the submerged information conveyed in so-called inclusive androcentric texts. Those passages of the New Testament that directly mention women cannot be interpreted as providing all the information on women in early Christianity. We can no longer simply assume that, for example, 1 Corinthians 11:2–16 speaks about women prophets whereas the rest of chapters 11–14 refer to male prophets and charismatics. The opposite is the case: 1 Corinthians 11–14 speak about the pneumatic worship of all Christian men and women. 1 Corinthians 11:2–16 mentions women explicitly because their behavior had become a special problem for Paul. However, if such a problem would not have arisen we would have no way to "prove" historically that the masculine terms of the letter must be read as inclusive language. Or, if the letter of recommendation concluding Paul's letter to the Romans were lost to us, we no longer would know much about women's early Christian leadership—mentioned here only in passing. These references to early Christian women therefore should be read as the tip of an iceberg indicating how much historical information we have lost.

In short, a historically adequate reading of androcentric language and sources must not only reject the topical approach but also shift the burden of proof to those who would understand masculine inclusive language as exclusive of women. A historically adequate translation and interpretation of androcentric texts therefore must not view the texts referring explicitly to women as patchwork pieces within an androcentric design, but must articulate a feminist model of historical reconstruction that can understand them as the highlights and colors within a feminist design.

Second: It is therefore important to spell out what kind of feminist design, pattern, or model one uses for stitching the scattered pieces of information together into an overall feminist historical reconstruction. In my work I use patriarchy as such a feminist heuristic model or concept. It therefore becomes necessary to clarify here the way in which I use it. I do not understand patriarchy in a general sense as a societal system in which all men have power over all women but in the classical sense as defined in Aristotelian philosophy. Just as feminism is not only a worldview or world-construction in language but a women's movement for change and liberation, so patriarchy in my understanding is not just ideological dualism or androcentric world-construction in language, but a societal-economic-political system of graded subjugations and oppressions. Therefore I do not speak simply about male oppressors and female oppressed, or see all men over and against all women. Patriarchy as a male pyramid specifies women's oppression in terms of the class, race, country, or religion of the men to whom we "belong."

Patriarchy as the basic heuristic model for feminist analysis allows us to conceptualize not only sexism but also racism and property-class relationships as basic structures of women's oppression. In a patriarchal society or religion all women are bound into a system of male privilege and domination, but impoverished Third World women constitute the bottom of the oppressive patriarchal pyramid. Patriarchy cannot be toppled except through the destruction of the bottom of the patriarchal pyramid where exploitation of triply oppressed women occurs. All women's oppression and liberation is bound up with that of colonialized and the most economically exploited women. This was already recognized by one of the earliest statements of the radical women's liberation movement: "Until every woman is free, no woman is free." In other words, as long as societal and religious patriarchy exist, women are not liberated and must struggle for survival and self-determination. Women's experience of solidarity as a social group is not rooted in our biological differences from men but in our common historical experiences as a group struggling against patriarchal oppression and for survival as historical subjects. Such a theoretical framework allows us to locate women's strength, historical agency, pain, and struggle within our common historical experience as women in patriarchal society and religion. In short, I understand patriarchy as a complex political-economic-legal system that found its systematic articulation in Aristotelian philosophy.

The classics scholar Marilyn Arthur has discovered that the articulation of the polarity between the sexes and the difference in male and female nature was not explicit in the writings of the Greek aristocratic period but emerged only with the introduction of Athenian democracy.[6] She argues that in Greek as well as in Roman aristocratic society the household was coterminous with the public realm and rule, and that therefore aristocratic women had relative freedom and control of their property and rights. While in aristocratic society family status defined more than gender roles, in Athenian democracy the political and legal structures of the state prescribed women's subservience and excluded freeborn women from citizenship. Explicit articulation of the specific natures of the subordinate members of the household was occasioned by the contradiction between the social-political structures of Athenian democracy restricting full citizenship to free propertied male heads of households and the democratic ideal of human dignity and freedom first articulated in the middle-class democracy of the city-state. In short, ideological polarity and misogynist dualism as well as the philosophical justification of social-patriarchal roles as based on distinctive human "natures" of slaves and freeborn women seem to be generated by a social-political situation in which the equality and dignity of all humans is articulated, but their actual participation in political and social self-determination is prohibited because they remain the economic or sexual property of freeborn male heads of households.

In the Hellenistic period women gained public influence and citizenship not on the grounds of their family status, as in aristocratic society, but by virtue of their wealth. In the Hellenistic age, women gained citizenship for outstanding public service, and some of them as benefactors held public office. While for classical Greek culture sexual dimorphism and the dichotomy between the public and private spheres were characteristic, in the Hellenistic period ideologies of sexual dimorphism no longer needed to be generated because the dichotomy between private and public were relativized for women who were wealthy and owned property. However, it must not be overlooked that such a dichotomy was never operative for lower-class and rural women.

According to Arthur, the early Roman empire resembled Athenian democracy more than Hellenistic society. She points to the legislation of Augustus, which sought to strengthen the family by giving the state more control over it. Moreover, she argues, Roman writers such as Tacitus or Juvenal saw women again as a threat to culture and produced misogynist diatribes. However, she has to concede that the similarities to classical Greek society are upset by the influence of Hellenism on Roman society and by the much greater economic and legal independence of Roman women despite the traditional legal concepts of *paterfamilias* and guardianship. Far from strengthening the patriarchal family, Augustean legislation undermined it by giving women the possibility of *de facto* emancipation even from formal legal guardianship.

Although in lesser numbers, women of the Roman empire held public office just as men did. They functioned as benefactors *(euergeteis* or *patronae)*, although they could not hold official political office on their own. It seems therefore that misogynist and literary texts about women are best understood as attempts of men in power to curtail the public, legal, economic, and cultural freedom and influence of propertied women and to establish definite boundaries between the public male and the private female spheres. It is therefore not accidental that Aristotelian patriarchal philosophy regained currency in the first century at a time when women's social, economic, and educational status was relatively high. Such misogynist or even "liberal" male texts must therefore be seen as prescriptive texts rather than as descriptive of the actual situation of women.

In Hellenistic as well as in Roman society, so-called mystery religions such as the cult of Isis, Judaism, or the cult of Dionysus emerge as a middle zone between the public male and the private female domain of household and state. Although traditionally religion encompassed both the public and the private spheres, according to Roman law slaves' and women's religion was determined by the religion of the *paterfamilias.* Insofar as the participation in mystery cults and philosophical schools depended on a personal decision for a religious way of life, in Hellenistic-Roman times such religious cults became a third, middle ground between the public and private spheres. Women's participation in mystery religions, ecstatic cults, and philosophical schools was therefore considerable. However, such religious cults and associations were considered potentially subversive to the order of the patriarchal household and state. Thus Greco-Roman literature polemicized against such cults because they corrupted the morals of well-to-do women and allowed them to go out by themselves at night. However, for economically and socially independent women who were marginal in the dominant culture and religion, such religious associations provided a means to overcome their status discrepancy.

This possibility for overcoming such status dissonance, I submit, and not their social marginality as childless women or widows attracted such women to the oriental cults, among them Judaism and the early Christian missionary movement. Insofar as the early Christian movement admitted individuals as full members independent of their gender or their social and economic status in the patriarchal household, it was a movement that produced conflict between its members and the dominant patriarchal society and religion. Yet the ethos of early Christianity, which was subversive of the patriarchal family, would be misunderstood if it were construed as antisexual and antiwoman. The marriage-free option developed for women in the early Christian movement is best understood as a "role revolt,"[7] which on religious grounds allowed women to move out of the confines of the patriarchal family and to center their lives on spiritual self-fulfillment and religious independence that gave them greater respect, mobility, and influence. Finally, insofar as the early Christian movement gathered in house churches and small groups, the dichotomy between the private sphere of the house and the public sphere of the church was nonexistent. As an emergent movement it allowed freeborn women as well as slave women and others who were marginalized by the dominant society to develop public ecclesial leadership and religious influence. Later New Testament writers sought to lessen the structural tension between the Christian discipleship communities of equals and the dominant patriarchal society.

Phoebe was one of the leading women in the early Christian movement who has been almost completely eradicated from our historical consciousness. Whereas Mary Magdalene, Martha, or Thekla have been celebrated in liturgy and art, Phoebe has not been remembered as clearly. As with most of the women in the circle of Paul, we know of her only by accident. Paul mentions her only briefly in Romans 16:1–2: "I recommend to you our sister Phoebe, a deaconess of the church of Cenchreae, that you may receive her in the Lord as befits the saints, and help her in whatever she may require from you, for she has been a helper of many and of myself as well." If Paul's and Phoebe's ways had not crossed, she would have been totally shrouded in historical silence like other early Christian women leaders. The first lesson to learn from her is to write one's own letters and biography, or at least to become friends with someone who does.

Romans 16 is a letter of recommendation for Phoebe that is addressed to the community in Rome, or if it was originally an independent letter, most likely to the community in Ephesus. Traveling Christian missionaries and church leaders used such letters of recommendation in order to receive access and hospitality in communities where they were not known personally. Phoebe's example testifies that women officially represented early Christian communities and that their travels served the communication between them.

Who is this woman Phoebe? It is as important to note what is not said about Phoebe as what is said of her. Although in antiquity, just as today, women were characterized by their relationship to men, through their family status as virgins, wives, or widows, Phoebe is not defined by her gender role and family status but by her ecclesial functions. Her position in the early Christian missionary movement is named with three titles: she is "our sister"; the minister or leader of the church at Cenchreae, a seaport of Corinth; and benefactor or *patrona* of many, and even of Paul himself.

It is interesting to note that the Greek terms *diakonos* and *prostatis* are often translated by patriarchal exegetes as the verb form: for example, "she serves" the community of Cenchreae and "she has assisted or helped many." If *diakonos* is understood as a title it is translated as "servant, helper, or deaconess," and it is interpreted in terms of the later institution of deaconess. Phoebe is then understood as one of the first pastoral assistants helping Paul in his missionary work. For example, H. Lietzmann understands the office of Phoebe by analogy to the later institution of deaconesses which, in comparison to that of the male deaconate, had only very limited functions. He characterizes Phoebe as "an apparently well-to-do and charitable lady who because of her feminine virtues worked in the service of the poor and of the sick as well as assisted at the baptism of women."[8] Already in the second century Origen had promoted this interpretation of Phoebe as an assistant and helper of Paul. From this he concluded that women who do good works can be appointed as deaconesses. Similarly, the Greek term *prostatis*, usually translated "leading officer, president, or benefactor," has been here translated "helper" or "assistant," since exegetes cannot imagine that Paul could be supported or outranked by a woman. Recently Ernst Käsemann again has reviewed the arguments for understanding Phoebe in terms of Greco-Roman patronage. He concludes: "There is no reference then to a 'patroness.' Women could not take on legal functions, and according to Revelation only in heretical circles do prophetesses seem to have had official ecclesiastical powers of leadership. . . . The idea is that of personal care which Paul and others have received at the hand of the deaconess."[9]

It is obvious that an androcentric perspective on early Christian history has to explain away the literal meaning of both words because it does not allow for women in church leadership, or can accord them only "feminine" assisting functions. Since this traditional interpretive model takes for granted that the leadership of the early church was in the hands of men, it assumes that the women mentioned in the Pauline letters were the helpers and assistants of the male apostles and missionaries, especially of Paul. Such an androcentric model of historical reconstruction cannot imagine or conceptualize that women could have had leadership roles equal to and sometimes even superior to those of men in early Christian beginnings. The much-invoked objectivity of historical-critical scholarship has a difficult time prevailing when the texts speak about women in a way that does not fit into the traditional androcentric models of historical reconstruction.

What can we say about Phoebe when we do not attempt to fit our information about her into an androcentric but into a feminist model of historical reconstruction? The early Christian missionary movement was spread by traveling missionaries and organized in house and local churches similar to other private associations and religious cults. Whereas a woman such as Priska engaged in missionary travels and founded house churches wherever she went, a woman such as Phoebe was the leader of a local community. Her "ministry" or "office" was not, as that of the later deaconesses, limited to women, but she was the *diakonos* of the whole church in Cenchreae. Paul uses the same Greek expression when he characterizes his own ministry or that of the charismatic missionary Apollos, whose teacher had been Priska. The word cluster *diakonos, diakonia, diakonein* is found most often in 2 Corinthians, and it characterizes the so-called pseudoapostles who were charismatic missionaries, eloquent preachers, visionary prophets, and spirit-filled apostles. Paul seems to have been criticized in Corinth because he was not an impressive figure or eloquent preacher and miracle worker as well as because he did not have support of the community or letters of recommendation. Such an understanding of the title in terms of preaching and teaching is justified since it is used also in extrabiblical sources to refer to preachers and teachers.[10]

Phoebe has the same title as these charismatic preachers in Corinth. Yet, rather than opposing Paul, she had a friendly relationship with him. She was acknowledged as a charismatic preacher and leader of the community in Cenchreae, who like the members of the house of Stephanas had dedicated herself "to the *diakonia* of the saints" (cf. 1 Cor. 16:15). Just as the closest coworker of Paul, Timothy, is called "our brother" and "God's *diakonos*" (1 Thess. 3:2), so Phoebe is not only introduced as *diakonos* but also as "our sister," a title characterizing her as a coworker of Paul's. In a similar way

the author of Colossians recommends a man by the name of Ty-
chikos as "our beloved brother" and "faithful *diakonos*" (Col. 4:7).

The significance of Phoebe's leadership is also underlined by the
third title *prostatis,* a word found only in Romans 16. The usual
meaning of this term is "leader, president, superintendent, or patron," a translation that is supported by the verb form found in 1
Thessalonians 5:12 and 1 Timothy 3:4 and 5:17. It refers in 1 Thessalonians to the leadership of the community and in 1 Timothy to
the leadership functions of bishop, deacons, and elders. Such an
understanding of the word in terms of leadership does not rule out
its understanding in terms of the patronage system of antiquity,
since patrons and benefactors could also take over leadership in the
associations and cultic groups supported by them.

The motif of reciprocity stressed by Paul speaks for an understanding of the word in the technical-legal sense of the Greco-
Roman patronage system.[11] Phoebe's patronage was not limited to
the community of Cenchreae but included many others, even Paul
himself, who stood with her in a patron-client relationship. Therefore Paul asked the community in Rome or Ephesus according to the
"exchange law" of Greco-Roman patronage to repay Phoebe the
assistance and favors that Paul and other Christians owed her as
clients. Those who joined the Christian community joined it as an
association of equals in which, according to the pre-Pauline baptis-
mal formula found in Galatians 3:28, social status stratifications in
terms of the patriarchal family were abolished. This is the main
reason why the early Christian movement seems to have been especially attractive to those who had little stake in the rewards of
religion based on either class stratification or on male dominance. It is obvious why well-to-do women were among its leading
converts.

Although we have little evidence for all-women associations, we
have sufficient evidence that women joined clubs and became
founders and patrons of socially mixed associations and cults. They
endowed them with funds for specifically defined purposes and
expected honor and recognition in return for their benefactions. The
well-to-do converts to Christianity must have expected to exercise
the influence of a patron in the early Christian community. Christians such as Phoebe acted as benefactors for individual Christians
and church leaders. In dealings with the government or the courts
they represented the whole community. With their network of

connections, friendships with well-placed persons, and public influence, benefactors such as Phoebe eased the social life of other Christians in Greco-Roman society.

Women such as Phoebe found possibilities of communal leadership and religious influence in the early Christian missionary movement that were not open to them in their dominant society and
official religion. Their leadership and contributions to early Christianity can, however, become historically visible only when we abandon our outdated patriarchal-androcentric model of early Christian
beginnings that conceives of early Christian women only as marginal figures or in subordinate feminine roles. We have to replace
it with a historical model that makes it possible to conceive of the
early Christian movement as a discipleship of equals. Such a model
allows us to imagine that women's leadership and contributions
were central to this movement. Rather than abandoning the struggles and achievements of our foresisters against societal and religious patriarchy, we have to reclaim them as our own heritage. A
feminist reconstruction of early Christian history is not just an
academic affair; it seeks to recover women's past for the sake of our
present struggles and the possibility of a feminist future for all of
us.

NOTES

1. See my book *Bread Not Stone: The Challenge of Feminist Biblical Interpretation*
   (Boston: Beacon Press 1983).
2. Author unknown. Submitted by Kay Brodie for use in S. Davy, ed.,
   Women, Work, and Worship in The United Church of Canada (Toronto: The
   United Church of Canada, 1983), 135.
3. See G. Leff, *History and Social Theory* (Anchor Books,), 13f.
4. J. Kelly, "The Social Relations of the Sexes: Methodological Implications
   of Women's History," *Signs* 1(1976): 809.
5. *In Memory of Her: A Feminist Reconstruction of Early Christian Origins* (New York:
   Crossroad, 1983).
6. M. B. Arthur, "Women in the Ancient World," in *Conceptual Frameworks for
   Studying Women's History* (Bronxville, New York: Sarah Laurence College,
   1975), 1–15.

7. For such an interpretation see also J. McNamara, *A New Song: Celibate Women in the First Three Christian Centuries,* Vol. 6/7 of *Women and History* (New York: Haworth Press, 1983).

8. H. Lietzmann, *Geschichte der alten Kirche* (Berlin: De Gruyter, 1961), 1:149.

9. E. Kasemann, *Commentary on Romans* (Grand Rapids: Eerdmans, 1980), 411.

10. See A. Lemaire, "The Ministries in the New Testament: Recent Research," *Biblical Theology Bulletin* 3 (1973): 133–66.

11. See S. C. Mott, "The Power of Giving and Receiving: Reciprocity in Hellenistic Benevolence," in *Current Issues in Biblical and Patristic Interpretation,* ed. G. E. Hawthorne (Grand Rapids: Eerdmans, 1975), 60–75.

CHAPTER 3

Reverence for Life: The Need for a Sense of Finitude

CAROL CHRIST

At any moment this earth and all who live upon it could be destroyed in nuclear war. One of the reasons we face nuclear destruction is that we do not recognize our connection to the earth. We fail to acknowledge our own finitude and death, and the potential finitude and death of the earth. Our religious and philosophical traditions since Plato have attempted to deny these limits and hence have prevented us from fully comprehending our connections to nature. We must challenge these traditions and provide alternatives. Feminist thinkers who remind us of our mortality and emphasize our connections to the earth have much to contribute to our survival.

As a thealogian, I share with Gordon Kaufman the conviction that "there is no question that the possibility of nuclear holocaust is the premier issue which our generation must address."[1] I agree further with Kaufman that as interpreters of our religious heritage, "we must be prepared to enter into the most radical kind of deconstruction and reconstruction of the traditions we have inherited, including especially their most central and precious symbols."[2]

One of the ways our religious and philosophical systems have contributed to the threat of extinction is that they have cut us off from our connection to nature and from the full experience and acknowledgment of our finitude. Our political leaders can think about fighting a nuclear war only because they don't really think they (and almost all other human beings and life forms) will die. They imagine a nuclear war to be "survivable" despite all the evidence to the contrary. Most of us are probably familiar with the story that became the title of Robert Scheer's book *With Enough Shovels*. Scheer reports that a government official told him that the way to survive a nuclear war is to dig a hole, climb into it, and pull a door down over it. The absurdity of this scenario, which reportedly was taken from a Russian survival manual, should not blind us to the fact that all schemes to survive a nuclear war are just as absurd.[3]

Paradoxically, the denial of finitude and death may express an even more profound failure of our culture, the failure to affirm life as it is lived, this life, on this earth, in these bodies. The underside of the denial of death may be despair about the meaning of life that ends in death. And thus the very politicians who assert that "we" will "survive" nuclear war may not really care whether we do or not.

It might be argued that the denial of finitude and inevitable death expresses an affirmation not a denial of life. But this life, bounded by finitude and death, is the only life we know, the only life we can know for certain to exist. To deny finitude and death is to deny the limitations of life as we know it in favor of an idea of life without death. We must learn instead to love this life that ends in death. This is not absolutely to rule out the possibility of individual survival after death, but to say that we ought not interpret our task in this life in light of such a possibility. Our task is here.

I feel and know my connection to earth more deeply than I feel or know anything. My spirituality stems from my sense of connection to this earth, to its cycles of changing seasons, to oceans, rivers, mountains, trees, grasses, birds, deer, roses, daffodils, and to my grandparents, to my mother, my father, my family, my friends, my dog, and to all the others whose lives have been intertwined with mine on this earth. With Alice Walker I pray: "Surely the earth can be saved for [these]."[4]

The inability to revere our connections to the earth has deep roots in our culture, roots that go back at least to Plato and are intimately bound up with the denial of finitude and death. The "finite" is defined as "having boundaries; limited; capable of being bounded, enclosed, or encompassed; being neither infinite nor infinitesimal; existing, persisting, for a limited time only; impermanent, transient."[5] This definition encompasses the major reason finitude has been denied in most of the philosophies and theologies influenced by Plato. For Plato, that which is limited by time or space was imperfect. In *The Symposium* Plato argued that our true home is not this finite, imperfect world. He described the journey of the soul from love of beautiful bodies, to love of beautiful souls, to love of beautiful laws and institutions, to love of science and knowledge, until finally the soul ascends to the vision of the good, which is described as "neither words, nor knowledge, nor a something that exists in something else, such as a living creature, or the earth, or the heavens, or anything that is—but subsisting of itself and by itself in an eternal oneness, while every lovely thing partakes of it in such sort that, however much the parts may wax and wane, it will be neither more nor less, but still the same inviolable whole."[6]

For Plato, "the good" is not affected by time (it does not come into being or die), and it is essentially unaffected by relationships (it is an inviolable whole). The vision of the good as totally transcending finitude is fundamental to Platonic philosophy. Susan Griffin aptly characterizes the Platonic vision when she writes, "It is decided that matter is transitory and illusory like the shadow on a wall cast by firelight; that we dwell in a cave, in the cave of our flesh, which is also matter, also illusory; it is decided that what is real is outside the cave, in a light brighter than we can imagine, that matter traps us in darkness. That the idea of matter existed before matter and is more perfect, ideal."[7] Griffin alludes to the *Republic* where Plato argues that just as the shadows on the wall of a cave are poor reflections of physical objects, so our physical bodies are poor reflections of ideas or forms, which are eternal.

Since Plato, Western thinkers have shared a dualistic philosophy in which mind and body are perceived as separable, and in which body and nature (because impermanent, finite) have been perceived as less than mind and the realm of ideas (imagined to be eternal, infinite). The contrast between finite and infinite is at the heart of Platonic dualism. Change and dependence are considered impediments to the soul's journey. Platonic thought asserts that man is not essentially finite, that his mind or soul partakes in the infinite. (I use the male generic here and elsewhere in describing dualistic thought, not only because this way of thinking is the product of male minds, but also because philosophers and theologians have never been certain that women have minds or souls with the same rational

capacity as the minds of men.) In denying finitude, man has proposed that he is not limited by time or space. When we are aware
of our bodies, we are aware of limitation: we cannot be everywhere
and we will surely die. We cannot live in our bodies without eating,
drinking, sleeping, and going to the bathroom. We know our bodies
to grow and change, whether we want them to or not, no matter
how we try to deny it. And one day our bodies will die. We will
not live forever. And yet man has sought to deny that he is limited
by his body. He has asserted that his mind or soul is eternal. He has
attempted through ascetic practices to deny that he is his body, to
free his soul. "I think, therefore I am," he has said, and he tells
himself that he is not even certain that other minds exist.

Much Christian theology is built on the denial of finitude and
death. The Platonic vision of the good as immaterial, unchanging,
and essentially unrelated to any other entity became the philosophical basis for Christian theology's doctrine of God. In classical
Christian theology, God is declared totally or absolutely transcendent of creation, the earth, and all creatures in it. God's absolute
transcendence becomes the basis for doctrines such as God's aseity
(or inability to be affected in his essential nature by what happens
to creation), God's omnipotence (or total power), and God's omni-
science (or knowledge of everything). The doctrine of God's absolute transcendence, like Plato's notion of the good, correlates with
a theology in which this earth, the body, and this life are despised,
and in which the spiritual goal is to transcend the flesh and its
desires and to seek a life after death in which the limitations of
finitude are overcome.

Theologians sometimes assert that the doctrine of the incarnation is an affirmation of finitude, and thus that Christianity cannot
properly be accused of denying finitude. The incarnation, the doctrine of God's full presence in the body of Christ, is said to be an
affirmation of the body. That God entered into this life is said to be
an affirmation of it. That God died on the cross is said to indicate
acceptance of death. But at best the incarnation is a partial affirmation of finitude. The doctrine of the incarnation was developed by
church fathers influenced by Platonism, who believed that the finite
and the infinite are essentially opposed. For them it was the highest
paradox that the divine could be fully present in human flesh. There
would be no paradox if the finite were understood to be the natural

home of the spirit or the divine. Because they polarized the finite and the infinite, the church fathers could not fully affirm finitude.

Nor could they affirm death. The denial of finitude within Christianity is encompassed in the phrase "he is risen." Without addressing the complex theological disputes about the nature of the resurrection, let me state the obvious: the statement "he is risen" is a denial that death marks the end of the individual life. The hopes of Christians throughout the centuries have been based upon the expectation of an individual life after physical death in which the limitations of finitude are overcome.

The Christian doctrine of original sin asserts that since the fall, since Adam and Eve, we no longer have the choice not to sin, or, as it is often put, "we cannot *not* sin." Whatever we do, this doctrine states, is tainted with evil. This doctrine imposes an infinite standard on our finite lives. We are made to feel guilty for being human, and we are told to long for a salvation that will release us from bondage to the finite. According to traditional theology, "the wages of sin is death." Because Adam and Eve sinned, death has entered into the world as punishment, it is said. Instead of being understood as an ordinary, and accepted, part of life, death is set up as an enemy of life, as something to be feared and avoided. But to understand death as punishment for some defect is to completely misunderstand the nature of life. Death is implicit in life. And we would do better to recognize and accept that fact. The cycles of nature include birth, fruition, and decay. We all die so that others may live. This is neither punishment nor sacrifice. It is simply the way things are.

Asceticism, the practice of self-denial, is a reflection of the Christian denial of finitude. Extreme ascetics deny themselves food, sleep, sex, comfort, baths. The number of vermin falling from an ascetic's body was once said to be a way of determining his holiness.[8] Self-flagellation was also practiced. The theory behind asceticism is dualism. It is said that the body is at war with the soul, and that by denying the body, one frees the soul.

While extremes of asceticism are frowned upon in most circles today, celibacy is still required of Catholic priests and nuns. The ascetic attitude toward the body has been reaffirmed in Pope John Paul II's teachings on sexuality, marriage, and celibacy. While these teachings take a more positive attitude toward sex within marriage than some earlier ones, they still affirm the traditional view that celibacy is a higher calling than marriage.[9] Although Protestantism abolished the celibate ideal, ascetic attitudes remain. Many Protestants are taught that pleasure is a sin and are urged to practice mental asceticism by constantly dwelling upon their imperfections.

Apocalypticism takes the denial of finitude and death a step further. Apocalyptic visions claim that the whole finite world will come to an end but affirms that God will create a new order. The Gospel of Mark states the apocalyptic view, "There will be such a distress as until now has not been equaled since the beginning when God created the world, nor will there ever be again. . . . Heaven and earth will pass away, but my words will not pass away" (Mark 13:19, 31). The book of Revelation likewise envisions the destruction of this earth. "Then I saw a new heaven and a new earth, and the first earth had disappeared, and now there was no longer any sea" (21:1). These writings are inspired by a mentality filled with disgust for this earth and this life. To envision destruction of this earth and its re-creation by God is to imagine that the limitations of finitude and death can be transcended in a new creation. New fundamentalist movements, which have had a great influence on American politicians and policy makers, accept and promulgate apocalypticism, tying the possibility or even inevitability of nuclear war to God's will.

Modern science is also the product of a culture that denies finitude and death. Carolyn Merchant, in *The Death of Nature,* argues that prior to the advent of modern science in the sixteenth and seventeenth centuries, people viewed "the earth as geocosm . . . as a nurturing mother, sensitive, alive, and responsive to human action." Because earth was viewed as being alive, it was understood that there were limits to man's attempts to control or master her. Human beings understood themselves to be part of a finite system; there were limits to their ability to control nature. As Merchant establishes, this view of nature as a finite system was not compatible with modern science. She writes, "The changes in imagery and attitudes relating to the earth were of enormous significance as the mechanization of nature proceeded. The nurturing earth would lose its function as a normative restraint as it changed to an inanimate dead physical system."[10] Scientists declared the earth "dead matter" to be controlled by "man." Modern science is based upon the correlative notions that the powers of the human mind are unlimited and that the mind can fully control and manipulate nature.

A nuclear mentality is built on the denial of finitude. It believes that man in his infinite wisdom can control forces far more powerful than himself. Plutonium 239, one of the substances created in nuclear power plants and used in the making of nuclear bombs, is deadly even in small amounts. Its radioactivity could contaminate the earth for 500,000 years.[11] Even if all nuclear bombs were dismantled and all nuclear power plants were closed tomorrow, we would still have to find a way to safely store radioactive material for half a million years. Scientists assume that when the time comes, other scientists will find a way to clean up the mess they have created. They deny that the time is now: today's containers in which nuclear waste is being stored are leaking into the ground and into the ocean. Scientists fail to contemplate the possibility that there is no way to control a deadly substance for 500,000 years. They do not accept finitude—their own or that of the earth. They deny the fragility of the ecosystem, the limitations of our minds, and our powerlessness to control nature. They do not face the very real possibility that the human race and most complex species of plants and animals would be destroyed in a nuclear war.

Politicians share the denial of finitude. The architects of nuclear policies imagine that nuclear war can be justified to preserve an abstraction called "our way of life." Robert Scheer asked the following question to Eugene Rostow, one of the architects of American nuclear policy: "Would it be fair to say that you feel that the dangers inherent in the arms race, the dangers of accidental war, the dangers brought about by more and more weapons piling up, are a less serious threat to peace than the danger of not controlling the Soviets and of having the Western alliance break up?" To this question Rostow answered, "That is absolutely correct." He acknowledged that the damage that would be brought about by a nuclear war would be "worse" than that caused by the two world wars, yet he stated that Soviet expansionism posed a greater threat. He has apparently deceived himself into believing that a nuclear war is different only in magnitude, not in kind, from World War II. Louis O. Giuffrida, appointed by Ronald Reagan in his first administration to run the Federal Management Agency, said to ABC News about the consequences of nuclear war, "It would be a terrible mess, but it wouldn't be unmanageable." He apparently expects to be around afterwards to clean up the "mess." Caspar Weinberger's statement to Scheer is even more frightening. In his conversation with Scheer about nuclear war, he admitted that he expects this world to come to an end. "I have read the Book of Revelation, and yes, I believe the world is going to end—by an act of God, I hope. . . . I think time is running out, but I have faith."[12] Weinberger seems not to take seriously the threat to survival posed by nuclear war, since he believes God is planning to bring this world to an end in any case.

These men have not allowed consciousness of the finitude of life on this earth to affect their thinking about nuclear policy. They deny that nuclear war is likely to mean the end of civilization, the end of humanity, the destruction of all but a few species of plants and animals. Jonathan Schell's vision of the survivors of a nuclear war as a "republic of insects and grasses"[13] seems to me to be a more realistic assessment of the consequences of nuclear war. According to Schell, the short- and long-term effects of nuclear war would probably mean the destruction of all the complex species of plants and animals. Yet, those who are making the decisions about the life and death of our planet seem to believe that they are not finite, and that human life and all life is not capable of being "bounded, enclosed, or encompassed." Most frightening are those who contemplate total destruction but imagine that such might be the will of God.

It is easy to dismiss these men as madmen. Indeed, they seem to have lost touch with reality. But these men are not aberrations within Western civilization. They are its products, and their visions of reality are considered sane within a culture founded on the denial of finitude and death, a culture that clings to ideas about life, to ideologies, rather than to life itself. I am not suggesting that Platonic dualism as represented in theology and philosophy is the sole cause of these men's views. But the cultural habit of denying finitude and death, which is deeply embedded in Western thought, makes it easier for them to deny that nuclear war could destroy almost all the life on this planet.

The crisis of our times calls upon us to point out the roots of our peril in the denial of finitude and also to begin to depict a religious vision compatible with the preservation of this finite earth. We must envision a spirituality that acknowledges finitude and death and encourages us to affirm rather than deny our connections with the earth and all life on earth. From the perspective of our religious heritage it might seem that such a spirituality is a contradiction in terms. What is spirituality, it may be said, if not an answer to questions we have about finitude and death? What is religion if not a call to deny our limitations, to strive for a "more perfect way"? The spirituality we need for our survival is precisely a spirituality that encourages us to recognize limitation and death, a spirituality that calls us to celebrate our connections to all that is finite.

There are many resources for such a religious vision. The indigenous preurban traditions of Africa, Asia, America, and Europe all have much to teach us about a spirituality that connects us to earth. Feminist thinking and spirituality also have much to say about the overcoming of the Platonic legacy of the denial of finitude.

Feminist thinkers remind us that our ideas about the body and nature are bound up with our ideas about women. As Rosemary Ruether, Mary Daly, and others have shown, in Western philosophy and theology women are associated with the negative side of Platonic dualisms. Women are associated with the body, nature, and finitude, while males (and the male God) are associated with the mind, the spirit, and the infinite. These attitudes, which are prevalent in Western philosophy and theology, reach their apex in the following charge found in the *Malleus Maleficarum,* the book used as a "hammer" against "witches": "All witchcraft comes from carnal lust which in women is insatiable."[14] The root of the equation of women with the body, nature, and finitude can be found in the fact that those doing the equating were men. Male theologians, philosophers, and scientists have viewed women's cycles of menstruation, pregnancy, childbirth, lactation, and menopause as manifestations of our carnal nature, while conveniently denying their own bodily processes, which just as definitively mark them as carnal. Recognizing the damage that has been done to women by dualistic philosophies that equate us with the despised body, some feminist thinkers have begun to question the equation of women with that which is despised. We have asserted that women's rational and spiritual capacities are equal to men's. And some feminist thinkers have also begun to question the dualistic patterns of thinking that separate mind and body, spirit and nature, finite and infinite.

One thinker who has questioned dualism in her writing is Adrienne Rich. In her book *Of Woman Born: Motherhood as Experience and Institution,* Rich is forced by her position as a thinker who is also a mother to question the dualistic patterns that equate women with the body. She chooses to affirm both her mind and its creative capacities *and* her body and its creative capacities as equally relevant to her task of understanding motherhood. She therefore acknowledges herself as an embodied female thinker. She cannot accept the denial of the body in the work of some feminist thinkers who affirm women's minds. She writes that she understands why "many intellectual and creative women" have "minimized their physicality" in their affirmation of women's rationality. But she urges feminist thinkers to move beyond this dualism.[15]

When Rich writes that we must learn to "think through the body" (and I assume she means all of us, not just women), she is fully aware that she is proposing a fundamental break from the dualisms of Western thought. She is saying that we must recognize that all thought is finite. Thus she is denying the Platonic view that the mind can separate itself from the body in order to perceive and participate in the unconditioned.

Susan Griffin, another feminist writer whose work challenges the underlying metaphysic of Western thought, documents "how man regards and makes use of woman and nature."[16] She shows how man has categorized both woman and nature as inferior to himself, as matter to be shaped and controlled by his mind and will. The central movement of Griffin's book occurs when woman strips away this false naming. When she recognizes that she is more than matter to be shaped by man's will, woman finds herself in a cave where she has a vision. Griffin's vision in the cave provides us with a model for a spirituality based on the acceptance of finitude and death. Griffin's vision provides a clear alternative to Plato's. In her vision the ego is transcended, but the earth and the body are not transcended. Socrates' vision as recorded by Plato was of the union of the soul with that which is unchanging, independent, and immaterial. Griffin's vision is of the connection of the body and spirit to that which is changing, dependent, and material. Socrates wanted to transcend the body and nature; Griffin experiences deeply her connection to body and nature. To Socrates the shadows on the wall of a cave are a metaphor for the illusory nature of material reality. In Griffin's vision the cave represents the reality of the material world.[17]

Griffin goes on to say, "We know ourselves to be made from this earth. We know this earth is made from our bodies." She challenges the Platonic longing for permanence when she writes, "Everything moves, everything changes." She bridges the gulf between "man" and "nature" when she insists, "We are nature."[18] When she says this, Griffin challenges the classical legacy, which insists on a categorical distinction between the human mind and what is called nature, namely finite, embodied, impermanent reality. When she says "we are nature," Griffin is not saying, as the romantics might say, that the human ego encompasses the whole. Her suggestion is much more humble. She is asking us to consider that we are as much a part of nature as are plants, stones, and other animals.

Griffin acknowledges that we "see" nature (a capacity we share with most other animals), that we have a concept of nature (a capacity that may be uniquely human), and that we speak of nature. But she does not conclude that we are set apart from nature by virtue of having a concept of it. Rather, she insists that "we are nature." This statement sounds paradoxical to us because the idea that nature is one thing and we are another is deeply embedded in our thinking. Griffin asks us to reconsider one of the fundamental and unquestioned assumptions of our thought.

It would be a mistake to conclude that Griffin "reduces man to nature." In asserting that we are nature, Griffin asks us to accept our finitude and our temporality. Like the cave, we are changing and continually changed. We too are made from other creatures; one day our bodies will become food for other creatures; our molecules will become something other than what we are today. But Griffin does not deny our ability to perceive, to think, to conceptualize. Rather than reducing us to "brute" nature, Griffin asks us to expand our concept of nature to include all that we are. It is important to stress this point, for it is easy to misread feminist thinkers like Griffin as denying the human capacity for self-reflection and our limited freedom to shape our relation to the earth. Rather, Griffin is calling us to redefine self-consciousness and limited freedom within, rather than in opposition to, our fundamental grounding in nature.

In *Diving Deep and Surfacing,* I discussed visions like Griffin's as examples of nature mysticism, and I named nature mysticism as one of the sources of women's spiritual vision.[19] I confronted the fact that nature mysticism (if it is discussed at all by theorists of mysticism) is denigrated as an inferior form of mysticism. This is because nature mysticism has been defined as union with the finite world, while so-called "higher mysticism" has been defined as union with the infinite, that which utterly transcends the finite, sometimes called the Void, or God. In my book I argued that nature mysticism is an important source of spiritual insight. Now I ask us to consider whether there is any reality "higher" than the finite, the earth, that which changes. I believe that we cannot know such a reality if it exists, and that it is destructive to the reality we do know to focus on an imagined reality that is superior to the finite, embodied, reality we do know.

During the past two summers, while visiting the alleged birthplace of Sappho, I had visions similar to Griffin's. My visions came in the cave at "Minerve's point" in Skala Eresos. I share these visions because I take seriously theology's starting point in our own experience. We will be faithful to that starting point only when we reflect on our own experience as well as that of other women. This vision in Lesbos is not the only nature mystical experience I have had, but it is one of the most intense. I refer to the cave as "She" in the words that follow, because for me (as for Griffin) the cave resonated with my knowledge that caves once were known as the womb and birth canal of earth, her opening.

She appears to me while I am floating in the embrace of the azure sea, rising up from the water in the shape of an enormous vagina. I swim her mouth and climb over anemone- and urchin-covered rocks to her opening. I see that iron ore has stained her mottled granite and sandstone folds the color of blood. I am startled, yet comforted, by a strong smell of salt and fish within. Watching the water flow in and out of her, I feel drawn to her center. I climb back and lean into the crevice. As my body relaxes, I feel a surge of energy, the life force flowing through me. My rhythms merge with hers, the shapes of the rock become the shapes of my body pulsating with energy, flowing into the sea. When I stand up I feel dizzy.

Near the cave is a tiny white church, dedicated to Panaghia, All Holy Mary. I know the church is here because once people knew the cave to be Panaghia, All Holy Mother. I am struck by the contrast between the enormous cave formed by the sea, changing with it, and the small church enclosed against the sea, constantly in need of repair. And I know which place is for me the more holy.

Although these visions come to us through women, visions such as these do not belong to women exclusively. They offer a vision that is essential to us all. These visions in caves contain a clue to a spirituality that can reawaken our sense of connection to all living things, to the life force within and without us. If we experience our connection to this finite and changing earth deeply within ourselves, then we must find the thought of its destruction or even mutilation intolerable. When we deeply and fully affirm this finite changing earth as our true home and accept our own inevitable death, then we must know as well that spirituality is the celebration of our connection to all that is and is changing. Then we will also know that there is no cause or ideology more precious than life itself. Such visions might undergird our survival. With every bone in my body, I pray, "Surely the earth can be saved for us."[20]

NOTES

1. G. Kaufman, "Nuclear Eschatology and the Study of Religion," *Journal of the American Academy of Religion* 51 (March 1983): 14.
2. Kaufman, "Nuclear Eschatology," 13.
3. R. Scheer, *With Enough Shovels: Reagan, Bush, and Nuclear War* (New York: Random, 1982), 18–19.
4. A. Walker, *Horses Make a Landscape More Beautiful* (New York: Harcourt Brace Jovanovich, 1984), 70.
5. W. Morris, ed., *The American Heritage Dictionary of the English Language* (New York: American Heritage Publishing Co., Inc. and Houghton Mifflin Co., 1973), 493.
6. E. Hamilton and H. Carins, eds., *The Collected Dialogues of Plato Including the Letters* (New York: Pantheon Books, 1966), 562.
7. S. Griffin, *Woman and Nature: The Roaring Inside Her* (New York: Harper & Row, 1978), 5.
8. M. Daly, *Pure Lust: Elemental Feminist Philosophy* (Boston: Beacon Press, 1984), 37.
9. See, for example, "Address to a General Audience about Marriage and Celibacy," *Osservatore Romano* (English edition) 27 (741) (July 5, 1982), 3ff.
10. C. Merchant, *Death in Nature: Women, Ecology, and the Scientific Revolution* (San Francisco: Harper & Row, 1980), 22–23.
11. H. Caldicott with N. Herrington and N. Stiskin, *Nuclear Madness: What You Can Do!* (Brookline, MA: Autumn Press, 1978), 67.
12. Scheer, *Shovels*, 210, 3, xi.
13. J. Schell, *The Fate of the Earth* (New York: Avon, 1982). This is the title of the first chapter of *The Fate of the Earth*.

14. *The Malleus Maleficarum of Heinrich Kramer and James Sprenger,* trans. M. Summers (New York: Dover, 1971), 47.

15. A. Rich, *Of Woman Born: Motherhood as Experience and Institution* (New York: W. W. Norton, 1976), 39.

16. Griffin, *Woman and Nature,* 3.

17. Griffin, *Woman and Nature,* 160–61.

18. Griffin, *Woman and Nature,* 226, 224, 226.

19. C. P. Christ, *Diving Deep and Surfacing: Women Writers on Spiritual Quest* (Boston: Beacon Press, 1980), 20–23.

20. Walker, *Horses,* 79.

CHAPTER 4

Spirit and Matter, Public and Private: The Challenge of Feminism to Traditional Dualisms

ROSEMARY RADFORD RUETHER

Christian feminist liberation theology is necessarily interconnected with theologies representing all other movements for human liberation, whether from a class and Third World perspective, a racial or ethnic minority perspective, or perspectives critical of militarism and the abuse of the environment. Feminist theological critique, nevertheless, insists that sexism be recognized as a specific structure of marginalization and oppression that cannot be subsumed under any other category. Sexism requires its own distinct analysis, and women's liberation requires its own distinct dimensions of social transformation. Stated more concretely, what links Christian feminist liberation theology to other liberation theologies is a refusal to separate the material from the spiritual order, but feminist liberation theology focuses specifically on women's work inside and outside the home and the relation between these two spheres of women's lives.

Christianity has, in its New Testament foundations and radical historical traditions, theological principles that should affirm the equality of women in the image of God and their restoration to full personhood as essential to the meaning of redemption. Yet, the church has seldom challenged either the socioeconomic and legal subordination or the personal abuse of women. Throughout much of Christian history, equality in Christ has been understood to apply solely to a redeemed order beyond creation and history, to be realized in heaven. Only with the Enlightenment is there a shift to an egalitarian concept of nature, which challenges the natural and divinely ordained status of hierarchical social structures.

Liberation theologies, theologies that reaffirm the social and historical dimensions of redemption in Christ, have come about through an integration of the biblical messianic symbols with their secular interpretations in liberalism and socialism. But liberation understandings of Christianity continue to be under attack by conservative Christians who wish to invalidate any theology, whether from a feminist, class, or racial minority perspective, that would make socioeconomic liberation an intrinsic part of the meaning of redemption. Such Christians would claim that redemption is a purely "spiritual" matter and has nothing to do with socioeconomic changes.

This privatizing and spiritualizing of salvation is the other side of the individualizing of sin. Sin is recognized only in individual acts, not in structural systems. One may be called to examine one's sinfulness in relation to self-abuse or personal unkindness to the neighbor, but not in terms of the vast collective systems of militarism, racism, poverty, and sexism. Liberation theologies reject this split between private religiosity and public neutrality as based on a faulty anthropology and a misinterpretation of scripture. The privatized self is an illusion. In fact, as persons we exist and have our being in social networks. We cannot understand the full dimension of sin, that is, alienation from God, self, and neighbor, and salvation, or reconciliation between God, self, and neighbor, apart from these social networks that bind us across space and time to the social order.

In its scriptural understanding, sin is not simply a matter of private or personal evil (sexual sin), but it is primarily the great social and historical constructs of evil, although persons also buy into these social constructs on an individual level. The Hebrew prophets even include sexual and religious violations as public evil, the violation of the covenant that binds society together with the cosmos and with God. Much of their attack is directed against the rich and powerful who oppress and defraud the poor, who write oppressive laws, steal the land of poor farmers, and cheat widows and orphans. Even such matters as unjust weights and inflated prices come under their judgmental eye.

The vision of salvation in the prophets is also social and historical, rather than spiritual and otherworldly. Their vision of redemption is one of a new era of peace and justice, when all these wrongs will have been righted, "when each may sit under their own vine and fig tree and none be afraid" (Mic. 4:4). The same perspective is continued in the New Testament in the preaching of Jesus in his hometown synagogue, where he announces, in the language of the prophet Isaiah, that he has come to "preach good news to the poor, release to the captives, the recovering of sight to the blind, to set at liberty those who are oppressed" (Luke 4:18). In the Lord's Prayer, Jesus' definition of God's kingdom come is God's will done on earth (Luke 11:2).

Christian feminist liberation theologians share this general perspective on the social dimension of sin and redemption, except that we stress the dynamic interconnection between personal and political life. Feminist liberation theology bases itself on the dynamic unity of creation and redemption. This means that we as theologians reject the dualism of nature and spirit. We reject both the image of nature or matter as static immanence and the concept of spirit as rootless or antinatural, originating in another world beyond the cosmos, ever repudiating and fleeing from nature, body, and the visible world. This means that we also reject the false conflation of nature or created being with the ontological foundations of the existing oppressive social order. Feminist theology affirms a vision of exodus, of liberation and new being, but emphasizes that these must be rooted in the foundations of being and body, rather than as an antithesis of nature and spirit.

The quest for the good self and good society exists in unbreakable dialectic. One cannot neglect either pole. One cannot assume with social managers, whether socialist or liberal, that reorganized social relations on a structural level will automatically produce a "new humanity." And one also cannot suppose that simply building up an aggregate of converted individuals will cause them to act differently such that society will be redeemed without any attention to structures of power. This is the delusion of revivalism. Instead, we must seek that vision of the liberated self and the liberated society that best promotes the open dialectical interplay between the two.

The dialectic of liberated self with liberated society begins with a critique of modern patriarchal industrialism as manifested by both capitalist and socialist practices regarding women's work. This critique requires in addition not only analysis of both conservative Christian and male liberation theologies and politics but also white middle-class feminist presuppositions. In order to see the total picture of gender oppression in modern patriarchal industrialism we have to look at the dual roles of women in the home and in the public work force and the interconnections between the two. Instead of making the male sphere the human norm and attempting to assimilate women into it, we need to ask whether it is not necessary to move in the opposite direction. We should take the creation and sustaining of human life as the center of that which binds liberated self with liberated society, and reintegrate the alienated work world into it.

Feminists are all too accustomed to efforts to colonize their movement and thus to declare that feminism is unnecessary because the national liberation movement or the socialist movement will "take care" of the women's issues. Black activists have in the past derided feminism as a white women's movement and declared that black women do not need feminism because black liberation liberates all black people without special attention to gender. Similarly, Third World liberation movements condemn feminism as middle-class and claim that the revolution of the workers or of the oppressed nation will simultaneously liberate women. All of this is of a piece with the historic inability of patriarchal thinking to recognize women as autonomous persons in their own right, rather than appendages of a male social system.

In addition to lack of support from the left, feminism today is under renewed attack from the right, which simply and openly asserts that any personal or socioeconomic autonomy of women threatens the organic fabric of the social order. According to George Gilder, social psychologist for Reaganomics, males are incapable of entering civilized or responsible relationships unless they are dominant and women are dependent. Faced with an independent woman with whom he must enter into a covenant of equals, the male ego collapses, the male flees from settled familial relationships, and all social order disintegrates into chaos.[1] (If such an immature male ego is indeed the glue holding together the social order, then human society is certainly in trouble.) The right-wing profamily movement focuses on efforts to legislate the patriarchal family by making feminism illegal in the schools, withdrawing funds for battered women's shelters or day care centers, defeating equal rights amendments ensuring female unemployment or exploitative wages—all this so women will be forced back into personal and economic dependency on males.

These strategies are totally misguided, even from the point of view of their own proclaimed goals of supporting families. Women's liberation did not create the rootless and mobile nuclear family, the woman worker, the unparented child, the high divorce rate, or the need for birth control. Modern technology and capitalism have created this new face of the family. Feminists have tried to respond to the contradictions imposed on women by the dual systems of patriarchy and capitalism.

Feminists must indeed recognize the inadequacy of any movement for women's liberation carried out solely in a white middle-class framework. Such a movement tends to ignore the underclasses of women, the armies of unpaid and underpaid domestic workers, service workers, clerical workers, and factory workers who service the physical and social machinery of the reproductive and productive systems. In practice, the rights won by women for women within a middle-class context have not been available as tools of liberation for masses of women. For example, if entrance into law school presupposes wealth, leisure, independence, money for household help or child care, then the right to enter law school does not change the lives of most women, including most women whose middle-class status derives from economic dependency on middle-class husbands.

In practice, the rights won for women in a white middle-class context become class privileges of elite women, which integrate them in a token way into the educated and professional ruling classes but have little effect on the overall class and gender structures that confine most women to exploitative relations both in the family and in the work world. This is to say, a feminism that concentrates only upon token participation of women in male professional elite circles does not address the total system of gender dependency that affects all women as women, including this apparently exceptional class. It is a truncated and partial understanding of the total system of gender oppression as this actually exists in the interlocking systems of patriarchy and capitalism.

Capitalism and Working Women

Working women in industrial society are oppressed workers both within the family and in the public world of paid labor. They are, therefore, doubly handicapped by the difficulties of connecting the two spheres. In the home, women function as the unpaid "re-producers" of the work force. This role refers not only to the physical reproduction, nursing, and nurturing of children as the future work force; it also means that they service the adult workers, that is, the husband and sometimes grown children or other working family members, who repair to the home both for their physical needs, such as rest, food, and laundry, and for their psychological needs created by the frustrations of the job. This vital role of reproduction and recuperation of the work force is the indispensable base of the entire economic system, although its value remains invisible and unaccounted for in the GNP. Although grown daughters or other females in the household may share this role with the wife-mother of the family, this is generally regarded as uniquely "women's work," so much so that men feel their masculinity demeaned when asked to participate in it to any extent. Even in American society today, which prides itself on the sharing of domestic roles between men and women, evidence shows that when women work outside the home, the family adjusts primarily by skimping on this work or rushing it into the after-work hours, rather than by shifting any significant portion of this work to the males of the household.

This domestic role also conditions fundamentally the sort of work to which women are directed in the paid labor force. In this sphere, women are disproportionately structured into the areas of service, clerical work, and rote manual labor. Women make up the vast majority of those who serve the food, clean the buildings, and type and file the papers of the industrial complex. Ninety percent of the women who work outside the home work in sex-segregated occupations with low status, low pay, and low job security and benefits. Within these occupations, they are treated as a secondary and marginal work force with rapid turnover. As a secondary labor force, they are also viewed as a group that can be drawn into the work force in greater numbers in time of need, such as the periods of rapid industrialization, or in times of war.[2]

Wartime in particular reveals the expedient nature of the prevailing ideology about womanhood in patriarchal society. In war, women are needed to hold many jobs normally held by men. All the ideological systems of socialization such as government, church, and public media suddenly reverse their usual messages and urge women to become truck drivers and workers in heavy industry, to take over the empty seats in the university, and even to preach from the pulpits in the churches vacated by males, as their "patriotic duty." When the war is over the messages are again reversed. Women are urged to return home to their true "womanly" duties in order to provide places for the men. The operative assumption that remains intact behind this whole process is male priority in the right to the public job.[3]

Women are seen essentially as dependents whose work in the public sector can be activated or dismissed according to male needs. Even today, with so much emphasis on women in leadership positions, less than three percent of working women are found in traditionally male, high-status professions, such as medicine, law, the clergy, and academics. Among the ten percent of working women classified as professionals, most work in female stereotyped professions, such as primary school teachers, nurses, and librarians. These professions are characteristically much lower paid and have much lower status than male professions with comparable educational requirements. Generally, women do not even control the leadership positions of these professions, that is, grade school principal or head librarian. The domestic stereotype of women as playing an auxiliary and service role in relation to men fundamentally conditions paid female work on every level.[4]

Women not only play the service roles in both family and paid labor, but they are fundamentally handicapped in both spheres by untenable demands to carry both roles fully. The working woman is constantly harassed by lack of time and energy to fulfill the middle-class ideal of mother and homemaker. All manner of social evil, from male impotence to juvenile delinquency, is blamed on her role in the work force, even though this work is an essential part of the family income. In addition, the working woman is fundamentally handicapped on the job by the need to provide for the domestic servicing of her own work role and that of her family. The home-work split is designed to free the male worker from servicing his own labor, so that he can devote his energies "full-time" to the job. The woman, by contrast, has to be her own "wife," not to mention wife and mother for others in the family. The disappearance of domestic servants or relatives from the modern middle-class family is only partially compensated for by mechanization of housework.

What this means concretely is that working women have a second job. They put in several hours each day shopping, cleaning, cooking, caring for children, something their male counterparts in traditional marriage do not do. The ambitious woman who seeks to compete with men in high status careers must then consider relinquishing marriage, or at least children, since these relations handicap her ability to work, while the male is assumed to be supported in his job by a wife. In addition, the male who also shares domestic work with his wife is handicapped in his job vis-à-vis his male colleagues with conventional marriage relationships.

There are further, even more serious, problems in the interconnections of the domestic and paid work roles of women in industrial society. The home is designated as a realm of compensatory status and ownership for males who are denied ownership and control over the means of production on the job. Protest against or even awareness of lack of ownership of the work world is suppressed by directing each worker to think of his home as the sphere of his pride in ownership and personal possessions. His wife and children are themselves seen as a part of this ownership. His ability to decorate his home with conspicuous objects of consumption is the measure of his status in a capitalist society. Lack of home ownership indicates lack of status and creates thereby a further cause for alienation.

Whether the home is owned or rented, women and the home not only decorate and service male work, they provide an outlet for male frustrations on the job. In a capitalist work structure where men are so alienated from their work, they are often humiliated by their subservience to their bosses. Once they are home they may unleash anger, suppressed on the job, by verbally and physically abusing their dependents. Women and other family members must absorb, physically and psychologically, these outbursts of frustrations that spill over into the home from the job.

The ideology of femininity and female subordination supports the basic structures of such a capitalist society and keeps women in place in their service role in the home. No matter how many women actually work and must work, no matter how few members of the society actually live in the nuclear, heterosexual monogamous family with sufficiently paid husband and unpaid wife, this still remains the ideological norm, rendering any other roles of women or any other type of family nonnormative and questionable. This domestic ideology continues to socialize men and women to think that men should rule and women should serve, not only at home, but on the job as well.

This ideology of femininity includes the sexual subjugation of women. Women's bodies are viewed as sources of sexual relief for men and of baby making, whose fruits belong to men, not to women themselves. The renewed struggle of the conservative forces of American society against birth control and abortion shows that patriarchal culture has by no means abandoned the basic premise that women should not be allowed primary decision-making powers over their own reproduction. The ideology of femininity is designed to idealize women as the passive nurturers and supporters of men and children; to praise women who make themselves passive victims; to rebuke those women as unnatural and "unfeminine" who put their own needs and personal development first.

The Christian churches continue to play a key role in this ideology of the feminine. They exalt the feminine as the true Christianity. At the same time, by reproducing the dominance of males over females in the symbolism and hierarchy of the church, they make clear that their version of the idealization of service sacralizes the hierarchy of dominance and servitude, rather than subverting it. Women are the "highest" Christians by acquiescing to be the "lowest." Rather than fostering liberation, the gospel is used to sacralize servitude.

Socialism and Working Women

This fundamental handicap of women in industrial society has been modified, but not fundamentally changed, in socialist societies whether secular or religious. A few years ago Hilda Scott published a book titled *Does Socialism Liberate Women?* This work was based on studies of sex hierarchy in employment in Czechoslovakia. Despite efforts in the Communist Party to include women fully in higher education and professions, and to provide child care in order to free women for employment, women were still generally found at the bottom of their professions, receiving lower pay and fewer benefits than men on the same level. After all the studies were completed, the author concluded that the single basic cause underlying this lower status of women on the job was the handicap of the "second shift."

On an average, women worked four hours a day beyond their paid work role by providing domestic services. This extra time sent women scurrying to shops, nurseries, and kitchens after work, while their male counterparts had the time to volunteer for party offices, take refresher courses, or go to the gym or the bars where many of the vital links between male colleagues were forged. This extra work role not only left women more tired on the job than men, but it also eliminated them from many of the processes by which men advanced themselves in the "meritocracy." This domestic role of women also kept the same psychological and cultural model of male-female relations intact in the whole society. Women on the job ran every race with their male colleagues as persons who both couldn't and shouldn't advance too high up the ladder.[5]

Thus when a feminist liberation theologian turns to socialism as a key to what liberation for women might be, she discovers that socialism also promotes a certain male bias. This bias disposes socialist theorists to think primarily of the oppression of men in the workplace. It assumes that women are included in socialist analysis without considering the hidden economic and cultural connections linking women's subordination on the job with their service role in the home. More recent socialist feminist thought has focused particularly on the unpaid roles of women in the home and the way this affects the relation of women to the paid labor force, but the implications of this have yet to be fully explored. For example, is it enough simply to think of increasing collectivization of the work of the home through communal nurseries, communal kitchens, or laundries in order to free women for equal status on the job? If collective control means *state control,* this may be experienced as progressive alienation of areas of one's own life for external power. Socialist theorists thus need to ask in new ways what it means to restore ownership of the means of production *to the people.*

If the state itself becomes an expression of a bureaucratic ruling class, this only exchanges one master for another. Returning ownership of the means of production to the people must mean restoring primary control and decision making to the base communities of workers. If we include the questions of women and the economic role of the home in this perspective, new aspects of the communal base of a libertarian socialist society come into play. We might think of such things as primary collectives of households for housing or child care where ownership and decision making remain with the people involved. We might think of new and more flexible social patterns to link home and work spaces in more organic ways. For example, worker-managed nurseries in the workplace could create a new relationship between parents and children by relating family and work in less alienating ways.

Thus a feminist critique, when directed toward socialist theory, explodes the limits of dominant socialist traditions and suggests that issues unique to women cannot be solved within the limits of a socialist system. Instead, we are forced to consider, in a much more fundamental way, the difference between women's role as child-bearer and nurturer and the male economic and political sphere that has been defined over and against it. As I have already suggested, this entails a shift in what we view to be normative and central to human society, namely, a focus upon the creation and sustaining of human life and the reintegration of an alienated work world into it.

Visions of a New Society

What, then, is the society that we seek? We seek a society that affirms the values of democratic participation, of the equal value of all persons as the basis for their civil equality, and of their equal access to the educational and work opportunities of the society. But more, we seek a democratic socialist society that dismantles sexist and class hierarchies, that restores ownership and management of work to the base communities of workers themselves who then create networks of economic and political relationships. Still more, we seek a society built on organic community, where the processes of child raising, of education, of work, of culture have been integrated in such a way as to allow both men and women to share child nurturing and homemaking, on the one hand, and creative activity and decision making in the larger society, on the other hand. Finally, we seek a nonmilitarist society where human and nonhuman ecological systems have been integrated into harmonious and mutually supportive, rather than antagonistic, relations.

We need a concept of deity that best organizes and integrates the religious significance and value of the relation between human life and human work.[6] The Holy One who is the foundation both of our being and our new being embraces both the roots of the material matrix of our existence and also its endlessly new creative potential. The God/ess who is the foundation of our being and new being does not direct us back to a stifled, dependent self, nor uproot us in a spirit trip outside the earth. Rather, s/he leads us to a converted center, the harmonization of self and body, self and society, self and cosmos. We cannot split a spiritual antisocial redemption from a human self as social being who is embedded in sociopolitical and ecological systems. Neither can we imagine that a reconstructed public order is possible without converted selves. Rather, we must recognize that sinfulness exists precisely in this splitting and deformation of our true relationships to all the networks of being with which we are connected. We must find liberation in an authentic harmony of all with all that is incarnate in social, historical life.

The issue of the liberation of women restores to center stage the basic questions about the meaning of an unalienated, humanized life in postindustrial society. How can we make the social and technological machinery of human life a means to humanized living, rather than making human life the servant of its own machinery for the sake of the profits of the few? This is the critical question. It is also the question on which feminism, socialism, and liberation Christianity can converge in a common quest.

NOTES

1. G. Gilder, *Wealth and Poverty* (New York: Bantam, 1981).
2. E. Leacock, "History, Development, and the Division of Labor by Sex: Implications for Organization," *Signs* 7 (1981): 474–91.
3. L. J. Rupp, *Mobilizing Women for War* (Princeton: Princeton University Press, 1978), 137–491.
4. Leacock, "History," 474–91.
5. H. Scott, *Does Socialism Liberate Women? Experience from Eastern Europe* (Boston: Beacon 1974), 191–208.
6. For a discussion of the symbol of the goddess, see Starhawk, *The Spiral Dance: The Rebirth of the Ancient Religion of the Goddess* (San Francisco: Harper & Row, 1979).

Part Two

EMBODIMENT, COMMUNICATION, AND ETHICS

CHAPTER 5

Problems with Feminist Theory: Historicity and the Search for Sure Foundations

SHEILA GREEVE DAVANEY

Feminist theology represents a radical departure both from more classical modes of theological discourse and from most contemporary theological options. Convinced of the oppressive character of male-conceived theology, feminists have undertaken the critical task of uncovering the patriarchal features of male theology and the constructive task of developing alternative theological frameworks responsive to women. While diversity and degrees of radicalness characterize feminist theological endeavors, feminist theology as a whole, from its most accommodating to its most uncompromising rejection of male theology, stands as a fundamental challenge to the methods and contents of many contemporary theological options.

While affirming that this turn to women represents a revolution within theological discourse, it is also my contention that in important ways feminist theology does *not* stand outside of the developments that have shaped modern thought, but that we have inherited, along with men, certain uniquely modern problems and that our work is an example of the contemporary struggle with these issues. In particular, I believe that two central issues have bedeviled the modern period. These are the Enlightenment-inspired quest for certain truth and the countermodern recognition of the historical and, hence, relative character of all claims to truth. This essay will argue that these themes have reemerged in feminist theology's claim of a normative vision and in its assertion of the perspectival and conditioned nature of all human knowledge. Further, I will suggest that these assertions stand in problematic and unresolved relation to one another within much feminist thought and that what further alternatives may emerge in feminist theology will depend, in good part, on how these tensions are confronted and resolved and moved beyond. By way of setting forth this line of argument I will offer a brief rendition of the historical foundations of these issues, followed by an exploration of how feminist theological options are presently being portrayed, and I will close with an examination of how these options might be reconsidered in light of the discussion concerning historical relativism and the quest for truth.

From the late medieval period onward, Western theology and philosophy witnessed and contributed to the steady demise of the traditional authorities upon which earlier theological frameworks had depended for their justification. In particular, the church's role as source and arbitrator of truth came under compelling and ultimately fatal attack as thinkers sought to articulate new foundations for claims to knowledge and truth that were not predicated on appeals to supernatural or religious authorities.[1]

This quest for new foundations for certitude became a driving force within the seventeenth and eighteenth centuries, culminating in what has come to be known as the Enlightenment's Ideal of Reason. Eschewing appeals to tradition and religious authority, Enlightenment thinkers proposed reason as the proper source of knowledge and adjudicator of truth claims. For them, reason was an autonomous means of understanding reality and discovering the structure of nature. Assumed to be substantially the same in all persons, reason offered a source of knowledge not tied to the privileged realms of revelation or ecclesiastical proclamation. The proper workings of reason were thought to provide several important steps to knowledge: universally valid criteria for assessing claims; objectivity, both in the sense of impartiality and adequacy to reality; and a means for the continued progress of humanity epitomized in the advances of the natural sciences. In an age of the erosion of traditional foundations, reason appeared to offer a new basis for certitude and a firm grounding for the optimistic hope in progress.

With this progressive elevation of reason coalesced conceptions of knowledge and truth whose impact has reverberated through the modern world. Philosopher Richard Rorty, in his work, *Philosophy and the Mirror of Nature,* traces the development of the central metaphor of reason as the mirror of nature, that which reflects and reproduces reality. With reason interpreted in this fashion, Rorty argues, knowledge came to be understood as representing reality, and truth referred to the accuracy of such depiction. That is, truth finally consisted in the correspondence between the reflection and that which was, or the *correspondence of thought to reality*. [2] This search for a common ground, beyond privileged authorities, that offers certitude and a normative perspective and can provide true access to reality is a hope that still finds expression in much of contemporary thought, including feminist theology. However, further developments have called the foundations for such a hope into question.

The seeds for the critique of the Enlightenment-inspired ideal of reason can be found within the Enlightenment itself. In particular the foundations of what is now labeled as historical consciousness can be located within this age of rationality. A central example of this is the commencement of historical criticism in relation to biblical sources in the eighteenth century. During this period and later, many rationalists turned to historical analysis and criticism as an ally in their opposition to ecclesiastical authority and the appeal to revelation and tradition. Not only would historical criticism, as it developed in the nineteenth and twentieth centuries, continue to raise problems concerning the relation of scripture to dogma, but it would lead as well to questions concerning the reliability and status of the biblical material itself. Furthermore, while reason and history were interpreted by many rationalists as allies, insofar as biblical criticism shared in the development of historical consciousness in general, it contributed not only to the undermining of traditional authorities, but also to the eventual historicizing of reason itself and thus to the erosion of reason's own claims to universality, neutrality, and objectivity.

Further sources for the historicizing of reason can be found within the Enlightenment's own attempt to analyze reason's working and to delineate the limits of human reason. The very examination of the limits of reason laid the basis, whether wittingly or unwittingly, for rejection of that universal character of knowledge. In the words of philosopher Steve Doty, "It is the very recognition of the finitude of human reason which opens up the possibility of taking history seriously. Modern historical consciousness arises with the discovery of the limitations of human reason, a discovery which calls into question the ideals of the Enlightenment."[3]

While other thinkers, including the Romantics, suggested a critical stance toward the Enlightenment, the most crucial challenge in the nineteenth century to those ideals came in the work of Friedrich Nietzsche. Nietzsche not only wholeheartedly denied the Enlightenment's quest for certitude and its aim for universal, necessary knowledge, but also countered the assumptions underlying these quests with the claim that all knowledge was perspectival and that such perspectives were the expressions of the will to power. With his analysis Nietzsche undermined the confidence in reason's neutrality and objectivity and with it the conviction that transperspectival criteria for assessing the validity of claims could be discovered. For many who followed Nietzsche, the assurance that truth was indeed the correspondence of thought to reality was lost forever and was replaced with a vision of competing perspectives, each embodying and serving its own will to dominance.

Many developments in the twentieth century rejected the rising tide of historical consciousness or sought ways around the dilemmas raised by the recognition of humanity's fundamental historicity. Philosophical positivism continued the search for a scientific form of knowledge, and in theology, Karl Barth's theological positivism accepted the limitations placed upon reason in the arena of normal knowledge while arguing for absolute truth and valid knowledge found in faith and grounded in an ahistorical revelation.[4]

If some continued to embody, albeit in a transformed fashion, the convictions of the Enlightenment, other persons and movements took the problem of human historicity as a central concern. This can be seen most clearly in what has come to be known as the critique of ideology. A number of schools of thought can be brought under this rubric, including Marxism, critical theory, and the sociology of knowledge. While offering distinctive analyses, these schools share the basic insight that individuals, communities, institutions, as well as ideas, symbols, and myths, are all influenced and given shape by their locus in history and by the temporal and social setting in which they take place. There is, according to this view, no such thing as objective, universally valid experience or knowledge. Human beings and our knowledge are irrevocably historical and hence conditioned by time and place.

The critics of ideology did not stop with the assertion that all knowledge was perspectival. Rather, in a manner reminiscent of

Nietzsche, they argued that such perspectives are not innocent but inevitably reflect the interests of the knower. Thus, they envisioned as central to their task the unmasking of those perspectives that asserted universal validity, that claimed to represent neutral and objective truth while, in fact, they embodied the interests of one class, race, or sex.

Yet, while the practitioners of the critique of ideology affirmed the perspectival and relative character of knowledge, and while many of them accordingly renounced any claim to absolute truth or moral certitude, they often rejected the full nihilistic implications of this direction of thought. Central figures suggested that while all views are historical and conditioned, some perspectives are more valid than others. Whether in the form of Karl Marx's "proletariat" or Karl Mannheim's "unattached intellectual" or, more recently, liberation theology's "poor," many have suggested that *thoroughgoing* nihilism, in which all values are commensurate and hence indistinguishable, need not be the conclusion of the historicizing of knowledge and truth.

In recent years, these critics of ideology who both accept a form of relativism and deny that such acceptance entails nihilism have been severely criticized by the French philosopher Michel Foucault. Arguing that knowledge and interests are fused in all situations and not just in the distortion of ideology, Foucault suggests that the search for a perspective beyond ideology, illusion, and error is fruitless and wrongheaded; indeed, it represents a kind of nostalgia, a false longing for innocence.[5] Rather than truth being a pure, nondistorted reflection of "the way things really are," truth is that which in any given historical moment can make its will felt, can bring about its effects. The distinction between truth and falsehood is not a question of ontological validity but of which forms of discourse are *accepted* as truth, both by virtue of coercion and because of the possibilities such realms of discourse bring into being.

This perspective linking truth and power entails the profound questioning of the correspondence theory of truth in all of its forms. Both on the level of historical claims and on the level of metaphysical or ontological assertions, this perspective argues that the grounds for delineating error and truth can no longer be made by appeal to "adequacy to reality." Instead, a thoroughgoing analysis must be undertaken to determine how in specific situations certain "regimes of truth" (Foucault) have come to be accepted as the norms for societal organization and practice. That is, not an ontology of truth but a politics of truth is what is demanded today.

It is this progressive loss of norms for evaluating claims to truth that we face in the twentieth century, and it is precisely this loss and its implications that feminist theology has yet to confront fully in its critical and constructive endeavors. The remainder of this essay will explore how feminist theologians have come to delineate the various strands of feminist theology; it will argue that present distinctions do not adequately uncover the understandings of truth and knowledge operative within feminist theology; and finally, it will raise the queston of what feminist theology would look like if it were more fully cognizant of and responsive to the dilemmas arising from a radical historical consciousness. In order to facilitate this exploration, I will concentrate on the recent work of reformist Christian theologians Rosemary Ruether and Elisabeth Schüssler Fiorenza, and of revolutionary Mary Daly.

Within feminist theological circles, the current means of locating women along the feminist spectrum is to refer to the division between the "reformists" and the "revolutionaries," the Christian or Jewish feminists and the adherents of a women-centered Goddess religion. This distinction has been fruitful in that it has illuminated the diversity of basic commitments, of assessments of Western religious traditions, and of strategies for the transformation of culture and society that characterize feminist theology. However, by stressing the differences between these approaches, this mode of analysis has failed to recognize the profound similarities shared by these perspectives, in particular, the often unexamined assumptions concerning the character of truth and the relation of reality and thought. As a means of uncovering this other level of feminist discourse, I will first concentrate upon the open divisions among these feminist thinkers and then explore their often covert similarities.

Rosemary Radford Ruether[6] and Elisabeth Schüssler Fiorenza,[7] while offering distinctive alternatives, have much in common. Each acknowledges the patriarchal history and character of Christianity, arguing that from its earliest roots in Hebraic religion to its contemporary setting, the social contexts within which Christianity emerged and developed have embodied an androcentric ethos and value system and that Christianity has incorporated this ethos in its texts, doctrines, and practices (IM, xv, 3, 20). Hence, according to

Schüssler Fiorenza and Ruether, a major task of reformist theologians is the unmasking of this masculine bias and the rejection of patriarchal assumptions.

However, neither Schüssler Fiorenza nor Ruether concludes from her analyses that Christianity should be left behind. A major reason neither jettisons Christianity is that both are convinced certain elements within this tradition challenge patriarchy. Ruether, exploring what she labels the prophetic-liberating tradition originating within Hebrew religion and finding expression in Jesus' alliance with the powerless, speaks of "intimations of alternatives" where one can glimpse not the sanctification of male dominance but a vision of "equivalence and mutuality between men and women, between classes and races, between humanity and nature" (SG, 22). Schüssler Fiorenza, while critical of Ruether's appeal to the prophetic tradition as too idealized and lacking in historical acuity, proposes her own intimations of alternatives. Recognizing the androcentric character of biblical texts, Schüssler Fiorenza argues that feminist criticism must go behind the texts to the sociocultural world of the Jesus movement and the early Christian community, and that in so doing women will discover traces of "the equalitarian inclusive practice and theology of early Christians" (IM, 56) and of a "discipleship of equals" (IM, 35). By referring to these traces, neither thinker claims to have discovered a pristine essence of Christianity that is "really" liberating to women. Instead, they view Christianity as a historical phenomenon that bears the marks of its patriarchal milieu but also contains alternative visions that resonate with the feminist quest for wholeness (SG, 22).

A second central reason for remaining within the Christian tradition lies, according to Schüssler Fiorenza and Ruether, in the historical character of human nature; humans are products of their histories, and unless they acknowledge and confront those histories and claim them as their own, they will continue to be their victims rather than their heirs (IM, xix). Further, this history is *women's* history; women, despite androcentric renderings of history, have been central to Christian life and community, and to leave Christianity is both to deny that centrality and to abandon the memory of earlier women who struggled for wholeness in a world where male power reigned. Hence, for both these reformists a major task is the rejection of the peripheral status given to women and a reclaiming of the center of the Christian tradition.

Radical feminist Mary Daly concurs with Schüssler Fiorenza and Ruether that patriarchy was the social context within which biblical religions arose and developed.[8] However, she draws more comprehensively negative conclusions from this insight and offers a more radical proposal for feminist response to this history of misogyny. First, Daly interprets biblical religion as having as a central dynamic the destruction of what Daly believes were earlier women-centered traditions; at heart these religions seek the literal control and extinction of the female spirit (G/E, PL, passim). Further, where the reformists find intimations of liberation and wholeness, Daly sees only pseudoalternatives that really function as more subtle means of furthering the oppression of women. Daly concludes from her analysis that Christianity (like all other male-produced religions) is a form of phallicism, that is, the worship of male power and the negation of female potency, and that therefore patriarchal religion is not reformable and women who engage in such revisionist activities are expending much-needed energy in the service of those who ultimately seek the destruction of women.

Thus, Daly urges women to step outside the traditions and mindsets of patriarchy and to create new space, new community, new ritual, and new language. Her recent work has focused on this latter concern with language; contending that language both creates reality and participates in it, she undertakes the task of developing a language and worldview that flows from and shapes anew the experience of women no longer affiliated with or loyal to the traditions of patriarchy.

These diverse options represent real alternatives; the import of the division between reformers and revolutionaries and the intellectual and existential choices such a division entail cannot be ignored. However, in our present context, it is important to ask whether this is the *only* model for distinguishing feminist theological alternatives, whether it does not mask other important issues by its concentration on the question of whether one has remained a Christian or Jew or opted for a women-centered religious vision. At this juncture, I will turn again to the issue of relativism and the question of truth and reconsider the positions developed by Schüssler Fiorenza, Ruether, and Daly in light of these concerns rather than according to the question of allegiance to or rejection of inherited religious traditions.

Building on the analysis set forth above, Elisabeth Schüssler

Fiorenza appears clearly within the camp of those who are convinced of the historical character of thought and hence the relative, conditioned nature of all texts, worldviews, and belief systems. Trained in the methods of historical criticism, Schüssler Fiorenza asserts that biblical texts are neither the products of verbal inspiration nor pristine doctrinal formulations but rather historical documents forged in concrete situations, reflecting the struggles of particular communities (IM, vx). Moreover, Schüssler Fiorenza insists that present interpretation of these texts and their social milieu is also an interest-laden process and that all claims to so-called scholarly "objectivity" are a failure to admit one's presuppositions and commitments (IM, xvii). Schüssler Fiorenza seeks to avoid such obfuscation by stating that her commitments are to women's struggle against patriarchal domination and that out of such commitments comes a normative stance that judges texts and traditions in relation to this clear feminist allegiance. Thus, she does not carry out historical analysis in order to discover the normative point in the past from which all else, including contemporary theological formulations, will be judged. Rather, she self-consciously seeks her norms for evaluation in the present movements of oppressed persons against domination.

Schüssler Fiorenza can thus be seen to resonate with those thinkers who take human historicity seriously and who have therefore engaged in the critique of ideology. However, she, like other critics of ideological distortion, does not carry her analysis through to a more radical Foucault-like conclusion; she rejects both a nihilism in which the distinction between truth and distortion no longer holds and also any strong relativism. The analysis is more difficult on this level, for Schüssler Fiorenza, like so many of the thinkers she repudiates, is not always clear about the assumptions that underlie her position. Nonetheless, it is important to delve into those deeper levels if we are to understand the full implications of her position.

The norm that Schüssler Fiorenza proposes for the theological evaluation of texts and traditions is the above-stated principle of how far and in what ways do these texts and traditions support women's struggle for liberation. It is against this "feminist scale of values" that the Christian tradition is to be judged. However, this norm is not only the interpretative principle for judging claims about women and human relationships; it is also the principle in relation to which assertions concerning the divine and the nature of reality are understood as valid, indeed revelatory, or not. In Schüssler Fiorenza's words, "Biblical revelation and truth are given only in those texts and interpretative models that transcend critically their patriarchal frameworks and allow for a vision of Christian women as historical and theological subjects and actors" (IM, 30).

Thus, on both a human level and a transcendent level, Schüssler Fiorenza rejects the notion that all views are commensurate. Instead, while all are historical and relative, some, in accordance with her feminist norm, are more valid than others. The all-important question is, why should this feminist scale of values be so normative? Is it because Schüssler Fiorenza believes this is the best human norm available at this historical point or simply that as a woman committed to women it is her stance? It is my contention that Schüssler Fiorenza assumes, though without explicit argument, that this feminist norm is not only historically compelling but also has ontological grounding; that is to say, it is also normative because it reflects divine reality and purposes and corresponds to "the way things are." In her work, Schüssler Fiorenza assumes the ontological reality of God and, further, that such divine reality is the source of the equalitarian possibilities she perceives in the Christian tradition. Alongside these assumptions, I suggest, is the implicit supposition that the principles or values that most closely correspond to this divine reality are the most normative and that it is precisely the feminist principle that fulfills this requirement. Hence, the feminist principle is normative both because it reflects a commitment to women and because it corresponds to the nature and purposes of the divine.

Schüssler Fiorenza can thus be seen to offer a somewhat uneasy combination of the insights of the historical consciousness and the continuing concern for a norm by which to ascertain truth and certitude. On an explicit level she works out of the traditions that take seriously historicity and the relative character of human life and thought. Yet she refuses to follow the logic of that position to the conclusion that all visions and assertions of validity are stripped of their claims to ontological truth. Instead she maintains, against patriarchal claims to truth and revelation, that the equalitarian vision is normative because it corresponds to her commitments to women and, implicitly, because it reflects the nature and purposes of ultimate reality itself. Radical relativism is ruled out.

Rosemary Ruether develops the same kind of implicit argument as Schüssler Fiorenza. She takes for granted that ideas, texts, and forms of human experience that have arisen within the confines of patriarchal history to some degree reflect the values of that socio-cultural context. Furthermore, she quite clearly speaks about historical particularity and limits in her rejection of any facile claims to universalism. However, she too refuses to take either the road of nihilism or radical relativism. This refusal can be seen most clearly in her distinction between false and true naming. Patriarchal views of the world and their concomitant understandings of male and female relations constitute not merely a competing interpretation to nonpatriarchal visions but a fundamental misnaming and distortion of reality. Furthermore, Ruether, as did Schüssler Fiorenza, links false and true naming with correspondence or lack thereof to divine reality. This divine reality Ruether labels the primal matrix and assumes, though without clarity about the bases for such an assumption, that this matrix is that which generates all things, is the source of new being, the one who opens up new possibilities of equality (SG, 38, 69, 85, 258). As such it is the ground of the hopes for mutuality and integrity that are at the heart of the feminist vision. Truth, then, is assessed according to the norm of the extent to which a vision promotes the full humanity of women, and such promotion is assumed to correspond to divine reality and its purposes (SG, 19).

Thus it can be seen that the two representatives of the "reformist" perspective propose as a critical norm for evaluating truth claims the furtherance of women's full humanity, but that accompanying this norm and giving it ontological status is the assumption that such female becoming corresponds to and reflects divine purpose and will. Hence, visions supporting feminist aspirations are not simply compelling human views, conditioned and relative, but indeed "true" if not absolute in that they bear the mark of divine validation and reflect the "true nature of things."

It is now important to turn to the work of Mary Daly and analyze whether her "revolutionary" stance entails a different interpretation of truth than her "reformist" counterparts. From her early work in *Beyond God the Father* to her more recent book, *Pure Lust*, Daly has had a sharp sense of the historical character of human worldviews, symbols, and belief systems. Her early critical material had as a central concern the unmasking of male claims to absolute truth and universal validity; with profound insight, Daly systematically unearthed the foundations of masculine power and purposes in doctrines and practices that purported divine sanction and revelatory certitude. Furthermore, in her creative efforts, Mary Daly has consistently maintained the constructive and imaginative nature of her and other feminists' work. Again and again she uses the language of artistic creation to describe the feminist task and has been adamant that the images and visions emerging in her work are ever-changing metaphors and myths rather than static attempts to capture and domesticate reality.

Despite her insistence upon the constructive/creative character of these symbols and visions, Daly, no less than Schüssler Fiorenza and Ruether, refuses to understand such feminist perspectives as merely alternatives to male-construed interpretations of reality. Indeed, in a manner far more explicit than either Schüssler Fiorenza or Ruether, Daly argues for the validity of feminist visioning on the grounds that it participates in and corresponds to ultimate reality.

In developing her argument, Daly uses theologian Paul Tillich's assertion that symbols, insofar as they are alive and vital, participate in the reality which they seek to symbolize (PL, 25). Women's symbols and visions participate in what Daly labels Ontological or Elemental Reality. Women, through their creative imaginations and their life-loving relationships are opened to the life-giving forces of ultimate reality. Women, furthermore, are capable of such knowledge of and participation in Elemental Reality because they possess, naturally and through experience, what Daly names female intuition and Realizing Reason; this connection is no supernatural conduit of revelation but "an Elementally natural process/unfolding." According to Daly, "the correspondence between her mind and deep reason has always been there" (PL, 163). Thus Daly proposes her own correspondence theory of truth, with truth residing in the dynamic correspondence between the creative, life-loving minds of "musing women" and the "intelligible structures of reality" as women seek to live out their commitment to themselves, each other, and the earth (PL, 163). Daly is careful to avoid claims of final truth; while she argues that radical feminists, or Nag-Gnostics, "sense with certainty the reality of transcendental knowledge" she advocates continual recognition of new awareness and transformed consciousness (PL, 12). Nonetheless, despite this dynamic dimension of her thought, she maintains, like Schüssler Fiorenza and Ruether, that Elemental, Ontological Reality is life-generating and that its purposes cohere with the life-loving commitments of radical feminism. Moreover, in a more radical form than Ruether and Schüssler Fiorenza, she suggests that women have a unique capacity to know and participate in this ultimate sphere.

Finally, Daly stresses this notion of correspondence between radical feminist consciousness and Ontological Reality by *denying* that such a correspondence exists between male consciousness and Elemental Be-ing. Throughout her work, Daly continuously refers to male visions, symbols, and beliefs as lies, deceptions, reversals, false perceptions, and fabrications. These products of the male imagination do not, as do women's symbols, participate in Being but in nonbeing, in "necrophilic nothing-loving" (PL, 79). Because they correspond to, reflect, and participate in nonbeing they are false in relation to true Be-ing, to Ontological Reality, and hence can make no claim to validity, truth, or certitude.

Thus, Daly, too, balances her fine sense of human historicity and insight into the constructed/imaginative nature of symbol with a rejection of relativism and a denial that all views are commensurate. While feminist symbols and visions are the products of female imagination, they are also true, if not final, reflections of ultimate Reality precisely because the feminist spirit resonates with the ontological structure of the universe.

The foregoing description of the distinction between the reformist stance and the revolutionary position, and the examination of feminist understandings of truth and the relation of human thought forms to ontological reality suggest that feminist theological options must be analyzed on a variety of levels. It is not the contention of this essay that the questions that have enlivened the debate between those who have remained within and those who have left the traditions of Judaism and Christianity are not central or important. It is, however, my assertion that other questions concerning the status of feminists' symbols and claims to truth are equally important and that when these are asked a different picture of feminist theology emerges.

What is revealed when these latter questions are focused upon is that feminist theologians, across the theological spectrum, continue to assume or make claims about the nature of truth and the character of ultimate reality, often without clear argumentation concerning the grounds upon which these assertions are based. Further, I would argue, many of these assumptions are in tension, if not outright contradiction, with the insights concerning the historicity of human experience and thought with which feminists have so strongly aligned themselves. That is to say, while on an explicit level these feminist theologians have embraced the canons of historical consciousness as a means of unmasking patriarchal claims to truth and validity, on another, often implicit level, they have continued to use the language of ontology and metaphysics, long in dispute in other arenas, as a way of contributing to the validity of the feminist vision.

By making these claims I do not mean to suggest that the feminist theologians examined in this essay have argued for a naive recapitulation of the Enlightenment ideal of reason as neutral, universal, and capable of an unmediated reflection of reality. It is clear that Schüssler Fiorenza, Ruether, and Daly have all assumed the historicizing of reason and concur that all knowledge is perspectival and conditioned by the locus of the knower. Nonetheless, each thinker has refused to sever the connection between knowledge and ontological reality, and each has sought to ground her position, to some degree, by asserting that it reflects such ontological reality and, hence, may lay claim to greater normativity and certitude.[9]

Thus, although feminist theologians have not returned simplistically to a repudiated correspondence theory of truth, they have continued to search for ontological validation for their positions. While there are important differences between women who stay within their inherited traditions and those who leave, there is also a profound similarity among many current feminist theologians in their continued assumption of the correspondence between feminist visions and ontological reality and the at least implicitly made claim that feminist-conceived symbols refer to such reality. When analyzed on this level, feminist theologians sound more alike than different.

This similarity suggests that the current delineation of feminist theologians as reformers or revolutionaries masks deep affinities between these perspectives. It also indicates the need for feminists to make explicit our unspoken understanding of the relation between conditioned knowledge and reality and especially what is conceived of as divine reality. As a way of sharpening this discussion, I would like to conclude this essay by suggesting what a

feminist theology might look like if we gave up the appeal to ontological reality as a grounds of validation for our positions.

First, feminist visions would be understood as thoroughly
human constructions sharing the same *ontological* status as male perspectives. The validity of these competing "regimes of truth" would
be judged not according to which was "closer to reality" but upon
the pragmatic grounds of what kind of existence these visions
permitted or inhibited. Thus, in place of the "objectivist illusions"
of a correspondence theory of truth, a new pragmatism would be
developed.

Second, the status of religious symbols would undergo thorough
reconsideration. While feminist theologians such as Ruether,
Schüssler Fiorenza, and Daly have all been aware of the role of
imagination in constructing religious symbols and hence have
avoided claims that these symbols refer directly to divine reality,
they have, nonetheless, continued to argue that there is indeed a
correspondence, if indirect, between feminist symbols and the divine. Thus, feminist religious and theological language has implicitly been assumed to be referential in character. In the alternative
approach being considered here, such a referential nature would be
denied. Instead, religious symbols would be interpreted, along with
the larger worldviews or visions that they center, as solely the
products of human imagination and the projection of human values
and desires. Hence, in place of a referential theory of religious
symbolism, a revitalized projection theory would be developed.[10]

The approach proposed here suggests that a feminist theology
that carries through the insights of historical consciousness more
consistently will move away from the appeal to ontological grounds
for its validity and will eschew referential models of knowledge.
Such moves, however, while perhaps more in line with the direction
of a radical historicity, raise difficult problems as well. In particular,
this approach raises the specter of a nihilism in which all perspectives are equal and all differences are leveled. Current feminist
theologians have rightly argued that such a nihilism is the weapon
of the powerful who can determine which interpretation will be
accepted as true purely on the basis of coercive capacity. Therefore,
they have insisted that liberating visions must be granted greater
ontological validity if they are to be understood as more normative
than others. The alternative suggested here will need to argue suc-

cessfully that grounds for adjudication can be discerned within the pragmatic and projectionist approach if its claims for the normativity of feminist visions will not be interpreted as special pleading or ineffective attacks on the prevailing position of the powerful.

The alternative sketched above does not propose to be fully developed nor without problems. The purpose of its presentation is to suggest that a feminist theology that resolves the tension between the quest for certain knowledge and the historicity of human visions in the direction of historicity will need to seek other grounds for its validity than the appeal to ontological reality. The analysis developed within this essay leads furthermore to the conclusion that no matter what grounds of validity to which feminist theologians appeal, there is a need to examine in a far more self-conscious manner our unexamined metaphysical assumptions. That is, I advocate a greater participation by feminists in the modern debate concerning truth and the status of knowledge. And I suggest that when we do enter this discussion more self-consciously, we may no longer be divided only along the lines of reformers and revolutionaries, but according to the status we give our symbols and how we understand our claims to truth.

NOTES

1. See J. Stout, *The Flight from Authority: Religion, Morality, and the Quest for Autonomy* (Notre Dame: University of Notre Dame Press, 1981).
2. R. Rorty, *Philosophy and the Mirror of Nature* (Princeton: Princeton University Press, 1979).
3. S. Doty, "Radical Hermeneutics and the Possibility of Critical History," unpublished manuscript, 1983.
4. See N. Haan, et al., *Social Science as Moral Inquiry* (New York: Columbia University Press, 1983) for articles on the parallel debate within the social sciences.
5. M. Foucault, *Power/Knowledge: Selected Interviews and Other Writings, 1972–1977*, ed. C. Gordon, trans. C. Gordon, et al. (New York: Pantheon, 1977), 117.
6. R. R. Ruether, *Sexism and God-Talk: Toward a Feminist Theology* (Boston: Beacon Press, 1983). Hereafter cited in text as SG.
7. E. Schüssler Fiorenza, *In Memory of Her: A Feminist Theological Reconstruction of Christian Origins* (New York: Crossroad, 1983). Hereafter cited in text as IM.

8. M. Daly, *Gyn/Ecology: The Metaethics of Radical Feminism* (Boston: Beacon Press, 1983). Hereafter cited in text as G/E. *Pure Lust: Elemental Feminist Philosophy* (Boston: Beacon Press, 1984). Hereafter cited in text as PL.

9. Schüssler Fiorenza may well argue that this analysis misconstrues her position. In the Introduction to her recent volume, *Bread Not Stone* (Boston: Beacon Press, 1984), xxii–xxv, she positively refers to the work of Richard Bernstein as one who rejects the dichotomy of objectivism and relativism without recourse to a new foundationalism. However, it is my contention that the feminist thinkers examined in this essay implicitly still assume such ultimate foundations and hence have yet to provide a way beyond the impasse of objectivism and relativism.

10. For an example of a contemporary projection theory of religious symbols, see R. Alves, *What Is Religion?* (Maryknoll: Orbis Books, 1984).

CHAPTER 6

Female Voice, Written Word: Women and Authority in Hebrew Scripture

CLAUDIA V. CAMP

At the heart of this essay lies this question: How does scripture serve, and how might it serve, as authority for people today? This difficult question includes the problem of interpretation—how we discern the meaning or meanings of a given text—but goes beyond it. It includes the ethical issue—how we use the Bible as a basis for decision and action—but goes beyond even that. It includes the theological concern—how we incorporate scripture into the vision of what it means to be the people of God—but is still more comprehensive even than that. All of these intellectual queries presuppose a nonintellectual commitment to scripture as somehow determinative for the personal and communal identity of Jews and Christians. The question of authority may, then, have most to do with why we bother with scripture at all. Why do we study scripture for any purpose except as part of our cultural heritage in the most general sense? This problem is particularly acute for women because of the patriarchal, androcentric pall that hangs over Hebrew and Christian scriptures. The spiritual journey of Mary Daly, for example, confronts every Jewish and Christian woman with another clear option that compels each of us to reassess our stand within the tradition.[1]

In defining the phrase *authority of scripture,* the word *authority* should be distinguished from *power* as coercion on the one hand and from *influence* on the other. To say that scripture has power over us would be to say that it threatens us with its inherent ability to carry out its warnings and promises. Fundamentalists who understand scripture as literally the word of God may experience it as having power over them. To say that scripture has influence would be to say that it has a persuasive potential, that it provides information about our environment and may help in the decision-making process, but that it has no more inherent value in such a process than any other worthwhile source of information or guidance. Susan Brooks Thistlethwaite correlates these perspectives with the "conservative" and "liberal" views on authority in general when she states, "The conservative view is that authority is always exercised through coercion and therefore that an authoritarian order must be hierarchical. The liberal view has been that authority is vested in an order of persuasion by reason and therefore must be egalitarian."[2]

To say that scripture has true authority over us, however, is to imply that we have, in some way, *freely* placed our decision-making processes into its hands. What it means to live within the jurisdiction of scripture will vary from person to person. What is constant is that an uncoerced acknowledgment of this authority has been made. Once authority is granted, one obeys without threat, promise, or argumentation from the source of authority. Thus obedience to true authority involves no loss of freedom.[3]

David V. J. Bell suggests that what induces this granting of authority is a set of shared values or beliefs held by both the one who gives and the one who takes authority.[4] Such "credenda" authenticate authority. To frame the primary question of this essay in these terms is to ask: What induces us to place ourselves freely in some way within its jurisdiction without need of threat or persuasion? More specifically, what are the credenda that women in the last quarter of the twentieth century hold in common with an ancient and androcentric text?

The process by which one grants authority to scripture and continues to live within this authority is a complex one. This essay focuses on only one aspect of this process in Jewish and Christian traditions by analyzing the three occasions in the Hebrew Bible where the process of such authority being created occurs. This study generates three models of authorizing fruitful for reflecting on the use of scripture today.

The authority of this scripture has long depended on the authority of the *persons* with whom given writings are associated. The authority of the Torah depends on its association with Moses, that of the Psalms with David, and that of the Latter Prophets with their respective historical personal referents. The only major body of literature that does not adhere to this general pattern is the Former Prophets. This material is the exception that proves the rule, however, because its authorization comes implicitly from its elaboration of the themes in the book of Deuteronomy, which fits the expected picture. Books like the Song of Songs and Ecclesiastes remained dubious for a long time, with respect to canonization, because of their unorthodox content. Although authorized by the name of Solomon, they evoke aspects of the tradition associated with him that tended to be on the theological and moral periphery of the Israelite value system. In all of these cases, the authorization by the persons involved (it might be more accurate to say "by the personae invoked") was an after-the-fact affair, evolving from a long history of traditional association of these names with the literary material.

Only three times in the Hebrew Bible do we glimpse the actual processes—and these processes varied greatly—through which a written word receives human authentication. Most remarkably, in all three cases, the authorizer is a woman or a female literary figure: Huldah (2 Kings 22:14–20; 2 Chron. 34:22–28), Esther (especially in 9:16–32), and the figure of Wisdom personified as a woman in several poems in Proverbs 1–9. These three provide three different models for the authorizing of a written tradition in a new context through the mediation of an authoritative human figure.

Huldah: Authority and History

Huldah, to whom King Josiah's servants took the Book of the Law for authentication after its "discovery" in the Temple, was clearly a recognized prophet. The king's words on hearing a reading of the book were, "Go and *inquire of Yahweh* for me, and for the people, and for all Judah concerning the words of this book that has been found. . . ." Huldah's voice was equated with the voice of the deity, and she responded as expected, "Thus says Yahweh, the God of Israel: 'Tell the man who sent you to me, "Thus says Yahweh: Behold, I will bring evil upon this place and upon its inhabitants, all the words of the book which the king of Judah has read . . ." ' " (2 Kings 22:15–16).

Huldah did not address herself directly to the matter of the book's authenticity. She simply echoed the realization already voiced by Josiah in verse 13: "Great is the wrath of Yahweh that is kindled against us. . . ." Whereas Josiah had located the guilt of the people in the past ("our ancestors have not obeyed the words of this book"), Huldah placed the burden on the present "inhabitants of this place" who, says Yahweh, "have forsaken me and have burned incense to other gods, that they might provoke me to anger with all the work of their hands." Huldah was not simply the authorizer of the book but its interpreter for the present day. If we consider her "hermeneutical principle," we find that she did not address the validity of the book for all time but rather set it as an announcement of doom impinging on Judah's current condition. The people's failure to examine with honest eyes their past and present lives was the basis for judgment. Only the king, who had not refused to hear the words of the book, would die in peace before the desolation of the land (vv. 18–20).

Huldah was actually wrong on this last point. Josiah died in battle at Megiddo in 609 B.C.E. In spite of this failure of prophetic foresight, the later editors of this material clearly accepted her judgment on their history and, by extension, on the book itself. Arlene Swidler comments,

This marks the first time any of the Hebrew scriptures were officially recognized as authentic. Josiah's acknowledgement of the Book of the Law, then, represents the first beginnings of our biblical canon. And the authority to pass judgment on this initial entry into the canon was given to a woman.[5]

Swidler is accurate in her assessment of this situation, but her observations can be sharpened. The context of the story gives insight into what it *means* to have written tradition recognized as "authentic," namely, that the tradition in question accurately describes the contemporary situation, including its nuances: the repentance of the individual human being as well as the hardness of heart of the many. It also means that the words of the traditions have power in the present situation, not in and of themselves, but insofar as they bespeak another potent reality when spoken by an authoritative person. Huldah spoke Yahweh into powerful existence through her interpretation of the book. This role of the prophet in the story is significant. To the scribe and the priest who brought the book to Huldah, it was, depending on one's interpretation of their intentions, either an obscure relic or a tool to be used for their own purposes. The king had greater insight: he saw the work of Yahweh behind what was written in the book. But the work of "authorizing"—creating as present reality by verbal invocation—was left to the prophet Huldah. Swidler's statement that "the authority to pass judgment on this initial entry into the canon was *given to* a woman" is an understatement. This authority was *created and claimed by* a woman, not "given" to her.

The story of Huldah, as a model of authoritative interpretation, reflects a dynamic, triangular interaction of a person, a text, and a history. It is too simplistic to say, as would someone working in Thistlethwaite's "conservative" model, that the text has the power to pass judgment on history. Rather, a *person* passes judgment on history *based on* a text. We speak of Huldah "authorizing" the text. This authorization process has three movements. Huldah began as an authoritative person, one who made a claim, recognized by others as legitimate, to speak for the deity. Regarding the text, she claimed the authority to declare it worthy of obedience and, more, to declare it representative of the effective will of God in the present. She judged the validity of the text vis-à-vis history by interpreting it in light of the present condition. As an authorized spokesperson for Yahweh, Huldah had another option. She could as easily have invalidated the text.

Huldah claimed authority not only over the text, but also, in a second authorizing movement, over the people's history insofar as she interpreted their contemporary situation in light of the text. Huldah placed herself and her people under the authority of the text by accepting its judgment against their history, past and present. An authorized person, she submitted to authority and received renewed authority at the same time. She both gave and took authority with respect to the text based on her own position and her understanding of history.

There is a third dialectical movement between the text and history. Huldah brought the text in judgment against history, not for all time, but for her own day. History will in the future, however, stand in judgment of the text. This is true in more than one sense. On a surface level, history will judge the accuracy of the text and

Huldah's interpretation of it, though this will not be its most important judgment. Allowances will be made for the fact that Josiah's righteousness did not save him from a violent and premature end. History's most vital judgment will be on the generative power of the text: Will it ultimately build up as well as tear down? Will a new community in a later day find in it a source of life? The character of Huldah presents a test for the life-giving power of the text in any contemporary community and for the liveliness of that community as well. The test is this: Will the text create the opportunity in history for another Huldah? Will it, in other words, continue not simply to take authority but also to give it to the one who stands in judgment both in history and on the text itself? And will the community hear this word of judgment?

Personified Wisdom: Embodying The Authority of a Text

The figure of Wisdom is personified as a woman in several poems in Proverbs 1–9 (1:20–33; 3:13–18; 4:6–9; 7:1–5; 8:1–36; 9:1–6).[6] This figure operates in conjunction with the concrete work of Wisdom, represented as woman's work in the concluding chapter 31, to provide a framework of authorization and interpretation for the proverb collection in the intervening chapters.[7]

The first nine chapters of Proverbs are often described by scholars as providing a "theological introduction" to the proverb collection in chapters 10–30. These proverbs represent "daily life wisdom": they are rarely explicitly theological and thus are thought to be in need of theological authorization. This analysis is accurate as far as it goes, but it does not tell the whole story.

A discussion of the role of personified Wisdom with respect to the proverb collection requires some background on the collection and the proverbs that comprise it. For the sages of ancient Israel, the proverb was the linguistic *sine qua non* of wisdom itself. Proverbs provided encapsulations of the collective experience of the community, past and present. The authority of a proverb depended, however, not only on its heritage, but also on its correct application by a person in a specific context of use. As the sages said, "Like a lame person's legs, which hang useless/is a proverb in the mouth of fools" (Prov. 26:7). A proverb was only fully meaningful if spoken "in season." Therefore, its authority depended as much on the verbal skill and timing of the speaker as on anything else. Proverbs in oral use are lively representations of tradition that both interpret and shape present experience.[8]

Once proverbs are put in written collections, however, their vitality ebbs away. Two factors contribute to this. One is the literary shapelessness of a proverb collection. There is no beginning, no end, no inherent unity. To the extent that form reveals meaning, a proverb collection is meaningless because formless. The timelessness they seem to assume constitutes a second problem. The "here-but-not-thereness" of their oral application disappears, and they take on the appearance of general moral principles. This combination of formlessness and timelessness undercuts the authority of proverbs in one of two ways. It either trivializes them as platitudes or inappropriately elevates them to doctrine.

Because so many of the proverbs deal with the ordinary, scholars have often postulated a conflict between the wisdom tradition and so-called "orthodox" religious Yahwism. It is not simply their origin in daily life that causes the problem, but also their doctrinal appearance that seems to set human wisdom in some way on a par with divine authority. Hence, the apparent need to "theologize" the collection with the voice of "divine" wisdom in Proverbs 1–9. The metaphor of Woman Wisdom in Proverbs 1–9 brings human and divine wisdom as two dimensions of knowing into a dialogue with each other that is *mutually* validating. The personification of Wisdom accomplishes this task through a process of *embodying*.

The process of embodying begins with the literary decision to personify Wisdom as a woman. The basic persona we meet in Proverbs 1–9 is that of a woman calling out in the public places of the city—the streets, the market, the gates, the walls—for people to follow in her way, the way to life and favor with Yahweh. The path itself is not explicitly laid out in Wisdom's speeches. Rather, we find a series of motifs through which Wisdom presents her claim to authority.[9] Remarkably, these authorizing motifs are drawn not from the sacred tradition but in large measure from the world of human experience, specifically, women's experience. Woman Wisdom takes her authority from her various characterizations as a prophet (Prov. 1:20–33) who condemns the mass of fools but offers hope to the individual righteous person (compare Huldah!), as a lover and wife (4:6–9; 7:4–5; 8:17), as a counselor (8:14–16), as a house builder and provider of food (9:1–6). It is, in other words, Wisdom's literary embodiment *as woman* that is the primary source of her authority.

Woman Wisdom does have a special relationship with the deity that is not insignificant in her claim to authority. The poem in Proverb 8 establishes her as the daughter of Yahweh, present at the time of creation and functioning as the joyful mediator between deity and humanity. Yahweh, moreover, brings forth Wisdom in labor, as *mother* to this illustrious daughter (8:24, 25). The meaning of Wisdom as the creative interaction between the divine and human spheres is completely embodied in female imagery.

When the formless collection of proverbs is given a beginning and an end, the word *embodying* takes on an additional nuance. Assuming chapters 1–9 to be the introduction to the book, the editors' intent seems to point the reader to the proverb collection in chapters 10–30 for the specific elements of Wisdom's way. The female guide and mediator, whose credentials are presented in the introductory poems, authenticates this path as the way of life (8:35–36). In terms of form, the collection is given structure by a framework of female images: the poems that personify Wisdom as woman at the beginning and the poems that represent the work of women as Wisdom's work in the concluding chapter 31.[10] In addition to the variety of tasks ascribed to personified Wisdom in chapters 1–9, this "work" includes the instruction given by a queen mother to her son (31:1–9) and the teaching of *hesed* (steadfast love) by the woman of worth (31:26). Beyond and including wise words the defining characteristics of Woman Wisdom are shared by the woman of worth. Both are more precious than jewels (3:15; 8:11; 31:10); both provide for their households (9:1–2; 31:13–27); both are recognized in the premier public space, the city gates (1:21; 8:3; 31:31). In providing the collection with a beginning and an end, the female imagery thus provides it with a hermeneutical key: wisdom is the work of women. The form gives meaning to the work. Not only the idea of wisdom but also the book of Proverbs itself—the way of wisdom—is embodied in female form. The literary figure of Wisdom accomplishes a literary task.

Embodiment also implies voice. When something is embodied, it has the possibility for speech. The written work of the proverb collection is not permitted to (or, perhaps, cannot) speak for itself. The ground of being of the collection is personified as a woman. The written word is channeled through a human voice that is in intimate connection with the world.[11] It is a voice that must be discerned from among the clamor of voices in the space of public life: from the voice of the violent and perverse man (1:8–19; 2:9–15) and from that of the strange and foolish woman (2:16–19; 5:20; 6:20–26; 7:10–23; 9:13–18). The proverbs are recontextualized as fundamentally oral through the representation of Wisdom's call. They are restored to life by her. In her, they become the possibility—the way—of life for women and men alike.

As with Huldah and the Book of the Law, the "giving" of authority that takes place in the book of Proverbs is a two-sided affair. Wisdom, personified as woman, gives authority to the text, recommends it as worthy of obedience, and offers warnings to the unheeding. But she also claims authority over the material by interpreting it. She does this by incarnating it, thus revealing its form. She humanizes and gives life to what is otherwise a "dead"—disincarnate—written word. Wisdom differs from Huldah in that Wisdom is a purely literary figure whereas Huldah is a historical personage. The historical, human hand behind Wisdom remains hidden. Yet, with her multidimensional human representation, she, like Huldah, insists that the validation of texts must always come from the world of lived experience and be spoken with a human voice.

Esther: The Authority For Celebration

The role of Esther in codifying and authenticating the practices of Purim, the Jewish festival on Adar 14–15 celebrating the Jews' deliverance from Haman, emerges as yet a third model. The flow of events in the book can be understood in two ways, depending on whether one takes the perspective of the historian or the literary critic. The source of the connection of Purim with the Esther story is historically irrecoverable. It is possible that the book was written to legitimate a popular festival whose origins are unknown to us today.[12] Such an origin is suggested by the fact that Esther 8:15–17 and 9:17–19 depict the Jews celebrating their victory before a written command is sent out from Esther and Mordecai. The people's eventual acceptance of the written word depends not only on the text itself, but also on their own experience, on "what they had faced in the matter" (9:26). Considered from a literary point of view, however, the narrative as a whole expresses the conviction that the *possibility* for the Jews' celebration existed only because of Esther's prior intervention before the king on their behalf. Esther took a double risk to her own life in so doing. In the first place, she took the initiative of appearing before the king knowing full well that "if any man or woman goes to the king inside the inner court without being called, there is but one law: all alike are to be put to death, except the one to whom the king holds out the golden scepter that he may live. And I have not been called to come in to the king these thirty days" (4:11). Surviving this first exposure, Esther took the second, equally great risk of identifying herself as a Jew in order to intercede for her people. Although it was too late to rescind the king's order to kill all the Jews of the empire, Esther won from the king a declaration of the right of the people to defend themselves in the face of the coming attack (8:3–8). The celebrations described in chapters 8 and 9 were the result of this successful defense.

If one assumes a literary point of view, as I do here, the epilogue to the story in 9:16–32 (especially v. 32) presents Esther as the one with the authority to codify and authenticate for later generations the celebratory practices begun by the Jewish populace at large.[13] This authority is based in part on her position as queen and also on her role as hero or role model for the Jewish people. Whatever the actual, historical antecedents of Purim may have been, and in spite of the narrator's perception that the Jews had to do a great deal to defend themselves even after Esther's work, the vitality of the celebratory tradition that became Purim depended on a story that could consolidate the immediate experience and shape it into a form with which future generations could identify. Esther's significance goes beyond the deeds she reportedly enacted. As a literary figure, she captures, embodies, and sustains the momentary experience of a large group of people, making it available to the memory of the future. She personifies the Jewish people.

There is, then, a transition that takes place in 9:16–32 from an oral to a written Purim tradition that is successful in part because of Esther's identification with her people and theirs with her. Her authority superseded their spontaneity, although not without recognition of their importance in the origination and ongoing life of the celebration of Purim (cf. 9:26–28). Just as Moses stressed to his followers in Deuteronomy 5:3, "Not with our parents did Yahweh make this covenant, but with us who are all of us here this day," so also the author of Esther 9:16–32 emphasized the immediate experience of the Jews and the active participation of their descendants as the vessels in which the tradition would be carried. In a similar manner, just as the law became identified with a single, authoritative individual, Moses, so also the written word regarding Purim acquired its lifeblood from Esther.

There is a dialectic of authority at work between the people whose lives were at stake, and who to some extent saved themselves, and Esther, who risked herself freely by identifying with them and representing them. She "saved" them by providing them the opportunity to save themselves. They "saved" her by remembering her life and story as their story and the means of their life. Esther's existence in the later tradition is possible only because of those who remembered her. The possibility of their memory exists only because of the one who saved them and who embodied them in story. Authority and life are bound together and shared in celebration.

Esther, like Huldah, authenticates a tradition's written form and bears witness to its continuing relevance and potency in that form. As a literary figure, however, Esther is even more closely identified with the tradition than Huldah. She is, in fact, a personification not only of the Jewish people but also of this tradition. The book *about* Purim is *named* Esther. In this sense, the literary function of this character parallels that of personified Wisdom, who also embodies the still-living and powerful quality of an oral-tradition-become-written and establishes its authority for future generations by giving it human voice.

Feminist Reflections

Consideration of these three biblical figures arises out of a concern for the question of the nature of scriptural authority. This large issue is part of a still larger one of the nature of authority in general. We face a crisis of authority today that stems from many sources. Not least among them is the wielding of authority by too few for too long, an abuse falsely legitimated by appeals to theologies that turn out upon examination to be only ideologies. Women have ceased to grant authority to men and the traditions controlled by men as readily as we once did. This refusal has caused this so-called authority to show its true colors as coercion masked by lies. Something, nevertheless, keeps drawing some of us back to the Bible. We are often angry and critical, yet we are still aware of the bonds that consist of something more than influence and different from power. The effort to balance this experience with a commitment to feminism has led some scholars to spend a certain amount of their academic energy attempting to justify scripture to women: by distinguishing a "usable tradition" and ignoring the "unusable." Elisabeth Schüssler Fiorenza has justly chastised us on this score.[14] Focusing upon these three female figures in the way I have while ignoring some of the blatantly sexist elements that are also found in these passages may seem like more of the same.[15] The central question raised here, however, is very specific: who authorizes written traditions and how is it done? The surprising answer is that *women* do it, and the variety of their characterizations—from historical to literary—is matched by the variety in their modes of authorization. What connects the models of authority the female figures present, in spite of variations, is the authority of the past taken and acted upon with authority in the present in such a way as to engender life for the future. This connection raises at least two more questions.

Do these texts provide models to inform our reading of scripture today? Although there is clearly no cause-effect relationship involved, two major trends have developed in contemporary feminist biblical scholarship that seem in certain ways to echo two of the voices we hear in scripture. I refer here to the "feminist theological reconstruction of Christian origins" of Schüssler Fiorenza, which might be correlated with the mode of Huldah, and to the feminist rhetorical criticism of Phyllis Trible, which resembles the mode of personified Wisdom.[16] The biblical "women" do not use "methods" in the same way that these women scholars use methods; rather, they provide images that lead to new imagination in dealing with the Bible. They suggest types of authorizing, of which the methods of Schüssler Fiorenza and Trible might be considered contemporary scholarly manifestations.

Like Huldah, Schüssler Fiorenza gives consideration to the text not as an end in itself, but rather as a focusing lens on history. The text is important not only for what it says, but for what has been omitted from the historical vision of the powers that be. These holes in the text allow space for judgment of the text, of history, and of the people who live and have lived this history. Her authority comes from who she is in her own setting, a woman who can see and give voice to what those in power have unwittingly ignored and even willfully suppressed when confronted with the knowledge of it.

Schüssler Fiorenza removes the notions of inspiration and authority from the Bible and places them with the "biblical people."[17] Authority must have a human voice. In this sense, she reverses the process begun by Huldah, though not in every sense. For Huldah, too, authority had a human voice. This prophet surely would have been hard put to imagine that her words to the king's servants on that fateful day in 622 B.C.E. would create a textual monster that men would claim could speak for itself as a ploy to mask their ventriloquism. In claiming the right to take authority away from scripture, Schüssler Fiorenza has in fact restored it to its rightful place. By reestablishing the dialogue between the text and history, she has actually taken away the capacity of the text to be manipulated coercively. Once again human history—the history of *all* humans—can stand in judgment on the generative power of the text.

The true authority of the text also reasserts itself as a primary conferrer of identity on those who claim to be Jews and Christians. Without the Bible, there are no "biblical people" to utter—and thereby make real—its otherwise meaningless words of life, none to mourn its "texts of terror,"[18] none to proclaim its judgment on oppressors, none to reconstruct theologically our origins. This also was the authoritative claim the text had for Huldah. As that which identified the people of God, it was to be a way of life, but they had chosen death. The text, then—in dialogue with a historical people to whom it provides a source of identity—generates a context within which a prophet does her creative work.

The text-centered work of Phyllis Trible stands in contrast to the orientation toward history of Huldah and Schüssler Fiorenza. Like personified Wisdom in Proverbs, Trible allows meaning to stand forth through her discovery and articulation of literary form. Even as she grants authority to the text by acknowledging the claim it makes on her to interpret it, the form of the text also gives her authority to speak for it. The form must be revealed by a human being, or it has no voice. Based on biblical models, Trible claims this authority as properly belonging to the work of women.[19] In a similar manner, the form and the authority of the book of Proverbs were represented as the work of women. In Trible's work, the text is re-incarnated, just as the originally oral proverbs were "re-heard" from out of their state of written death by the authoritative embodiment of wisdom as a woman. Authority rests in the interaction of the text and its interpreter.[20]

Although Huldah and personified Wisdom represent two modes of authoritative relationship with scripture that find expression in contemporary feminist biblical scholarship, the kind of model represented in Esther is found in the world of scholarship only by extension. This exchange of life and dialectic of authority resulting in celebration is potentially the work of all women in the world. It appears whenever a woman who is protected and safe risks herself for those unprotected, whenever she recognizes that *her* life depends on them as their lives depend on her. It is there when those who succeed in overthrowing their oppressors choose as the embodiment of their existence—as their authority—an image and story of one disenfranchised, "deauthorized" by society. It appears when this disenfranchised one is "reauthorized" by the work, life, and celebration—by the authority—of each new generation.

The second question raised by the authoritative interaction of the female figures in the Bible with the text is how to explain theoretically this role that women play. Is there anything about women that makes them essential to this process? Even though we do not see men actually authorizing texts, it is clear from the association of Moses with the Torah, David with the Psalms, and others that male images were even more prominent than female ones in this process. Furthermore, none of the modes discussed above are explicitly feminist, in the sense of being concerned with offering a critique of culture in light of misogyny (Trible) or being concerned with restoring the work and oppression of women to our historical memory (Schüssler Fiorenza). There were at least as many male prophetic critics of history in ancient Israel as female, and there are many male practitioners of sociohistorical criticism today (though few are either as critical or prophetic as Schüssler Fiorenza). Likewise, men shaped canonical books like Proverbs, even when they accomplished it with female images, and there are many men practicing literary criticism today. Hermeneutics is not comprised of method alone, however. It begins with a stance, a choice of a hermeneutical key, a decision about whose eyes with which to see the world and whose voice with which to speak. The three female figures and their modes are not, then, in any narrowly defined sense feminist. Nonetheless, they do speak with women's voices, and that is reason enough to consider whether or not they convey a message worthy of response.

Two notes sounded in these texts should be harmonized with any feminist appropriation of the authority of scripture or, for that matter, authority of any sort. The first is the nonhierarchical, *dialogical* nature of true authority. One who grants authority to someone or something else must first be acknowledged to have the authority to do so. Legitimate and uncoerced granting occurs from a position of strength, not weakness. This granting is, moreover, reciprocal. In the case of a text, this means that it must continually create new persons to participate in this ongoing interaction. Many of us who find our lives and vocation shaped by scripture have been created by the text in this way.

The question of how a text creates these new persons requires consideration of the second theme of the biblical texts we have considered: the fundamental interconnectedness of true authority and the giving of life, its quality of embodiment. What the three modes of authorization by the female biblical figures share is the bringing together of traditions with present circumstances to create the possibility of life for the present and future. This is true even when, as in the case of Huldah, it means the destruction of all existing institutions of power that have usurped authority. The product of true authority is life. On this its claim to freely given obedience rests.

What can we say about the shared set of values that are at work in the authority of scripture in the life of a feminist? The process begins with the experience of new life available in the text. However, having had one's self and one's history challenged by the text, one eventually turns to the task of challenging it, based on one's experience. The voice taken from the text becomes the voice that speaks to it. In accepting the authority of these three female figures, we appropriate the entire process of authorization including the responsibility to authorize, interpret, and, by inference, deauthorize the texts. The authority of women over scripture—specifically, the authority of prophetic, life-giving, embodying, celebrating women—becomes a primary credendum of scriptural authority.

NOTES

1. See M. Daly, *Pure Lust: Elemental Feminist Philosophy* (Boston: Beacon Press, 1984).
2. D. V. J. Bell, *Power, Influence, and Authority* (New York: Oxford University Press, 1975); S. B. Thistlethwaite, *Metaphors for the Contemporary Church* (New York: Pilgrim NY Press, 1983), 154–62, 155.
3. Thistlethwaite, *Metaphors,* 155.
4. Bell, *Power, Influence, and Authority,* 42–56.
5. A. Swidler, "In Search of Huldah," *The Bible Today* (1978), 17: 1783.
6. The personification of Wisdom produces a metaphor that scholars have often called "Lady Wisdom." Because of the class connotations associated with such terminology, I prefer to say "Woman Wisdom."
7. See C. Camp, *Wisdom and the Feminine in the Book of Proverbs* (Sheffield: Almond Press, 1985).
8. C. R. Fontaine, *The Traditional Saying in the Old Testament* (Sheffield: Almond Press, 1982), 43–71, esp. 50–52, 57–60.
9. M. Gilbert makes this point with respect to Proverbs without focusing as I do on the female imagery. "Le Discours de la Sagesse en Proverbs 8," in *La Sagesse de l'ancien Testament,* ed. M. Gilbert (Leuven: Leuven University Press, 1979), 202–18.
10. Gilbert, "Le Discours," 218; N. Habel, "The Symbolism of Wisdom in Proverbs," *Interpretation* 26 (1972): 133–57; Camp, *Wisdom and the Feminine,* chap. 6.
11. Solomon was traditionally cast as the mentor of wisdom in Israel; however, in Proverbs he appears "in name only," without development in "body" or "voice," and without any explicit connection drawn between him and the Wisdom figure.
12. See S. Berg, *The Book of Esther: Motifs, Themes, and Structure* (Missoula: Scholars Press, 1979), 1–11.
13. C. Camp, "The Three Faces of Esther: Traditional Woman, Royal Diplomat, Authenticator of Tradition," *Academy: Lutherans in Profession* 38 (1982): 20–25.
14. E. Schüssler Fiorenza, *In Memory of Her: A Feminist Theological Reconstruction of Christian Origins* (New York: Crossroad, 1983), 8–10, 14–21.
15. For further consideration of, for example, the "strange woman" who functions as the negative counterpart to personified Wisdom see Camp, *Wisdom and the Feminine,* chaps. 4 and 9.
16. P. Trible, *God and the Rhetoric of Sexuality* (Philadelphia: Fortress, 1978); *Texts of Terror* (Philadelphia: Fortress, 1984).
17. Schüssler Fiorenza, "Contemporary Biblical Scholarship: Its Roots, Present Understandings, and Future Directions," in *Modern Biblical Scholarship: Its Impact on Theology and Proclamation,* ed. F. A. Eigo (Villanova, PA: Villanova University Press, 1984), 22.
18. This phrase is the title of Trible's most recent book (see n. 20).

19. Trible, "Biblical Theology as Women's Work," *Religion in Life* 44 (1975): 7–13.
20. Trible made this statement regarding biblical authority in discussion following her presentation at the national meeting of the Society of Biblical Literature, Dallas, TX, December 1984.

CHAPTER 7

Softening the Hearts of Men: Women, Embodiment, and Persuasion in the Thirteenth Century

SHARON A. FARMER

One persistent gender stereotype in ancient and medieval literature entailed not the silence of woman, but the spellbinding power of her voice. This stereotype was usually a negative one. In Homer the "honey-sweet voice" of the Sirens enticed men to their own destruction. According to Hesiod, "lies and tricky speeches" were among the attributes that the gods, including "Queenly Persuasion," gave to Pandora, who brought "evil," "harsh labor," "cruel diseases," and "miserable sorrows" to the "races of men."[1]

Medieval Christian authors were remarkably similar to these Greek writers in attributing destructive powers to the female voice. According to twelfth-century theologians, Eve compelled Adam "to obey her voice rather than the word of God," and Eve's spiritual descendant—Everywoman—"induce[d] crime with her . . . voice and hand."[2] Abelard even declared that woman's tongue could be considered "the seedbed of all evil," and the fifteenth-century Dominicans who wrote the *Malleus Malificarum* thought that the power and destructive capacity of woman's voice helped explain her propensity for witchcraft.[3]

As I argue in the first part of this essay, the assumption that women have a special power in the oral sphere was related, in part, to a predominant Western tradition that placed women closer to the physical realm and men closer to the spiritual, rational, or cultural realm.[4] Because ancient and medieval societies were predominantly oral cultures, philosophers and theologians in those societies felt the full impact of speech as sensuous and physical phenomenon, and they therefore associated speech with the physical realm and with women. In the Middle Ages, moreover, the tendency to associate women with the power of speech was bolstered by the fact that there was a sharp division between the oral world of illiterate women and lay men and the textualized world of clerics.

Towards the beginning of the thirteenth century the boundaries between the physical and the spiritual and the oral and literate realms began to blur. Some theologians even began to encourage women to employ their persuasive powers to influence their husbands for the good. The physical came to be seen as an enhancement of the spiritual, and oral persuasion—more sensuous and embodied than textual communication—gained new importance. In the second part of this essay, I analyze the social and cultural developments that helped bring about these transformed perceptions.

Like the ancients, medieval men associated women with the power of speech in part because they associated both women and oral persuasion with seduction and magic. Men found women seductive because they projected their own sexual urges onto the objects of their desires. They found speech seductive, in a way that we do not, because they lived in an oral universe that knew the immediacy of the sensuous power of words as sounds, which "tend to evoke responses from outside [the producer of the sound] in a way that very few . . . visible or tangible activities do." Like men and women in preliterate cultures, those of ancient and medieval society, in which literacy existed within a still highly oral culture, experienced spoken words as charms and incantations. Spoken words, unlike written words, signify actual, existential present power because "sound must be in actual production in order to exist at all." This is of course always the case, but literate people think of words differently, as reduced to visual space; we are alienated from the full physical impact of words as sounds.[5]

Gorgias, the fifth-century Greek rhetorician, had praised the magical and seductive power of speech, and especially poetry, to charm men. But Plato, who drove a wedge not only between the body and the mind but also between form and content in discourse, denigrated oral rhetoric for the very reason that it had the magical power to charm men without communicating the truth. In Socrates, however, Plato saw at work a magic that differed from that of ordinary rhetoricians. Because Socrates had the power to convince men of the nature of ultimate, immaterial truths, his power of persuasion represented for Plato divine inspiration.[6]

Christian theologians, at least through the twelfth century, inherited Plato's preference for content over form, his discomfort with the rhetorical arts, and his assumption that what is truly real is immaterial and therefore disembodied. Moreover, elaborating Plato's dichotomy, Christian theologians associated false rhetoric— that in which men and women were persuaded of something that was contrary to Christian doctrine—with magic or seduction, while they associated true rhetoric—that which persuaded men and women to believe and obey Christian doctrine—with divine inspiration or assistance. Augustine, for example, described the "seductive" eloquence of Faustus, the Manichean leader whose oratory could "delight" but not enlighten. And while Augustine endeavored to instruct his fellow Christian leaders in the art of oral persuasion, he maintained as well that Christian persuasion could take place only when God had made the orator's audience receptive.[7]

In the twelfth century, and even into the thirteenth, Catholic theologians continued to distinguish in this way the "false" rhetoric of heretics from the "true" rhetoric of the church. While ordained priests had the right to preach and did so effectively because they had received the power of the Holy Spirit at ordination, lay persons and heretics had no such right.[8] Indeed, the effectiveness of their preaching was due to its demoniacal, seductive, or sexual qualities.

Several male clerics of the twelfth and early thirteenth centuries decried the fact that women were allowed to preach in some of the heretical movements. They also emphasized that women were preponderant in the audiences of male heretical preachers, and they pointed to this fact as a sign of the seductive nature of the heretics' teaching methods. In a passage that reveals his own subconscious association of persuasion with sexuality, one twelfth-century cleric moved from a description of the alleged sexual license of a heretic and his followers to the seductive and demoniacal nature of the heretic's preaching:

Matrons and adolescent boys (for he enjoyed the pandering of both sexes), attending him at different times, avowed openly their aberrations and increased them, caressed his feet, his buttocks, his groin, with tender hands. Completely carried away by this fellow's wantonness and by the enormity of adultery, they publicly proclaimed that they had never touched a man of such strength, such humanity, such power. By his speech [they claimed], even a heart of stone could be moved to repentance. . . . When rumors of this sort floated into our district, the people, applauding their own destruction with their peculiar fickleness, daily and every day longed to be beguiled by his discourse. . . . [When] he addressed the people, it was as if legions of demons were all making their noise in one blast through his mouth. Nevertheless, he was remarkably fluent. When his speech entered the ears of the mob, it stuck in their minds. Like a potent poison, it penetrated to the inner organs. . . .[9]

This passage reveals not only the clerics' typical attempt to denigrate heretics by imputing to them licentious behavior, but also an underlying recognition, fear, and awe of the copulative nature of oral communication. The author's metaphors emphasize, in a sexual manner, the penetrating nature of the heretic's speech. Walter Ong, a contemporary linguistic theorist, has drawn on similar images in his discussions of the potency of oral communication. "The word," Ong maintains, "and particularly the spoken word, is curiously reciprocating not only intentionally, in what it is meant to do (establish relationships with another), but also in the very medium in which it exists." While sights (and hence written words), "may reflect, from surfaces," Ong continues, "sound binds interiors to one another as interiors."[10]

Through the eleventh, and into the twelfth century, medieval thinkers were often aware of this power of sound and voice, but many considered it an affront, a sensuous imposition or seduction that turned the interior soul away from its silent, suprasensory conversation with God, the true source of knowledge. Because their epistemology was one of Platonic idealism rather than Aristotelian empiricism, they considered inferior the knowledge that the senses could impart.[11]

Medieval clerics were uncomfortable with oral persuasion because they recognized the sensual qualities of speech and the fact that it was conveyed through a natural and physical medium—the voice. In woman, moreover, male theologians saw the embodiment and essence of the baser—the sensual and physical—side of human nature.[12] It is not surprising, therefore, that women became associated with the sensual and physical qualities of speech. Women's intonation, moreover, is usually more emotive and dynamic than men's intonation, and for this reason, the female voice is frequently considered more "natural" than the male voice.[13] If medieval clerics feared the male voice because it conveyed words through a powerful, natural, and sensuous medium, they feared the female voice all the more, because they perceived it as even more natural than the male voice.

One characteristic that was peculiar to medieval society enhanced the clerical men's association of women with speech and with its powers. Medieval Latin—the language in which learned clerics communicated—was, as Ong has called it, a "fully textualized" language. Those persons who learned Latin—and they were nearly all male—did not learn it as they had their mother tongues, through total immersion in the oral-aural realm. Rather, they learned to read, write, and speak Latin simultaneously. For everyone who learned it, Latin was, from the beginning, a written language. Because they experienced Latin as a text, through a visual medium, its words were more removed for them than were the vernacular tongues from the potency of the purely oral-aural universe.[14] In gazing out from their world, which was celibate, male, Latin, and fully textualized, medieval clerical men were predisposed to associate the power and seduction of the spoken word with their mother tongues, and with women—who as mothers or nurses had uttered the first words that these men had heard and mimicked, and who as women were clearly absent from the realm of communication that they associated with Latin and textuality.

Although negative assessments of woman's seductive capacities and of her power with spoken language predominated in the imaginations of clerical males, a number of monastic and scholastic writers from the period between the mid-eleventh and early thirteenth centuries attributed to pious married women a positive power with spoken language. Only toward the beginning of the thirteenth century, however, did any of these authors openly encourage good women to be seductive in their use of spoken language. Around this time clerics began to discuss consciously the possibilities of persuasion within marriage and the special function of a wife's persuasion in influencing her husband's moral conscience.[15]

In discussing the wives of usurers, for example, Thomas of Chobham, who wrote a widely read *Manual for Confessors,* argued in opposition to some of his contemporary theologians that because they could exercise persuasion, usurers' wives should be allowed to stay with their husbands, even though by living off the profits of the sinful activity of usury they associated themselves with their husbands' sins. For Thomas, the potential good that the women's persuasive powers could bring about was the most important consideration, and he even associated the wife's persuasive activities with those of Jesus:

[The usurer's wife] is like the Lord, who ate with sinners and plunderers [Luke 19:2–7], and even though they gave him nothing except property that belonged to others, nevertheless, because he attended to the cause of the poor and persuaded the plunderers to restore the stolen goods, he freely ate their food. In a similar manner, the [usurer's] wife is able to persuade her husband that he should restore the income from the interest or accept a lower interest rate from the poor, and because she thus labors for them and attends to their cause, she is freely able to live from their property.[16]

Like Thomas of Chobham, Robert of Courson, another early thirteenth-century theologian, argued that the wife of a usurer could stay with her husband in order to "attend to the cause of the despoiled," and she would thus become an "advocate" of those victims. Furthermore, in a passage that presupposed the wife's use of oral communication, Robert described her potential effect on the usurer's moral conscience: such a wife could work at "softening the heart of her husband" and "inducing" him to restore the stolen property.[17]

Thomas of Chobham's advice concerning *all* wives, however, most fully articulated the positive potential of women's persuasive powers. Thomas offered no parallel discussion of the persuasive powers of husbands.[18] Moreover, he clearly associated the woman's powers with sexual seduction, and his language about greed and the poor—as well as words like *plundering* and *softening the heart,* which had arisen in the discussions of usurers—suggests that he associated the persuasive power of *all* wives with sins that occur especially in a money economy:

In imposing penance, it should always be enjoined upon women to be preachers to their husbands, because no priest is able to soften the heart of a man the way his wife can. For this reason, the sin of a man is often imputed to his wife if, through her negligence, he is not corrected. Even in the bedroom, in the midst of their embraces, a wife should speak alluringly to her husband, and if he is hard and unmerciful, and an oppressor of the poor, she should invite him to be merciful; if he is a plunderer, she should denounce plundering; if he is avaricious, she should arouse generosity in him, and she should secretly give alms from their common property, supplying the alms that he omits.[19]

The statements about women's persuasion in Thomas of Chobham, Robert of Courson, and others[20] are indicative of vast transformations in European society that began around the year 1000. A formerly rural, local, decentralized, and subsistence society began to give way, in the years between 1000 and 1300, to long-distance trade, commodity production, political centralization, and an urban and money economy.[21] These social, political, and economic changes fostered new attitudes toward nature and the realm of the physical, a growing dependence upon and interest in oral persuasion, and the rise of literacy. These cultural changes contributed, in turn, to the positive assessments of women's persuasive capacities.

In the early thirteenth century, men and women were not as threatened by the powers of nature as they had been in the year 1000. Increased productivity had rendered them much less vulnerable to the natural cycles that led to drought and famine; and some inhabitants of urban centers, like Francis of Assisi, were able to develop a lyrical appreciation for the beauties of the natural and physical realm.[22] Increased confidence, technological developments, and mounting intellectual inquiry led to a sense that nature was humanity's partner, that it was intelligible, and that its forces could be channeled to the benefit of society. Religious thinkers, even those still imbued with Neoplatonism, became increasingly affirmative of the realm of the empirical, declaring that men and women could begin their quest for knowledge and love of God by looking at the world: physical creation pointed to the existence of its creator; divine truth could be learned from nature; there was no insurmountable gulf between the material and spiritual realms.[23]

While the theology of Thomas Aquinas demonstrates the degree to which Aristotle's writings ultimately lent philosophical and scientific sophistication to the new attitudes toward the natural and physical realm and to the new empirical epistemology, those of Cistercians such as Bernard of Clairvaux and William of St. Thierry—mystical monks who wrote in the twelfth century, before Aristotle's writings had been fully assimilated—indicate that Aristotle's writings did not cause the new attitudes. Bernard expressed his mysticism in erotic and experiential language. While he was still deeply Platonic and Augustinian, he affirmed the realm of the material, undermining the dualism that had once divided personal choices into love of the good and love of evil. Knowledge of their concrete existence, Bernard maintained, should lead all men and women to love God; carnal love for oneself and for others were the first steps towards love of God; and love of God remained, in this life, carnal as well as spiritual.[24] Thirteenth-century female mystics went even further than Bernard in their eroticism, and their ideas indicate, as Caroline Bynum has argued, that "the theme of the positive religious significance of physicality runs throughout thirteenth-century theology."[25]

In his affirmation of the use of feminine wiles, Thomas of Chobham underscored the same message that twelfth-century Cistercians had already made, that female mystics were making, and that Thomas Aquinas would soon reiterate[26]—that the lessons and experiences of the natural, physical, and sensuous realm could be channeled to teach Christian truth. The voice and embraces of a wife, in Thomas of Chobham's discussion, were examples of the physical realm serving the purposes of the spiritual.

Thomas and other Scholastics in his circle were not merely interested in conveying knowledge about Christian truths. They wanted to change people's behavior, and to do that they had to exhort—to persuade. Social and economic changes, as well as a new attitude towards lay society on the part of the church, had fostered this new interest in exhortation.

The rise of commodity production and growth of urban centers went hand in hand with the growing value and experience of persuasion. In the subsistence and largely local economy of the early Middle Ages men and women had little opportunity to make economic choices—to compare prices or to weigh the advantages and disadvantages of buying one item rather than another. They largely bought or bartered for what they needed whenever and however they could. By the early thirteenth century, circumstances were quite different, especially in the urban settings where commodities were bought and sold. Men and women learned to negotiate, to argue, and to persuade.[27] Moreover, the greater complexity of twelfth- and thirteenth-century society both increased the importance of communication and rendered it more difficult. People's experiences were more diverse than they had been in small face-to-face communities. Attempts to communicate now had to begin in the perception of diversity and with the willingness to bridge the gulf between one's own experiences and those of others.

The new emphasis on persuasion was also related to the greater role that individuals were able to play in a more complex society in determining their life circumstances. As cities—as well as more extensive and bureaucratic governments—first grew in importance, new professions and crafts came into existence, and they drew their numbers from the countryside.[28] More men and women were able to make more choices than they could have in the early Middle Ages, and the experience and perception that people had options and that they could change carried over into the moral sphere, where preachers became increasingly interested in persuading lay people to follow the precepts of the church or to convert to a life of repentance.

Similarly, the greater complexity of urban life and of more extensive and centralized forms of government put a premium on the cooperation and self-monitoring of inhabitants of cities and extended political units. People were less likely to live in a face-to-face community, where the mere possibility of being observed and recognized served as a deterrent against violating the community's norms. Rather, urban centers lent greater anonymity to the individual's day-to-day activities, and the smooth functioning of society depended more on an interiorization of the community's norms. The theological literature of the twelfth century demonstrates a heightened interest in interior motivation, and the new concern with popular exhortatory preaching, which culminated with the founding of the preaching orders at the beginning of the thirteenth century, further indicates that the church wanted to inculcate the laity with its values.[29]

Persuasion, then, was at the heart of urban experience—in the marketplace and on the pulpit. It was a necessary form of communication in a society where individuals who could make choices had to cooperate, negotiate, and live together peacefully. It is not surprising, therefore, that theologians of the twelfth and thirteenth centuries became interested in the positive role that persuasion could play within marriage.[30] Nor is it surprising that Thomas of Chobham associated women's moral persuasion with the sins that men committed in activities related to the new money economy: money, commodities, urban life, and persuasion are closely connected.

Effective persuasion, as the theologians were learning and discussing, required not only a mastery of abstract truths, but also a sense for the concrete. A great speaker does not simply convey a disembodied message. He or she must embellish that message with style, delivery, and illustrative anecdotes, and he or she must adjust those techniques for different audiences. A good speaker has at least some knowledge of who is listening. The authors of manuals on the art of preaching—and Thomas of Chobham may have written one of the first—were aware of these aspects of good oratory, and they provided preachers with a sense for the concrete by suggesting appropriate sermons and subjects for people from various walks of life—soldiers, lawyers, princes, married people.[31]

This art of responding and accommodating to the laity was even more important in confession—the church's second strategy for encountering and influencing the laity—which became a mandatory practice in 1215, and which was often carried out by popular preachers. Here, too, a priest's task entailed persuasion, but in an even more concrete and particularized form than that of preaching, since confession took place in a one-on-one encounter between priest and confessee. Manuals for confessors, such as that of Thomas of Chobham, taught priests to consider not only an individual's walk of life, but also his or her sins, and the circumstances under which they had been committed.[32]

Nevertheless, as intent as they were upon considering the particular and concrete, manuals on the art of preaching and confession could deal with persons only as abstract types. Parish priests may have taken these lessons further in their personal interactions with members of their parishes, but the tasks of preaching and confessing were frequently performed by visiting friars who did not have time to come to know individual believers.[33] Their itinerant life would have inclined them to approach individual lay persons according to the typologies in their manuals. The absolute effectiveness of preachers and confessors was (and is) hindered by the fact that no priest can attain full empathetic understanding for every lay person who hears his sermons, or who speaks with him in confession.

In asserting that "no priest is able to soften the heart of a man the way his wife can," Thomas of Chobham both acknowledged the limitation of the priest's communicative role and proposed a supplementary forum of communication and exhortation in the wife's fully concrete and connected relationship with her husband. There is an element of dominance and manipulation in Thomas' advice; if it had been taken seriously, the bedroom would have become a vehicle for the church's control over private lives and a means of enhancing its public power.

There is a positive aspect, however, to Thomas's message in his recognition of the need for concrete connectedness in effective communication, and in his affirmation of the tangible embodiedness that is so closely related to reciprocal oral communication. Thomas recognized that the more intimately a speaker knows his or her audience the more effective his or her persuasion can become. In linking the "alluring" and "arousing" qualities of the woman's voice to her physical embraces he expressed—this time with approval—his underlying understanding that both are copulative. Oral communication, like sexuality, is relational and reciprocal. Both speaker and listener—like sexual partners—are grounded in actuality and simultaneity.[34] Only through the senses can a speaker appropriately know her audience and thus respond with the effective vehicle for conveying her message. In choosing to advocate the persuasive role of wives rather than husbands, Thomas remained consistent with the gender dichotomy that had already associated women with embodiment and the realm of the concrete. Unlike many male clerical authors, however, Thomas fully endorsed this realm and saw an advantage in women's association with it.

Thomas of Chobham's affirmation of physicality indicates, in part, the greater distance men and women had placed between themselves and the natural realm, and their confidence in their ability to become partners with its forces. Men and women could now appreciate and enjoy the natural realm because they did not feel overwhelmed by its power. In a similar way, Thomas's affirmation of women's words points to a sense of distance from the oral-aural realm, and to a budding confidence, on the part of churchmen, that the power of the spoken word could be controlled or brought into partnership with the rationality and orderliness of the written word. The growing importance of literacy had increased the importance of the visual realm, thereby diminishing the more threatening aspects of the power of the oral-aural realm.

Throughout the late twelfth and early thirteenth centuries the spheres of textuality and orality increasingly intermingled. Though most lay persons remained illiterate until after the invention of the printing press, from the twelfth century on their lives and modes of thought became increasingly affected by the existence of texts and written records. The bureaucratized governments, which began to replace personalized, early feudal forms of power, generated more and more written records. Written law replaced oral, customary law; written documents replaced oral testimony. With the appearance of vernacular literatures in the twelfth century the written/oral dichotomy ceased to be the central feature distinguishing Latin from vernacular language. And indeed, popular preaching and the church's efforts to reach out to the laity represent intense interaction between the Latin world of clerics and the vernacular world of the laity.[35]

This interaction began in the twelfth century, before the church had officially assumed the task of addressing the laity, and to a large extent it was the threat of the popularity of twelfth-century preachers, many of them declared heretical, that forced the church into this arena. Most of the heretical preachers of the twelfth century were learned men, often trained as clerics, who actualized written Latin scripture, originally the monopoly of the church, by preaching its message in the vernacular to illiterate audiences. The following of a preacher, as Brian Stock has pointed out, constituted a "textual community." Although themselves illiterate, heretical men and women were joined together by their interpretation of a text, and they employed that text in order to judge the very institution from which their leaders had seized it. Heretics claimed that they were true followers of Christ because they adhered more faithfully to the "apostolic life," as described in the New Testament, than did the wealthy and extravagant clergy. Words from the Bible, interpreted literally, were the heretics' source of authority.[36]

By the time Thomas of Chobham began to write, the church was regaining the upper hand over popular heretical leaders, not only through the use of force, but also by meeting popular preachers on their own turf. The members of the new preaching orders, notably, the Franciscans and Dominicans, led ascetic lives that were less offensive to the laity than were those of bishops and other members of the ecclesiastical hierarchy; and these friars considered evangelism a central part of their spirituality. Manuals for preachers and confessors (written in Latin) converted complex theological issues into practical moral terms, and the preachers who read these manuals transformed their ideas into vernacular sermons and dialogues with illiterate lay persons. The new preaching orders channeled the power of popular preaching to the church's own purposes; the new manuals helped assure that the oral message of popular preachers adhered to and remained under the influence of written doctrine. The spoken word had been tamed, and the bifurcation between written and oral, Latin and vernacular, broke down.[37]

At the same time, the spoken word was also losing its psychological impact, its magic. As a result of the growing importance of texts, the perceptual universe was shifting. Gothic architecture provides tangible evidence of the growing impact of the visual realm: geometry, underlying coherence, sequential divisions of space, light, and color gained new importance.[38] For Thomas of Chobham's contemporaries, the oral-aural realm was balanced by the visual realm, and for that reason, they responded to the spoken word with less intensity than had their predecessors. They could accept it as a natural phenomenon.

Although theologians continued to associate (partially for reasons of control) effective and official preaching with divine grace and the power of the Holy Spirit, Thomas, in his discussion of persuasive wives, whom he designated "preachers to their husbands," made no mention of divine grace or power. His choice of words about softening men's hearts established a positive affinity between the efficacy of the speech of wives and that of preachers,[39] but Thomas did not feel compelled to attribute any supernatural force to the wife's words. Her persuasion was seductive, but it was neither divine nor magical and demonic. For Thomas, speech that was grounded in the natural and material realm could be channeled, without fear, to serve worthy purposes.

The medieval gender stereotype associating women with the potency of the spoken word is indicative of an underlying logic that drew correspondences among various symbolic dichotomies. Just as the natural or physical realm was, before the thirteenth century, persistently considered inferior to the spiritual or rational realm, oral persuasion (which must respond to diversity and plurality among audiences) was persistently considered inferior to abstract, absolute truth. All of these inferior categories were joined together in the association of woman with the power of spoken language.

Thomas of Chobham's ideas do not represent a turning point in clerical male assessments of women and women's voice.[40] It makes perfect sense, however, that—at a time when theologians were affirming the natural and physical realm, and when they were developing a greater interest in oral persuasion—someone extended the implications, affirming both woman's seduction and her use of spoken language. Thomas's advocation of the proper uses of women's seductive speech suggests that he saw in it strengths that were lacking in the speech of priests. He understood that communication, which begins with a recognition of *who* someone else is and *where* he or she is situated, had to be grounded in the senses, and in attention to the concrete and particular. Such, Thomas assumed, was the nature of a wife's relationship to her husband.

Such indeed is the nature of the realm of experiences—of private, domestic, nurturing activities—traditionally associated with women. While Thomas of Chobham questioned neither the social structures that restricted women to this realm nor the gender stereotypes that ensued, his discussion of persuasive wives implicitly challenged the symbolic hierarchies that have frequently devalued and degraded sensual, concrete, and domestic life while valuing immaterial, abstract, and public existence.

It is possible to draw at least two implications for contemporary feminist thought from Thomas's discussion of persuasive wives. The first entails the need to analyze attitudes toward gender and embodiment with as much historical and cultural specificity as possible. Thomas of Chobham inherited a set of gender dichotomies that associated women with physicality and speech, but his evaluation of physicality, embodiment, speech, and women was not absolutely predetermined by a static, all-pervasive cultural patrimony. Rather, his values and intellectual formulations took root in the soil of his own historical epoch.

In order to analyze and criticize contemporary attitudes toward embodiment, feminists need to distinguish the various attitudes toward nature and the body that have predominated at various times in the West and to attempt to understand the historical contexts that gave rise to these attitudes. Christians have not been mere passive recipients of Plato's body/soul dualism, and Christianity has not taken a single, monolithic stance toward nature and the body. The welding of Christianity with Platonism, and the exacerbation, in the period between 200 and 400 C.E., of asceticism and otherworldliness must be understood in the particular historical context of the later Roman Empire.[41] Similarly, the attitudes toward nature, embodiment, and the material realm that we find in Thomas of Chobham must be understood in the context of the social, economic, and cultural developments of the twelfth and thirteenth centuries.

In our own day, we are heirs not only to Plato and the thirteenth century, but also to the scientific and industrial revolutions, which have created a chasm between our own attitudes toward nature and embodiment and those of Thomas of Chobham. An affirmation of nature as partner has given way to a desire to dominate; and a mechanistic view of the world pushes us, as Carolyn Merchant has asserted, "increasingly in the direction of artificial environments, mechanized control over more and more aspects of human life, and a loss of the quality of life itself." These domineering attitudes, moreover, have been assumed by women as well as by men. In their desire to transcend totally the limitations of the female body, existentialist feminists, such as Shulamith Firestone, have expounded views that could arise only in the twentieth century.[42] Only now has technology made possible this kind of transcendence of, and alienation from, physicality.

The second implication feminists can draw from Thomas of Chobham is that embodiment is not an issue for feminists alone. To be sure, women have been associated with the natural and physical realms, and for this reason many feminists approach the issue of embodiment with particular insight and commitment. Nevertheless, Thomas's discussion of persuasive wives, and the historical and social context in which it arose, suggest that in complex societies neither men nor women can afford to devalue the sensual realm. In order to communicate, we must *all* be grounded in the senses.

In the modern world, we are confronted, much more than were Thomas and his contemporaries, with the problem of diversity and with the potential, on a global scale, for misunderstanding. In order to avoid annihilation, we must keep channels of communication open, and we must maintain respect for the concrete and sensual experiences that make communication reciprocal. As Beverly Harrison has asserted, "bodily repression"—disdain for our embodied state—leads to *"loss of a sense of our connectedness* to the rest of nature, to the cosmos, and to each other."[43] Embodiment, connectedness, reciprocity, and communication are crucially linked. We cannot afford to devalue any of them.

NOTES

1. Homer, *Odyssey* 12:187, in *The Odyssey of Homer: A Modern Translation,* trans. R. Lattimore (New York: Harper & Row, 1965), 190; Hesiod, *Works and Days,* 42–105, trans. M. Lefkowitz, in *Women's Life in Greece and Rome,* ed. M. Lefkowitz and M. B. Fant (Baltimore: University Press, 1982), 13.
2. Rupert of Deutz, *De trinitate,* ed. J. P. Migne, *Patrologiae cursus completus: Series latina* (Paris, 1844–64), 167:295 (henceforth, PL); Hildebert of Lavardin, "Carmen CX," PL 171:1428, with corrections by M. Haureau, "Notice sur les mélanges poétiques d'Hildebert de Lavardin," *Notices et extraits des manuscrits de la Bibliothèque Nationale et autres bibliothèques publiés par l'Institut National de France* 28 (1887): 366.
3. Abelard, *Letter 7,* in *The Letters of Abelard and Heloise,* trans. B. Radice (Harmondsworth, England: Penguin, 1974), 188; *Malleus Maleficarum,* part 1, question 6, ed. J. Sprenger and H. Kramer, trans. M. Summers (London: The Puskin Press, 1948), cited in *Women and Religion: A Feminist Sourcebook of Christian Thought,* ed. E. Clark and H. Richardson (New York: Harper & Row, 1977), 123.
4. See P. Cooey, "The Word Become Flesh: Woman's Body, Language, and Value" in this volume, and n. 12 below.
5. W. Ong, *The Presence of the Word: Some Prolegomena for Cultural and Religious History* (New Haven: Yale University Press, 1967), 123, 113, 112, 111–75.
6. J. de Romilly, *Magic and Rhetoric in Ancient Greece* (Cambridge: Harvard University Press, 1975), 1–43.
7. "Seductorium," "delectabat," Augustine, *Confessions,* 5:6:44, 15, ed. Lucas Verheijen, *Sancti Augustini confessionum libri xiii,* Corpus Christianorum, Series latina 27 (Turnholt: Brepols, 1981), 62; Augustine, *On Christian Doctrine,* 4:16, trans. D. W. Robertson, Jr. (Indianapolis: Bobbs-Merrill Inc., 1958), 142; J. J. Murphy, *Rhetoric in the Middle Ages: A History of Rhetorical Theory from Saint Augustine to the Renaissance* (Berkeley and Los Angeles: University of California Press, 1974), 286–92.
8. Hugh of Rouen, *Contra haereticos libri tres,* 2:1–2, PL 192:1275–76; Stephen of Bourbon, *Tractatus de diversis materiis praedicabilis,* 4:7:342, in *Heresies of the High Middle Ages,* ed. and trans. W. L. Wakefield and A. P. Evans (New York: Columbia University Press, 1969), 210.
9. Description of Henry of Le Mans, *Actus pontificum Cenomannis in urbe degentium,* in Wakefield and Evans, *Heresies,* 109–110.
10. Ong, *Presence,* 125.
11. The *Rule of Saint Benedict* (chapters 6, 42) prescribed silence for monks: *RB 1980 The Rule of Saint Benedict in Latin and English, with Notes and Thematic Index*

(Collegeville, MN: The Liturgical Press, 1981), abridged edition, 38, 90. On sound and voice as impositions and seductions, see Augustine, *Confessions*, 6:8, trans. R. S. Pine-Coffin (Harmondsworth, England: Penguin, 1961), 122; William of St.-Thierry, *The Nature and Dignity of Love*, ed. E. R. Elder, trans. Thomas X. Davis, *Cistercian Fathers Series* 30 (Spencer, MA: Cistercian Publications, 1981), 75; Abelard, *Letter 7*, trans. Radice, 188.

12. Augustine, *The Trinity*, 12:7–14, trans. S. McKenna, *The Fathers of the Church* 45 (Washington, DC: The Catholic University of America Press, 1963) 348–356; *De genesi contra Manichaeos*, 2:11:15; 2:14:21, PL 34:204, 207. There were scientific as well as theological roots to the medieval gender stereotype: see V. Bullough, "Medieval Medical and Scientific Views of Women," *Viator* 4 (1973): 485–501.

13. S. McConnell-Ginet, "Intonation in a Man's World," *Signs* 3 (1978): 547–56.

14. W. Ong, "Orality, Literacy, and Medieval Textualization," *New Literary History* 16 (1984): 1–12; "Latin Language Study as a Renaissance Puberty Rite," in Ong, *Rhetoric, Romance, and Technology* (Ithaca: Cornell University Press, 1971), 113–41.

15. S. Farmer, "Persuasive Voices: Clerical Images of Medieval Wives," *Speculum: A Journal of Medieval Studies* 61 (1986): 517–43.

16. Thomas of Chobham, *Summa confessorum*, 7:6:11:3, ed. F. Broomfield, *Analecta Mediaevalia Namurcensia*, 25 (Louvain and Paris: Beatrice-Nauwelaerts, 1968), 506–7. For background on Thomas, see John Baldwin, *Masters, Princes, and Merchants: The Social Views of Peter the Chanter and His Circle* (Princeton: Princeton University Press, 1970), 1:34–36, 2:26 n. 216.

17. "Concilium Parisiensis, 1212," pt. 5, chap. 10, in *Sacrorum conciliorum nova et amplissima collectio*, ed. J. D. Mansi (Florence and Venice, 1759–1798), 22:852. For background on Robert of Courson, see Baldwin, *Masters*, 1:19–25.

18. For reasons why this was so, see Farmer, "Persuasive Voices."

19. Thomas of Chobham, *Summa*, 7:2:15, ed. Broomfield, 375.

20. Anonymous monk of Marmoutier (probably late twelfth or early thirteenth century), *Liber de restructione majoris monasterii*, ed. A. Salmon, *Recueil de chroniques de Touraine* (Tours, 1854), 343–73; Conrad of Eberbach (early thirteenth century), *Exordium magnum Ordinis Cisterciensis*, 5:12, PL 185:1147–49. For discussion, see Farmer, "Persuasive Voices."

21. See L. K. Little, *Religious Poverty and the Profit Economy in Medieval Europe* (Ithaca: Cornell University Press, 1978), ix–xi, 3–18; G. Duby, *The Early Growth of the European Economy*, trans. H. B. Clarke (Ithaca: Cornell University Press, 1974); M. Bloch, *Feudal Society*, trans. L. A. Manyon (Chicago: University of Chicago Press, 1961), 1:59–71; J. Strayer, *On the Medieval Origins of the Modern State* (Princeton: Princeton University Press, 1970).

22. Duby, *Early Growth*, 181–210; "The Canticle of the Sun," trans. B. Fahy, in *The Writings of Saint Francis of Assisi*, intro. and notes, P. Hermann (Chicago: Franciscan Herald Press, 1964), 130–31; L. White, Jr., "Natural Science and Naturalistic Art in the Middle Ages," reprinted in White, *Medieval Religion and Technology* (Berkeley: University of California Press, 1978), 23–41.

23. M. D. Chenu, "Nature and Man—The Renaissance of the Twelfth Cen-

tury," in Chenu, *Nature, Man, and Society in the Twelfth Century,* trans. J. Taylor and L. K. Little (Chicago: University of Chicago Press, 1968), 1–48; B. Stock, *Myth and Science in the Twelfth Century: A Study of Bernard Silvester* (Princeton: Princeton University Press, 1972), 3, 258, 278–79; T. Stiefel, "Twelfth-Century Matter for Metaphor: The Material View of Plato's *Timaeus,"* British Journal for the History of Science 17 (1984): 169–85.

24. Bernard of Clairvaux, *The Book on Loving God,* 2:2, 6; 8:23–25; 15:39–40, trans. R. Walton, in *Bernard of Clairvaux: Treatises II: The Steps of Humility and Pride/On Loving God,* Cistercian Fathers Series 13 (Kalamazoo, MI: Cistercian Publications, 1980), 95, 98, 115–17, 130–32; Etienne Gilson, *The Mystical Theology of Saint Bernard,* trans. A. H. C. Downes (London: 1940), 81; Colin Morris, *The Discovery of the Individual, 1050–1200* (New York: Harper & Row, 1973), 76ff.

25. C. W. Bynum, "Women Mystics and Eucharistic Devotion in the Thirteenth Century," *Women's Studies* 11 (1984): 200, 179–214.

26. Thomas Aquinas, *Summa theologiae,* 1:1:2:3, ed. Institute of Medieval Studies of Ottawa (Ottawa: Garden City Press, 1941–1945), 1:13–15.

27. Little, *Religious Poverty,* 197–99.

28. Little, *Religious Poverty,* 19–29. See also A. Murray, *Reason and Society in the Middle Ages* (Oxford: Clarendon Press, 1978), 81–109.

29. On the demise of face-to-face groups, see P. Brown, "Society and the Supernatural: A Medieval Change," *Daedalus* 104 (1975): 133–51; on intention and complex society, see C. Radding, "The Evolution of Medieval Mentalities: A Cognitive-Structural Approach," *American Historical Review* (vol. 83) 3 (1978): 591. For a review of the literature on twelfth-century interest in interior motivation, see C. W. Bynum, "Did the Twelfth Century Discover the Individual?" in *Jesus as Mother: Studies in the Spirituality of the High Middle Ages,* ed. Bynum (Berkeley: University of California Press, 1982), 82–109. On clergy inculcating values, see Little, *Religious Poverty,* 146–219 and Baldwin, *Masters,* 1:161–309.

30. See Farmer, "Persuasive Voices."

31. Murphy, *Rhetoric,* 303–26; Little, *Religious Poverty,* 173–96. Thomas of Chobham may have written the *Summa de arte praedicandi* in ms. 455 of Corpus Christi College: Murphy, *Rhetoric,* 317ff.

32. On the early history of lay confession, see P. Michaud-Quantin, "A propose des premières *Summae confessorum,"* Recherches de théologie ancienne et médiévale 26 (1959): 292 ff; Michaud-Quantin, *Sommes de casuistique et manuels de confession au moyen âge (xii–xvi siècles), Analecta médiaevalia Namurcensia* 13 (Louvain: Editions Nauwelaerts, 1962), 7–8; R. Rusconi, "De la prédication à la confession: transmission et controle de modèles de comportement au xiii siècle," *Faire croire: modalités de la diffusion des messages religieux du xiie au xve siècle, Collection de l'Ecole française de Rome* 51 (Rome: 1981), 67–68.

33. Little, *Religious Poverty,* 185–86, 200.

34. Ong, *Presence,* 128.

35. B. Stock, *The Implications of Literacy: Written Language and Models of Interpretation in the Eleventh and Twelfth Centuries* (Princeton: Princeton University Press, 1983), 3–87; E. R. Curtius, *European Literature and the Latin Middle Ages,* trans.

W. R. Trask, vol. 36 of the Bollingen Series (Princeton: Princeton University Press, 1973), 383–99; M. T. Clanchy, *From Memory to Written Record: England, 1066–1307* (Cambridge: Harvard University Press, 1979).

36. Stock, *Implications,* 88–240; M. D. Chenu, "Monks, Canons, and Laymen in Search of the Apostolic Life," and "The Evangelical Awakening," in Chenu *Nature, Man, and Society,* 202–69.

37. Little, *Religious Poverty,* 146–96.

38. Stock, *Implications,* 82.

39. Farmer, "Persuasive Voices."

40. G. R. Owst, *Literature and Pulpit in Medieval England* (New York: Barnes & Noble, Inc., 1961), 385–90, provides examples of the theme of the shrew in late medieval sermons.

41. E. R. Dodds, *Pagan and Christian in an Age of Anxiety* (New York: Norton Press, 1970).

42. C. Merchant, *Women, Ecology, and the Scientific Revolution* (New York: Harper & Row, 1983), 291; and, on dominance over nature, 164–90; Shulamith Firestone, *The Dialectic of Sex: The Case for Feminist Revolution* (New York: Morrow, 1970). For an alternative view see C. Christ, "Reverence for Life: The Need for a Sense of Finitude" in this volume.

43. B. Harrison, "Human Sexuality and Mutuality," in *Christian Feminism: Visions of a New Humanity,* ed. J. L. Weidman (San Francisco: Harper & Row, 1984), 148. See also Christ, "Reverence for Life," in this volume.

CHAPTER 8

Relational Love:
A Feminist Christian Vision

LINELL E. CADY

To develop effective alternatives to patriarchal visions of reality, feminist theology must maintain a critical relationship with the major religious traditions from which it springs. If it ceases to sustain a dialogue with its tradition, it risks becoming a marginal form of reflection, with negligible public impact. Alternately, if it abandons its thoroughly critical perspective, it will fail to offer a genuine feminist alternative to patriarchy. Avoiding these twin perils is not an easy task, as the often acrimonious debate between feminist "radicals" and "reformers" demonstrates.[1] To carry out the task of developing a feminist vision of reality that retains ties to a religious tradition, both ethical and theological forms of reflection are required. Instead of following the Enlightenment model, which maintains a disciplinary wall between theology and ethics, feminist reflection must develop a creative interplay between these modes of inquiry. Following this procedure, this essay endeavors to develop a feminist vision of reality rooted in the Christian tradition by exploring the theological implications of its central ethical motif: love. Drawing out the theological ramifications of a feminist interpretation of Christian love allows for the theological novelty demanded by feminist critique while preserving the continuity necessary for the effective transformation of our visions of reality.

Although all forms of feminist theology criticize existing religious traditions for their patriarchal bias, their assumptions about the nature and scope of that bias differ widely. As "radical feminists" have persuasively argued, too many fail to excavate the

deeper levels of patriarchal infection. Although institutional practices such as Roman Catholicism's prohibition of female priests and
traditional Judaism's exclusion of women from prayer quorums reveal most blatantly the secondary status of women, theologies that
struggle to redress the outward manifestations of sexism are focusing on the symptoms rather than the disease. Recognizing the complicity of scriptures in legitimating institutional discrimination,
other feminist theologies seek to make distinctions within a scripture while retaining its normative status: that which is supportive
of full human equality and liberation constitutes the genuine canon,
while that which impedes it is unauthoritative, the product of the
prejudices of an earlier age.[2] The pragmatic success of this methodological move effectively conceals its theoretical confusion. As
Orthodox Jews and Christian fundamentalists correctly perceive,
once such discriminations within scripture are made, its revelatory
status is undermined. Scripture no longer is functioning as the authority for theology, by supplying its warrants, when theology has
predetermined its canonical core. Continuing to refer to scripture in
this situation as an authority simply masks the circularity of such
appeals.

Perhaps more serious than the methodological muddle, this approach fails to be sufficiently critical of the patriarchal distortion
within religious traditions. Anxious to preserve the status of scripture, the approach assumes that scripture possesses a valid core, and
it thereby places too much emphasis upon an androcentric text. As
Elisabeth Schüssler Fiorenza has persuasively argued, feminist theology must not be bound by texts that were written by men and
reflect their biases and prejudices. Such androcentric texts fail to tell
the whole story; they present a selective, distorted version of the
past, which must not be confused with what in fact occurred. Given
the bias of the text within patriarchy, she proposes that Christian
feminists move behind the texts to uncover the community of
equals that has been present throughout Christian history but that
has been masked and marginalized by both scripture and the tradition.[3] Although making a very important and effective case for the
feminist deconstruction of scriptural authority, Schüssler Fiorenza
places insufficient emphasis upon the further need to explore critically the way in which patriarchal traditions have construed the
divine, if we are not inadvertently to transmit the content of the
patriarchal religious imagination. This is evident in her explanation

of her project: "My argument has been precisely that God and the Bible cannot be commensurate if we take the feminist hermeneutical insight seriously that the Bible is 'man-made,' written in androcentric language and rooted in patriarchal cultures and religions."[4] Although correctly regarding the Bible from a historicist perspective, that is, as the product of a particular time and place, she fails to consider the symbol of "God," the anchor for the patriarchal worldview, from the same angle. A thoroughgoing feminist critique of patriarchal religious traditions must extend to the fundamental religious symbols that structure these worlds.

Such radical critiques have been developed, of course, largely by those judging these traditions bankrupt. Persuaded that the basic symbol of "God" legitimates stereotypic masculine attributes, some women have sought to resurrect the symbol of the "Goddess" to supplement or replace it.[5] Although backed by strong arguments for the political and psychological importance of such symbolic transformations, these proposals fail to consider how symbolic visions orient human life. The symbolic webs within which we exist are not arbitrary creations imposed from without but the evolving products of many generations of human creativity. Their longevity confers upon them an "aura of factuality," which enables them to grasp the human imagination and function as orienting visions.[6] Proposing theological frameworks that have no connection to the historical tradition in which we find ourselves is useless; such proposals, despite their intellectual and moral merit, could not function properly as orienting visions. A set of religious symbols that appears as an arbitrary imposition upon experience fails to grasp human loyalties. The move to resurrect Goddess-talk suffers from this weakness. Despite the cogency of the arguments for employing Goddess imagery, the latter strikes many women as a highly artificial and hence unappealing alternative. Theology is not, as is fiction, the imaginative construal of a world that can be entered into by the few. It is, rather, the critical revising of the religious worldviews that people actually inhabit.

Ignoring this pragmatic constraint ensures that feminist theology will be a culturally marginal form of reflection, without the power to transform existing frameworks with their real social, political, and moral sanctions. If feminist theology is ever to have a broad impact upon the political and social configurations of our world, it will need to offer reconstructions of the extant religious traditions.

The magnitude of the influence that Christianity and Judaism continue to exert on this culture renders feminist analyses and reconstructions of biblical religion crucial. As Schüssler Fiorenza states: "We will either transform it into a new liberating future or continue to be subject to its tyranny whether we recognize its power or not."[7] Rather than opt for any romantic escape from the patriarchal traditions that continue to shape our culture, we must critically engage them, simultaneously defusing patriarchy's hold as we create workable traditions for the future.

Critically engaging a tradition does not entail according a fundamental consent to its basic scriptures, creeds, and symbols. It means, rather, extending a tradition according to current moral and intellectual lights. This may require novel reconstruction as certain features are emphasized, others ignored, and certain transformations introduced. This will certainly be the case in extending a tradition from a feminist perspective. For the patriarchal character of, for instance, Judaism and Christianity is not a function of selected institutional and ritual practices nor isolated scriptural passages that can be readily transformed or omitted. It permeates the entirety of these traditions, including the language and symbols used to articulate the nature of the divine.[8] It is because women have been excluded from the activity of "naming the divine" that the feminist extension of patriarchal traditions requires substantial theological reconstruction.

However, how does one begin to extend a patriarchal tradition from a feminist perspective without reiterating the biases of that tradition? Understanding how symbolic visions shape and give direction to human experience can help us resolve this problem. Using and extending Kant's insight that there is no perception without conception, research in a variety of disciplines has convincingly demonstrated that experience is always interpreted experience, that is, patterned by various symbols and myths that are historically and culturally rooted.[9] These symbols and myths function as frames of reference that give shape to reality, rendering certain virtues desirable and certain actions preferable. Following Clifford Geertz's formulation, there is an interdependent relationship between a worldview, a symbolic vision of the way things are, and an ethos, the attitudes and practices considered appropriate.[10] The interrelationship between worldview and ethos calls into question any sharp separation between the disciplines of theology and ethics. Ethical reflection is not a function of an ahistorical reason, able to intuit moral absolutes, as the Enlightenment would have it, but a form of reasoning informed by specific historical interpretations of human nature, the world, and the ultimate.[11] Conversely, our theological interpretations of human nature and the divine have direct implications for how we construe appropriate modes of human living. There is, in short, a dialectical connection between our interpretations of the moral life and theological visions that precludes isolating ethical and theological reflection. When there is a fundamental suspicion about the adequacy of a religious tradition, as is clearly the case in feminist theology, our reconstructive efforts will be aided by focusing upon our understanding of human personhood and the nature of the moral life before excavating their theological ramifications. Although this procedure will not produce consensus, such interpretations are more accessible for comparison and evaluation than are interpretations of the divine.[12] Furthermore, if we are suspicious of patriarchy's naming of the divine, focusing upon our normative anthropologies provides the necessary place to stand from which we can articulate our theological alternatives.

Interpretations of the moral life within the Christian tradition typically include an analysis of the meaning of love, arguably the primary Christian virtue. The central focus on love within Christian thought and piety is rooted within the earliest strata of the tradition. Jesus and Paul, for instance, elevated love above all other virtues; Jesus cited love of God and the neighbor as the two greatest commandments, and Paul insisted that, without love, all virtues are like the clanging of cymbals. In addition to regarding love as the primary constituent of the moral life, theologians including Augustine and and Pseudo-Dionysius considered it the most appropriate attribute for understanding the divine nature.[13] Although the primacy of love within the Christian tradition makes it the fitting focus of our moral inquiry, feminist reflection cannot uncritically appropriate its traditional meaning. Given the dialectic between symbolic visions and interpretations of the moral life, there is no reason to assume that the dominant interpretation of love escapes the patriarchal bias of the tradition.

Christian love has been most typically characterized as a radical conversion of the mind and will, resulting in a selfless concern for the needs of the other. It is a love that, abandoning all self-interest, is *for* the other completely. While other forms of love retain vestiges of acquisitive or selfish desires, Christian agapeic love alone is truly and fully self-sacrificial.[14] Based neither on the attractiveness nor worth of the other, Christian love is disinterested insofar as it is directed to all equally, without regard to distinguishing human characteristics. The crucifixion represents a primary symbolic vehicle for this interpretation of Christian love, by depicting the ultimate sacrifice of one's life as the cost of genuine love.

Christian self-sacrificial love has been increasingly criticized, especially by feminists, for various deficiencies. Perhaps its most serious drawback is, as the literature attests, its complicity in reinforcing social inequality.[15] By making self-sacrifice the primary criterion of the virtuous life, Christianity has given powerful religious validation to the situation of oppression. For those who lack power and status in a society, there is no motivational lever by which equality can be gained when the religious ideal is one of altruistic selflessness. Indeed, this ideal tends to foster the reverse dynamic: an inducement to remain subjugated in testimony to one's disregard for self.

In addition to its ideological legitimization of powerlessness, Christian self-sacrificial love fails to highlight the relational character of love. Insofar as it is defined in terms of the solitary individual, Christian self-sacrificial love can make little sense of the motives or the effects of love. Self-sacrifice comes to be seen as an end in itself, rather than as a means to the creation of some other good that might justify it. If we abandon the focus on the individual and consider love from a wider perspective, we reach a very different picture of its purpose and traits. This alternative picture of Christian love not only depicts our experience of human interaction more faithfully, but it avoids the unacceptable political repercussions of a love defined exclusively in terms of sacrifice.

Instead of construing love as a feeling or virtue of an isolated individual, we need to consider it from a relational perspective in order to understand its motivations and effects.[16] To love is to feel and to act in a way that takes account of the feelings, interests, and needs of the other. Such an orientation establishes a relationship between the self and the other that alters the basis from which the self acts. No longer operating from a narrow self-concern, the individual identifies the self with the relationship and seeks its continued existence and well-being. Through love, the other, in effect, becomes part of one's expanded self. Because of this self-expansion, acts of love are not due to heroic efforts of will, seemingly lacking in motivation, but are the outgrowth of the identification of self and other that occurs in and through love.

Love is a mode of relating that seeks to establish bonds between the self and the other, creating a unity out of formerly detached individuals. It is a process of integration whereby the isolation of individuals is overcome through the forging of connections between persons. These connections constitute the emergence of a wider life including, yet transcending, the separate individuals. This wider life that emerges through the loving relationship between selves does not swallow up individuals, blurring their identities and concerns. It is not, in short, an undifferentiated whole that obliterates individuality. On the contrary, the wider life created by love constitutes a community of persons. In a community, persons retain their identity, and they also share a commitment to the continued well-being of the relational life uniting them.

This can readily be seen in a successful marriage. Each spouse is loyal to the continued existence and well-being of their union, but such loyalty does not eclipse the distinct identities or diverse wants of each partner. To maintain a successful union each partner must take account of the other's interests and needs, along with his or her own, in determining which actions will be for the common good. This will certainly entail compromises and sacrifices, but if not mutually shared, the relationship of love will turn into a tyranny of one partner over the other. All relationships must, for limited periods, be able to withstand the refusal or failure of one spouse to act for the common good; but, if chronic, the union will inevitably fail.

Similarly, a larger communal whole based upon the love of many members depends for its continued life and health upon the members acting so as to further its cause. Although members do not ignore their own specific desires and needs, they do subordinate them to the needs of the wider life. All communities must deal with the failure of members to support the common good. Although a strong communal life can withstand such betrayals, if they become habitual and widespread, the life of the community inevitably withers and dies. Thus although love, by either a spouse or a member of a larger community, seeks to sustain and deepen a common life, it lacks the power to ensure that its goal will be reached. A successful marriage as well as a wider community cannot be secured by the efforts of one member. (It is, at the same time, a dangerous illusion to assume that genuine love attempts to maintain the relationship at all costs, even if it means subordinating the self to the demands of the other(s). Such love is spurious, resulting in despotism rather than a genuine communal life.)

Locating love within a wider context and identifying its communal aims allows for further specification of its nature. Two tasks must be performed by the lover if indeed love is to secure the wider relational life it seeks. First, in order to discover the integrating deed, the lover must come to see the other clearly. Without struggling to know the other in his or her situation, it is impossible to determine what action will be genuinely reconciling. This sounds deceptively simple; in practice it is extraordinarily difficult, even rare. Our selfishness, insecurities, and indifference corrupt our gaze, rendering the other, at best, a pale reflection of its actual state. Coming to see the other is, as Iris Murdoch has observed, an infinite task.[17] To varying degrees the self remains bound to its own perspective and concerns, unable and unwilling to confront the reality beyond its own carefully constructed borders. Truly to love involves the willingness and ability to risk the judgment and disequilibrium that transcending one's horizon entails. Nevertheless, "unselfing" in order to see the other without the distorting prism of one's own needs must be supplemented by the discernment that leads to an action that will achieve the desired reconciliation. Such action depends upon our capacity to imagine and courage to execute deeds that will help to secure and deepen the common life, toward which love aims. From this perspective it is clear that love, although certainly requiring a measure of selflessness, cannot be equated with it. Self-sacrifice is an abstraction from the largest set of characteristics needed to create, sustain, and deepen the relational life of love.

To function as the primary motif of the moral life, however, love must be defined more specifically than in terms of its capacity to create and sustain a common life. Love makes possible many forms of community including marriage, friendship, and a national life. Does one union better exemplify the nature of genuine love and hence serve as the more appropriate paradigm for the moral life? Seeking to articulate a feminist ethic, Eleanor Haney has proposed friendship as a primary model of the moral life. Friendship, ideally, involves a reciprocity and equality between the friends as well as a desire to nurture each other.[18] There is significant merit in her proposal. The paradigm of friendship not only captures the aim and characteristics of relational love, but it is especially apt as a counter-measure to the self-sacrificial love that has reinforced women's inequality and selfless devotion to others. However, friendship is, finally, too restrictive to convey the expanding dynamic of love. As the model of the moral life, friendship implies that love aims at maintaining a relationship of two persons who respect and nurture each other. Love, as described above, however, is continually seek-ing to create, deepen, and extend the bonds that unite self and others in more inclusive relationships.

By extending this expansive aim, the goal of love can be depicted more adequately through the paradigm of the universal community in which all being is interrelated in the most inclusive relationship possible. Although, unlike friendship, this is a vague and utopian metaphor for construing the aim of love, it is not thereby utterly vacuous and useless. Most importantly, it suggests that less inclu-sive relationships, such as friendship and marriage, although valu-able, are not the primary determiners or parameters of genuine love. They may be our most immediate and deepest experience of love, but they must be understood and valued within the eschatological context of love's final goal, which is the universal community of being.[19]

Furthermore, by emphasizing the universal community, the dis-interested character of Christian love is preserved. Christian love is not directed toward a select few whose personality or qualities attract the self. It is directed toward all persons regardless of their intrinsic worth or attractiveness. This disinterested or universal character of Christian love does not lead to the subordination of the self to all others but to an unceasing effort to include all persons in a reciprocal common life.

This form of love depicts the orientation of human life that most facilitates the emergence of greater being and value. It is through such love that the communal contexts that give our lives meaning and purpose are created and sustained. It would be misleading, however, to portray love as building community without also recognizing that it is responsible for building persons. The self is not an unchanging entity with fixed borders but a fluctuating conflu-ence of relationships. It is a dynamic integration that emerges in and through love. As Beverly Harrison puts it, "Literally through acts of love directed to us, we become self-respecting and other-regarding persons, and we cannot be one without the other." It is through acts of love that we "create one another."[20] Through love we both are empowered and empower others to extend the self beyond the limits of its immediate biological and experiential borders, thereby securing the wider purpose and meaning that humans seek. Consequently, interpreting love as *either* a virtue of the single individual or as a divine gift, as *either* a function of freedom or grace, is misleading. Neither taken alone does justice to the dialectic of love, to the mutual cocreation of self and community through the spirit of love.

Having sketched out, if only briefly, a blueprint for a normative anthropology, we are now in a position to consider its theological ramifications. If this portrait of love and personhood appears adequate in terms of its descriptive power to elucidate our experience, and in terms of its moral power to overcome patriarchal legitimations, what theological implications follow from it? It has often been noted that our conceptions of the human person and of God are dialectical, each being mirror images of the other.[21] Recognizing this point, Harrison writes: "By stressing that God is 'being itself' or is the 'wholly other' the Christian tradition implies that a lack of relatedness in God is the source of divine *strength*. And this image of divine non-relatedness surely feeds images of self that lead us to value isolation and monadic autonomy."[22] What theological vision correlates with the relational anthropology and interpretation of love set forth here?

The vision of human being and the moral life sketched out above does not lend support to traditional theism with its focus on an independent, transcendent divine being. I have been using love as a primary metaphor for depicting the orientation of human life that most facilitates the emergence of greater being and value. Incarnating this spirit is analogous to what traditionally has been understood as love of and relationship to God. However, important differences render the latter expression misleading. Most basically, the self does not relate to an independent divine being but embodies the spirit of the divine. Nor should this be understood as the creative work of God operating in human life, insofar as that formulation suggests the activity of an independent agent operating on or through humans. Such a vision is too mechanistic, failing to take account of the moral struggle that the activity of loving entails.[23]

According to this vision, the divine is not *a being* that exists and is unified but is, rather, the *unifying of being*. It is a symbol for directional, integrative processes in life that depend upon moral struggles to give and receive love. The divine spirit of love motivates and empowers humans to see more clearly and to act more justly by identifying the self with that which lies beyond its narrow borders. Notice the correlation between the self and the divine in this theological vision. From this perspective the self is no substantial entity, complete and defined, but a reality always in the process of being created through the dynamic of love, which continually alters its boundaries and identity. Similarly, the divine is not a perfected and completed being but processes that seek to expand and perfect being. Thus, the traditional conception of God modeled upon the single individual is inappropriate. Such a theistic model isolates and esteems autonomy and completion and fails to value the relational, emerging dynamic of life.

If our theological vision is to complement a relational anthropology, it will need to avoid images of divine reality suggesting a fully integrated autonomous being existing over and against us. Although theologians and philosophers have sought to reinterpret the conception of God, overcoming its anthropomorphism, it is doubtful that this symbol can shed its traditional connotations. The scriptures, creeds, prayers, and liturgies in Christianity continually reinforce the notion of a powerful, transcendent, and autonomous being, rendering conceptual reinterpretation rather ineffective. Indeed, an inability to avoid the negative psychological and political effects of traditional imagery leads some feminist theologians to consider discourse on the Goddess a necessary alternative to God-talk. Substituting or adding the symbol of the Goddess does perform the important function of legitimating and valuing female power and experience. However, it is an alternative that is overly determined by what it rejects. Goddess imagery responds to and fills in the gaps generated by the masculine symbol of God, thereby retaining some of the problematic characteristics of the latter. Although needing to escape from exclusively masculine imagery, such as Father, Lord, and King in our articulation of the divine nature, we must avoid the individualism that has always underlain Western theological frameworks. The symbol of Goddess, like the symbol of God, mirrors the single individual and fails to capture adequately the interrelated character of being. A more thorough revision of our theologies is called for, one that is developed not merely within the interstices of our inherited frameworks.

Nevertheless, if feminist theology is to have a significant impact upon social and political realities, it cannot propose theological visions that have no connection to currently inhabited symbolic worlds. In light of this constraint, I would propose that Christian feminist theology attempt to retrieve the symbol of the divine spirit, interpreting it in terms of the struggle of love to weave the fabric of more expansive selfhood and wider and deeper community. Not only would this theological focus reinforce the relational anthropology and interpretation of love described above, but it would be able to draw upon symbolism that has deep roots within the Christian tradition, by having already evoked rich imagery in scripture, theology, and prayer. Reappropriating this imagery from a feminist perspective would allow for a revision of Christian theology in a way that is not foreign to the symbolic and ritual life of a Christian community.

Clearly, much more needs to be done to spell out the details of this interpretation of human personhood and the moral life and to excavate its theological ramifications. In this essay I have suggested how feminist reflection should proceed to develop more adequate symbolic visions. The approach taken in this essay is rooted in a recognition of the historicity of human life and thought. Recognizing the historical and cultural influences that shape all religious activity and belief, this perspective refuses to consider any text, creed, ritual, or symbol system as normative. The entirety of a tradition must be subject to a "hermeneutics of suspicion," to a critical evaluation of its adequacy to illuminate and empower human flourishing in the present. The historicity of human life, however, makes the revision and extension of a tradition a more attractive option than the creation of completely novel alternatives. Carefully crafted theologies that lack connection with presently inhabited visions remain marginal to the life and thought of historical beings and hence are ineffective in bringing about the transformation of the political and social realities of patriarchy.

Acknowledging the importance of continuity in our lived worlds must not become an apologetic device for retaining the distortions of the past, particularly in their symbolic formulations. To minimize this danger we need to make explicit our moral and anthropological ideals and, from this vantage point, assess and, if necessary, revise the patriarchal naming of divine reality. Combining moral and theological reflection in this fashion allows for a more thoroughgoing critique and revision of a tradition. Following this procedure, this essay attempts to extend the Christian tradition from a feminist perspective by reinterpreting the meaning of love, one of its controlling ethical motifs. In place of the traditional Christian focus on self-sacrificial love, I have proposed an alternative interpretation of love in which the primary aim is the creation, deepening, and extension of communal life. This form of love suggests an understanding of the human and the divine that differs in important respects from the classical Christian vision. In place of the autonomous individual, which has been the paradigm for both God and the human person, this interpretation of love suggests that an expansive relational process constitutes the core of both the person and the divine. The Christian symbol most able to capture this relational life is that of the divine spirit, understood as the immanent power of love to create persons and communities. Resurrecting and refining this symbol can best illuminate and facilitate this form of life and thereby contribute to the feminist transformation of the Christian tradition.

NOTES

1. For a clarification of these two orientations, see *Womanspirit Rising,* ed. C. Christ and J. Plaskow (San Francisco: Harper & How, 1979), 9–11.
2. Examples of this approach include L. Russell, *Human Liberation in a Feminist Perspective—a Theology* (Philadelphia: Westminster, 1974) and V. Mollenkott, "Women and the Bible: A Challenge to Male Interpretations," in *Mission Trends No. 4,* ed. G. Anderson and T. Stransky (New York: Paulist Press, 1979).
3. See E. Schüssler Fiorenza, *In Memory of Her* (New York: Crossroad, 1983), chaps. 1–3; E. Schüssler Fiorenza, *Bread Not Stone* (Boston: Beacon 1984).
4. Schüssler Fiorenza, *Bread Not Stone,* 154.
5. Two of the strongest arguments on the importance of the Goddess for women are found in C. Downing, *The Goddess: Mythological Images of the Feminine* (New York: Crossroad, 1981) and C. Christ, "Why Women Need the Goddess: Phenomenological, Psychological, and Political Reflections," in *Womanspirit Rising,* ed. Christ and Plaskow.
6. For a discussion of this character of symbolic worlds, see C. Geertz, "Reli-

gion as a Cultural System," in *The Interpretation of Cultures* (New York: Basic Books, 1979) and P. Berger, *The Sacred Canopy* (Garden City, NY: Anchor Books, 1969), especially Part 1.

7. Schüssler Fiorenza, *In Memory of Her*, xix.

8. Given the extensive literature documenting the patriarchal distortion of Judaism and Christianity, this essay is not concerned with reiterating those analyses. The focus here is on the problem of feminist theological reconstruction of a tradition.

9. See, for example, S. K. Langer, *Philosophy in a New Key* (Cambridge: Harvard University Press, 1973); Berger, *The Sacred Canopy*.

10. See Geertz, "Religion as a Cultural System," and "Ethos, Worldview, and the Analysis of Sacred Symbols" in *The Interpretation of Cultures*.

11. See A. MacIntyre, *After Virtue* (Notre Dame: University of Notre Dame Press, 1981); J. Stout, *The Flight from Authority: Religion, Morality, and the Quest for Autonomy* (Notre Dame: University of Notre Dame Press, 1981). From a different perspective Stanley Hauerwas has explored this relationship in his concern with story in the formation of the moral life. See, for example, *Vision and Virtue* (Notre Dame: University of Notre Dame Press, 1981); *Truthfulness and Tragedy* (Notre Dame: University of Notre Dame Press, 1977).

12. Although my use of the term *divine* is not standard, there are certain advantages to using it in this fashion. First, its generality, indeed vagueness, enables it to avoid many of the historical associations conveyed through the symbol of "God." Second, insofar as it is an adjectival form, it resists the typical reification to which nouns are prone. Using *divine* alone without adding *person, being, reality,* or *nature* helps to avoid a dualistic worldview in which sacrality or divinity is other than this realm.

13. See Matthew 22:34–40; John 13:34–35; 1 Corinthians 13:1–13. The primacy of love was brought into the Christian theological tradition largely through the writings of Augustine and Ps. Dionysius. See, for example, Augustine, *The Trinity*, trans. S. McKenna (Washington, DC: Catholic University of America, 1963), 207, 492–94; Ps. Dionysius, *The Divine Names*, trans. C. E. Rolt (London: S.P.C.K., 1975), chap. 4.14.

14. Two important studies of the concept of Christian agape include A. Nygren, *Eros and Agape* (New York: Harper & Row, 1969) and G. Outka, *Agape: An Ethical Analysis* (New Haven: Yale University Press, 1972).

15. In addition to Nietzsche's scathing attacks on the Christian love ethic, recent theologians and ethicists criticizing Christian self-sacrificial love include: V. Saiving, "The Human Situation: A Feminine View," in *Womanspirit Rising*, ed. Christ and Plaskow; J. Plaskow, *Sex, Sin, and Grace: Women's Experience and the Theologies of R. Niebuhr and P. Tillich* (Washington, DC: University Press of America, 1980); M. Daly, *Beyond God the Father* (Boston: Beacon Press, 1973); B. H. Andolsen, "Agape in Feminist Ethics," *Journal of Religious Ethics* 9, no. 1 (1981) 69–83; and B. Harrison, "The Power of Anger in the Work of Love," *Union Seminary Quarterly Review* 36, Supplement (1981), 41–57.

16. Other thinkers who have developed interpretations of love along this line

include J. Royce, *The Problem of Christianity* (Chicago: University of Chicago Press, 1968); D. D. Williams, *The Spirit and Forms of Love* (New York: Harper & Row, 1968); and Harrison, "Power of Anger."

17. I. Murdoch, *The Sovereignty of Good* (New York: Schocken Books, 1970), 28–30.
18. E. H. Haney, "What is Feminist Ethics? A Proposal for Continuing Discussion," *Journal of Religious Ethics* 8, no. 1 (1980): 118–21.
19. My position is indebted to other Christian theologians who have interpreted the divine nature in terms of the universal community of being. Most influential in my thinking have been Jonathan Edwards, Josiah Royce, and H. Richard Niebuhr.
20. Harrison, "Power of Anger," 48, 47.
21. M. Taylor, *Erring* (Chicago: University of Chicago Press, 1984), 35.
22. Harrison, "Power of Anger," 48.
23. Harrison makes a similar point in "Power of Anger," 46.

CHAPTER 9

The Ethical Limitations of Autonomy: A Critique of the Moral Vision of Psychological Man

MARY ELLEN ROSS

In recent years, many ethicists have ceased to emphasize the moment of moral decision and have turned their attention instead to the construction of character and acquisition of virtue. These theorists argue that, long before a person faces a moral dilemma and decides either to maximize happiness or adhere to principles, she or he has developed a moral perspective that logically leads to that decision. That is, moral decisions are historical—they occur where the individual's specific past and her or his cultural traditions converge. So we cannot fully understand the decision to end an unplanned pregnancy, manufacture a defective car, or boycott South African goods without posing questions about character.

Here I intend to join this discussion by explaining why patriarchy—which I define as consisting of hierarchical social relations that allow men to dominate women—obscures our moral vision. I argue that this failure means that a feminist ethic should criticize patriarchy not only because of its hierarchical nature, but also because it gives rise to a kind of character lacking in the capacity for moral discernment. We can see the seriousness of this problem when we measure the moral stature of the modern North American against a contemporary moral crisis such as world hunger.

World Hunger and Our Moral Deficiency

We middle-class North Americans generally go about our daily business oblivious to the fact that in Africa, Asia, and Latin America, two billion people suffer from malnutrition. Moreover, ten thousand children, women, and men starve to death every day.[1] Occasionally, when this chronic hunger becomes so acute in a particular place that it qualifies as a famine, we turn our attention to the problem and analyze it in magazines, newspapers, and on television news programs. We may even initiate hunger relief drives. But our response is generally temporary, and when the famine subsides (or at least we grow tired of hearing about it), the problem fades in our consciousness and we behave as if it had never happened.

Americans treat the hungry in poorer nations as fundamentally different and separate groups of individuals. We seem to lack the willingness to enter sympathetically into their situation and to fully understand their struggle. Lacking this willingness, we fail morally, for the ability to identify with others is an essential component of the moral life: one cannot possess a moral vision without the capacity to move beyond the narrow boundaries of self-interest to concern for the whole human community.

Because we pay so little attention to the problem of hunger, we harbor serious misconceptions about its causes, readily accepting the most common analysis of famine that labels it the result of some natural disaster such as drought or flood. We also accept the usual explanation for the more chronic form of hunger: that it arises when runaway population growth strains already scarce resources. In fact, much—some food experts say most—of the poverty and hunger in the Third World results from patterns of consumption and economic imperialism originating in the First World. For example, the Dominican Republic exports two-thirds of its agricultural products. Of these products, sugar is the most important and nearly all of it ends up on First World tables. Moreover, the U.S.-based multinational corporation Gulf and Western, which controls more than ten percent of the arable land in the Dominican Republic, is the largest exporter of sugar. Thus the activities of an American business, in its effort to profit by serving First World appetites, cause the diversion of Dominican farmland from the cultivation of staples to the production of luxury export crops while half of the residents of the country suffer from severe malnutrition.[2]

Even those who have devoted considerably more effort than most Americans to exploring hunger can fail in their perception of the problem. Perhaps the best example of this failure is Garrett Hardin, a biologist who has written extensively on hunger. Hardin's analysis contains major distortions, for he ignores the role wealthy nations play in creating poverty and hunger in the poorer ones; he holds the poor nations entirely responsible for their plight. He claims that they have created their own suffering by failing to control population growth as well as by relying on financial assistance from wealthier nations rather than striving for self-sufficiency. He concludes that the wealthier nations have no obligation to aid the hungry, further arguing that such aid would place so great a strain on our natural resources that we would instigate an environmental disaster. Hardin advises us to let the hungry starve, and the skewing of moral perception thus becomes an exhortation to avoid moral action.[3]

Before turning to Hardin's analysis, I will consider what makes possible this attitude, which I see as representative of a broader cultural problem.

Psychological Man: The Ascendent Character Type in Contemporary American Culture

To explore this question, I turn to the issue of character formation. In so doing, I shall look to the psychoanalysis of Sigmund Freud, a theory designed to help individuals cope with the modern world. Several recent commentators have recognized that Freud's work suggests a specific character type—what sociologist Philip Rieff calls "psychological man"[4]—as an appropriate model for those struggling to negotiate the demands of modernity. Freud thus bears the same relationship to current American life that Calvin bore to an earlier age: by constructing a theory that addresses the fundamental dilemmas of our culture, he has played a critical role in determining who we are. This is true even though Freud's theory is often appropriated in a mutilated form and "psychological man" assumes shapes that Freud himself would find distasteful.

The concept of psychological man emerges from Freud's meditations on the problem of authority. Freud, in focusing his attention on neurosis—both personal and communal—concludes that the clash of repressive cultural authority with the instinctual nature of human beings causes sickness. More specifically, the ethical ideals, religious norms, and legal restrictions that Western culture imposes on its members ignore the instincts and their resistance to social control. This conflict expresses itself as neurosis, which contains elements of both prohibition and resistance to prohibition.

Aware that the demands of cultural authorities are too high, Freud provides a theory that describes how to recognize these demands as excessive and to live without being enslaved by them. The secret lies with the adoption of what Freud calls the analytic attitude:

It consists simply in not directing one's notice to anything in particular and in maintaining the same "evenly suspended attention" . . . in the face of all that one hears. . . . For as soon as anyone deliberately concentrates his attention to a certain degree, he begins to select from the material before him; one point will be fixed in his mind with particular clearness and some other will be correspondingly disregarded, and in making this selection, he will be following his expectations or inclinations. This, however, is precisely what must not be done.[5]

Freud here describes the detachment of evenly suspended attention as an attribute of the practicing analyst, but such detachment also serves as the foundation of psychological man's approach to life. With the help of the analytic attitude, psychological man has overcome irrational loyalty to church, state, and all the institutions wielding social power that ask for more than anyone can give.

The most powerful authorities present all-encompassing worldviews—the Calvinist doctrine of predestination and Catholic moral theology, for example—in which unreachable standards of conduct are embedded, and psychological man must detach himself from the worldviews as well as the authorities. With the analytic attitude, he reduces every Weltanshauung to its origins in the human desire for protection and security and thus exposes it as wish rather than reality. As a result, psychological man accepts life as meaningless, for only a coherent worldview, built on the foundations of unassailable authority, can give life meaning.

Without a coherent worldview, what organizes psychological man's life? According to Rieff, the self is the only sound organizing principle for occupants of the modern world. Psychological man eschews grand schemes of meaning that call for virtue, even heroism, and concentrates on living as comfortable and stable a life as possible. He allows himself periods of instinctual release and no longer feels guilt over this. But he makes sure the times of release are controlled and calculated, so as not to sabotage the possibility of pleasure in the future.

Psychological man lives in what Rieff calls a "negative community."[6] Positive communities are based on faith, on belief in some authoritarian doctrine of salvation. Psychological man has no desire and no need to commit himself to such a community. He lives among other psychological men, pursuing pleasure and avoiding pain, asking for little and giving little. He learns nothing from the past and is relieved to have escaped repressive traditions. He does not think much of the future, for it holds no real hope for him. He exists in the present, anticipating the future only enough to maximize the possibility for a prudently pleasurable life.

Rieff asserts that the ethic of psychological man, although created in Europe, has flourished in the soil of American competitiveness and individualism. He states correctly that psychological man is becoming our dominant national character type.[7] At this time, the burden of proof is on anyone who would dispute that the reigning American cultural theme is the prudent pursuit of pleasure, entailing both the command to be disciplined and controlled—eat right, exercise, work hard, don't waste any time—and the exhortation to consume a universe of products, most of which advertising links to sex and aggression. Even those who see themselves as opposed to this theme in its most obvious forms end up subscribing to some version of it: the religious right, for example, fuses a restrictive morality on issues like abortion and homosexuality with permissive silence on the subject of uninhibited consumption.

Freud's reflections on authority and his recommendation of the ethic that Rieff calls psychological man are not only statements about modernity; they are above all concessions to patriarchy, for they focus on *paternal* authority, on the concrete manifestations of paternal power—from that of the deified father (God) to the internalized father (the superego). More specifically, Freud's discussions of authority are always cast in terms of the Oedipus complex, the drama of the father-son struggle for supremacy. The sons can be actual biological progeny or symbolic offspring, as in the case of the relation of god to believers or a great man to his followers. But no matter what form it takes, the Oedipus narrative is always a tale of hierarchy and domination. So Freud ends up recommending the character type Rieff calls psychological man largely because of his ambivalence toward patriarchal authority: he both distrusts it and views it as inevitable. Freud's thought therefore contains two opposing trends.

The first trend, the critical one, is evident in both his clinical and cultural writings. In the clinical writings, the critique of authority occurs in several references to the superego, the part of a boy's psyche that forms when he identifies with his father. This identification is built on fear of authority, for the boy believes that the consummation of his desire for his mother would lead to mutilation at the hands of his father. The process of identification includes internalization of his father's moral commands. These commands represent social morality in general, which becomes an integral part of the boy's character after he has passed through the oedipal period.

Many of Freud's clinical writings examine the role an overly demanding superego plays in the creation of an obsessive neurosis. Freud speculates that an obsession evolves in this way: First, a person develops a particularly harsh superego that represses an instinctual impulse. A ritualized activity then arises as a way of diverting attention from the impulse. But the impulse doesn't go away, and frustration intensifies its force, so that the obsessive activity—the symptom—occupies more and more of the neurotic's time and energy. The impulse to masturbate, for example, may bring on the response of handwashing, and as the impulse gains power through frustration, the handwashing becomes more frequent and disruptive of other activities.[8] Since psychoanalysis, when confronting the case of an obsessive patient, attempts to banish symptoms by taming the demands of the superego, a central task of Freud's method is the diminishment of the power of authority in the life of the individual.

Freud's cultural writings engage in a parallel struggle. Most of these writings focus on religion and either imply or explicitly argue that social authority should not reside with religious institutions. Freud argues that the concept of God arises in response to regressive needs and prevents believers from achieving any independence of thought or action. *The Future of an Illusion* concludes that

in the long run nothing can withstand reason and experience, and the contradiction that religion offers to both is all too palpable. Even purified religious ideas cannot escape this fate, so long as they try to preserve anything of the consolation of religion. No doubt if they confine themselves to a belief in a higher spiritual being, whose qualities are indefinable and whose purposes cannot be discerned, they will be proof against the challenge of science; but then they will also lose their hold on human interest.

Religion may console, but it also interferes with one's ability to exercise powers of reason because it involves deference to an illusory god. Science, on the other hand, defers only to verifiable human experience.[9] In this sense, science is nonhierarchical, for it considers data available to everyone.

Although Freud criticizes authority, he believes in the inevitability of hierarchical power arrangements: he claims only to instruct the individual concerning how to achieve a measure of psychological autonomy within hierarchical structures. Returning to Freud's extended discussion of the superego—conducted within dozens of essays—this trend in Freud's thought is evident: while Freud does believe in diminishing the savagery of the superego, he is also certain of the necessity of the superego's existence.

For Freud, this necessity arises from the fundamental problem of civilization: instincts pit human being against human being and must be controlled. In *Civilization and Its Discontents,* Freud hypothesizes that, in the state of nature, men would fight ceaselessly for the possession of women—in this scenario, he gives women the status of property—and life would be intolerable. He observes that, fortunately, aggression within civilization is relatively controlled. During the oedipal period, a boy is assisted in controlling his aggression toward his father by the formation of his superego. The superego is a segment of the ego that separates from the ego and, energized by aggression, turns that aggression on the ego in the form of guilt, rather than directing it outward in the form of patricide: "Civilization, therefore, obtains mastery over the individual's dangerous desire for aggression by weakening it and disarming it and by setting up an agency within him to watch over it, like a garrison in a conquered city."[10] While Freud prefers that this garrison be merciful, he has no doubt that its presence is necessary.

We can find further confirmation of Freud's recognition of the necessity of the superego in his writings on women. Here he argues that females, who do not fear castration, have no real motive for moving completely beyond the Oedipus complex and adopting a well-defined superego: "Their superego is never so inexorable, so impersonal, so independent of its emotional origins as we require it to be in men."[11] Freud values the qualities of an autonomous super-ego and concludes that the moral level of women is below that of men.

Signs of this more positive attitude toward authority emerge in the writings on religion as well. For example, in *Moses and Monotheism* Freud does not conceal his admiration for Moses, whom he credits with presenting the concept of monotheism to the Hebrews. Freud's discussion of Hebrew monotheism makes clear his assessment of Moses' religion as far superior to the Baal worship that preceded it and the Christianity that followed it, due to the Hebraic renunciation of polytheistic sensuality and magic. According to Freud's interpretation, Moses almost singlehandedly led his recalcitrant people to intellectual and psychological maturity.[12]

Freud's ambivalence toward authority yields an image of the good man—and I use the term advisedly, since Freud's theories deal almost exclusively with male development—who is neither conservative nor radical. He is a compromise figure who exhibits neither deep loyalty to a hierarchical social order nor any intention of dismantling it, for he views that order as necessary and thus inevitable. And while he will never be guilty of blind, fanatical loyalty to a cause, he also lacks the hope that society can survive beyond the death of hierarchy.

Of course, the possibility of the demise of hierarchy is the main hope and primary article of faith among feminists. Psychological man, insofar as he capitulates to asymmetrical power arrangements, violates the fundamental impulse of feminism. Moreover, psychological man presents another ethical problem: he cannot accurately perceive the moral crises that face us in the latter half of the twentieth century. Because he cannot perceive them, he cannot begin to address them. The case of world hunger provides a specific example of this moral failure.

Psychological Man on Hunger

Earlier I referred to Garrett Hardin's position on hunger. Now I would like to return to his argument and examine it more carefully to show how thoroughly it expresses psychological man's attitudes and how seriously it fails as a response to the crisis of world hunger.

Hardin's best-known discussion of hunger is "Lifeboat Ethics: The Case against Helping the Poor," in which he suggests we use the metaphor of the lifeboat to help us think through the hunger issue. He says that each wealthy nation resembles a lifeboat with limited supplies. Hordes of the needy from poorer countries surround every boat, and these needy are begging those in the lifeboats to let them climb aboard. Hardin warns that we cannot allow them on; if we do so, our boats will sink and everyone will drown. If we refuse their pleas, at least we in North America and Europe will stay afloat. Thus the lifeboat metaphor reveals the nature of our dilemma and its solution: we must let the needy starve, for there aren't enough resources to go around.

In addition, Hardin uses the metaphor of the commons, by which he means communal grazing land, to describe our situation. He depicts "the tragedy of the commons," which occurs when one herdsman, who feels no responsibility for preserving the land, allows his cattle to overgraze and destroy it, thwarting the other more careful herdsmen. Thus only one irresponsible person can ruin everything when property or goods are held in common. Hardin uses this image to argue against the establishment of a world food bank, which would take donations from the countries that have produced a food surplus and give supplies to those countries that have suffered a deficit. Hardin calls this bank, which "liberal international groups" and politicians such as Edward Kennedy and George McGovern have proposed, a "commons in disguise."[13] Like the irresponsible herdsman, the poor nations would abuse the privilege of the bank and draw from it year after year without attempting to limit their population growth and without learning to feed themselves. Such an asymmetrical situation would persist until uncontrolled population growth had disastrously depleted the earth's resources and radically diminished the quality of life in both rich and poor nations.

Hardin also takes on the issue of immigration. He sees this as related to food aid, for while food aid brings food to people, liberal immigration laws bring people to food. Both cases have the same result: misguided idealism does more and more damage to the earth by trying to care for everyone. In the end, such idealism will backfire, causing the destruction of our environment and making human survival difficult, even impossible.

But Hardin is not only against a world food bank and liberal immigration laws. He also opposes development aid such as the provision of farm machinery and fertilizers or the sending of agricultural advisers to the Third World. Because he believes that Third World population growth will continue at its present dangerous rate, he asserts that helping the hungry feed themselves is as harmful as giving simple handouts. Either way, the population of the poor countries will increase so quickly that it will bring on environmental ruin and make it impossible to pass a tolerable world on to our descendants.[14]

The attitudes of psychological man appear throughout the case Hardin presents: Hardin *is* psychological man in that he regards survival and comfort as his highest value. Ethicists call the stance Hardin takes "prudential," because it involves a careful weighing of options with the intent of selecting the one that affords the individual the greatest balance of pleasure over pain. Hardin's prudentialism spares him the difficulties entailed in swearing allegiance to a heroic ethic including excessively high-minded ideals like justice or the sanctity of life. These ideals would interfere with psychological man's antiheroic commitment to self-protection, since they often call for sacrifice.

Hardin also seems to accept the proposition that life is ultimately meaningless, for his belief that his personal survival must be his highest good prevents him from accepting a worldview that might provide meaning. He explicitly repudiates Marxism and Christianity, and we can surmise that he would reject all other worldviews organized around demanding moral principles.

Moreover, all major Western worldviews include the element of hope or a sense of futurity, and Hardin's view of life duplicates that of psychological man in its lack of hope and futurity. He does not believe that a fair or humane distribution of world resources is possible, and he is convinced that to attempt such a distribution would be disastrous: "complete justice—complete catastrophe."[15] His conception of the future is really a projection of the present— with all its inequalities and injustices—and is therefore not a conception of the future at all. This failure of imagination gives his thought a deeply conservative cast: unable to envision alternate worlds, he assents to a status quo of authoritarian social structures and hierarchical relationships. This leads him to argue that if we in the First World give up some of our power, privilege, and wealth, we will hasten the ruin of our environment.

In addition, Hardin embodies psychological man in his extreme isolation. This isolation leads him to choose the lifeboat metaphor over the spaceship metaphor many environmentalists prefer. Hardin implies that the spaceship image depicts human beings as equal and as sharing a common fate, whereas a truer depiction indicates a division between wealthy and poor, a fundamental separation between "them" and "us." As his argument proceeds, the reader can see the separation grow wider and wider, with Hardin falling just short of saying that those in the Third World are irresponsible and untrustworthy and consequently don't deserve any assistance.

But even those within the hypothetical lifeboats appear to have little binding them together. In fact, their only connection appears to be the capricious good fortune that put them inside and everyone else outside. Those on the inside thus constitute a negative community of those who find themselves in the same situation but otherwise have no ties to one another. Thus when Hardin raises the issue of our obligations to posterity, his statements lack conviction: if he experiences no connection with the hungry and no true bonds with his neighbors, how can we believe that his expression of concern for future generations is anything but an extraneous point he has tacked onto his argument in an attempt to give it extra persuasive force? In short, a careful look at Hardin's arguments reveals the reasoning of psychological man.

Further inquiry reveals the inadequacy of this reasoning. That Hardin does not understand the hunger dilemma is evident from his use of metaphors that fail to comprehend the issue. One of his weakest images is his primary metaphor, the misleading picture of the lifeboat with a few passengers inside and hordes of the drowning outside begging to be allowed on board. Hardin's conviction that we must protect ourselves from these overly fertile masses is based on two assumptions. First, he believes that food is scarce. However, if such a scarcity exists it is much less serious than Hardin will allow, and many experts on hunger, including Frances Moore Lappé, Joseph Collins, Susan George, and Suzanne Toton argue that no shortage exists at all. Rather, they contend that what appears to be shortage is actually a complex system of unequal distribution of the world's resources. This inequality works to the advantage of those in the First World and helps perpetuate hunger and poverty in the Third.

In *Food First,* Lappé and Collins examine the myth of scarcity and its sources. One source is the misleading nature of hunger statistics. For example, while acre-to-person ratios are often presented as evidence that there are too many people and not enough land in major portions of the world, such ratios actually tell us little. We need to know instead how efficiently a particular country uses its land and how its agricultural products are distributed. The situation in Bangladesh illustrates this point. Although most of us assume that extreme scarcity prevails there, Bangladesh actually has twice the cultivated land of populous Taiwan, which has no difficulty feeding its people. Unfortunately, though, land ownership in Bangladesh is highly concentrated, with seven percent of the farms comprising thirty-one percent of the farmland. The absentee landlords who possess most of the land prefer either to grow jute for export to the First World or grain for export to India, where it commands a higher price than it would in Bangladesh. Bangladesh also has rich inland fishing grounds—perhaps the richest in the world—but these, too, are controlled by absentee owners content to raise relatively few fish and sell them for a large profit on the world market.[16]

Moreover, what appears to be scarcity may actually be surfeit. Since the Depression, when overproduction of farm goods, along with other factors, exerted a disastrous effect on the American economy, the U.S. government has tried to control overproduction by ordering cutbacks, recommending the planting of animal food and nonfood crops, and devising less efficient ways to use produce. For example, the elevation in food prices on the world market in 1972 resulted from the Food Power policies of the United States, which increased demand for certain kinds of produce and then raised the prices of the commodities to increase U.S. export profits.[17]

Hardin's second assumption, that overpopulation is the fundamental cause of hunger, is also incorrect. While rapid population growth undoubtedly will eventually strain the world's resources, focusing solely on this growth causes confusion. Hunger and rapid population growth are not related as cause and effect, but as twin symptoms of fundamental economic inequalities. People are hungry because they are poor, and they have many children for the same reason: "Another baby for a poor family means an extra mouth to feed—a very marginal difference. But by the time that child is four or five years old, it will make important contributions to the whole family—fetching water from the distant well, taking meals to fathers and brothers in the field, feeding animals." Later on the child helps with more complicated household chores in a house without the simplest appliances or running water. In their old age, the parents can rely on support from their children—unnecessary in more prosperous countries that have some sort of social security system.[18]

The answer, then, is to treat not merely the symptom; passing out contraceptives to the poor has generally proven unsuccessful. What curbs population growth is economic reform—most importantly, land reform. As we can see from the example of the Western European countries, Taiwan, and Korea, among others, a high per capita income usually means a lower birth rate.[19] Whereas children are a financial benefit to the poor, they are a financial liability to the prosperous, as many North American parents struggling to provide their child with a college education can testify.

Hardin's lifeboat image also implies that the First World bears no responsibility for the hunger of the Third; it suggests that we are merely trying to protect our own cache of food, which we have wisely avoided squandering. It further suggests that those outside the lifeboat are asking for what is rightfully ours. But this ignores the history of our relations with the Third World, particularly as manifested in colonialism.

With colonialism, indigenous development in most colonized Third World countries was derailed and replaced by forms of production and trade that served the colonizing powers. Production of food and other goods necessary to maintain life locally was disrupted in favor of cultivation of crops for export, and trade routes for internal food distribution fell into disuse while trade mechanisms for export were enhanced.

This emphasis on exportation transformed native economies. Under colonial rule, the notion of private property was instituted, and, due to the introduction of a money economy and a tax system, the small landholders gradually lost their land and were forced to live on the plantations of the rich local elites and the colonists. For example, in India before British rule, debt was common but the moneylender had little power. Land could not be lost through indebtedness because land was not privately owned. But the British instituted private ownership to make tax collection easier, and the smallholders suffered as a result, for they were expected to pay their taxes in cash and on time. When harvests were bad and the small landholder could not pay taxes, he was forced to borrow money, using land as collateral. If his harvest continued to be poor, he lost his land.[20]

The type of overt political colonialism that the British Empire represented is rare today. But this form of colonialism helped create conditions for the neocolonialism of multinational corporations, the First World–based conglomerates with branches all over the world. Like the traditional colonizing powers, multinationals encourage the cultivation of a single crop in individual countries and foster a system of land ownership that allows a few local elites to control vast areas of land. Landless peasants therefore have no other choice than to harvest bananas, coffee beans, sugar, or other export crops for minimal wages. Although the multinationals argue that they further economic development by investing in the Third World, little evidence supports this. These corporations invest their Third World profits almost immediately in their First World base countries. Moreover, the related claim that they provide jobs should be questioned. While this is true in the literal sense, the jobs they do provide seem hardly worth having, with wages dipping as low as fifty cents an hour. In addition, the multinationals automate production whenever possible, and increased automation in the coming years will inevitably result in fewer jobs.[21]

But the multinationals not only pursue their goals by sponsoring cash crop cultivation; they also use the Third World to extend the market for their candy bars, baby formulas, soft drinks, and other products once their First World market has been saturated. They do this primarily through vigorous advertising that links particular products with the prosperous "good life" in the First World, obscuring the fact that these products often have low nutritional value compared to locally grown foods. For example, in Brazil Coca Cola markets Fanta Orange drink, the second most profitable beverage that Coca Cola sells in that country. But the name "Fanta Orange" is misleading, for it contains no orange juice. While individual Brazilians drink great quantities of Fanta Orange, their country exports nearly all its indigenous orange crop, and many Brazilians suffer from a deficiency in vitamin C.[22]

Thus the phenomenon of multinational colonialism impugns the innocence of the First World and calls Hardin's image of the lifeboat into question. A more accurate picture would depict the lifeboats of the affluent nations loaded with supplies snatched from the drowning. This image would also more accurately depict other aspects of First World–Third World relations, including unfair terms of trade that keep the prices of Third World products low and development programs that serve First World businesses more than the hungry.[23]

Hardin presents a second problematic image, the metaphor of the commons. He argues against any shared property—and ultimately the idea of a food bank—by resorting to generalizations about essential human nature: "In a crowded world of less than perfect human beings, mutual ruin is inevitable if there are no controls."[24] Here Hardin operates on the assumption that human beings are always and everywhere motivated by self-interest and unable to work together for a common good. The well-known perils of arguing for the constancy of human nature bear repeating: no evidence to substantiate such an assertion exists, and the assertion itself serves as an excuse to inhibit constructive change because it presents the current social order as the only possible order. Where belief in "human nature" prevails, the unequal relationship between the advantaged and disadvantaged remains secure.

The Demise of Psychological Man

Thus Hardin has presented a fatally flawed case. But to understand the significance of this fact, we must acknowledge that Hardin's understanding of the crisis of world hunger is no aberration but draws on rationalizations common to us all. Hardin differs simply in raising these rationalizations to the level of an explicit and relatively coherent argument. In other words, the prevailing American character type is blind to the complexities of a moral problem like world hunger. But can a different society that would engender a new character type with more acute moral perception be conceived?

Certainly this vision is elusive. But if we look carefully, we can find intimations of a more morally sound order. I have already cited some examples: the writings of those who have not been satisfied with the usual explanations for hunger but have insisted on pursuing the problem to its roots and reflecting on its implications. These writings present a vision of a world in which we can overcome hunger through the just distribution of resources and the leveling of unequal power relations. This vision of an altered world implies a new character type as well: one willing to accept responsibility for inequalities and to redress past injustices. In her or his emotional engagement, acceptance of binding moral principles, and sense of futurity, this type would be psychological man's opposite.

We can perceive intimations of this world and character in other places as well. Freud's theory rests on his multiple interpretations of the Oedipus complex, the central and most vivid experience for men in contemporary Western culture. But, as many feminist psychoanalytic theorists have pointed out, the period of mother-infant unity prior to the oedipal period provides the primary developmental experience for women in our culture. Whereas most men have had their characters formed in an oedipal struggle with a patriarch, women's character formation is more directly tied to the memory of interdependence and harmony in relation to a mother.[25] Women, therefore, have character resources to counter the isolation and detachment of psychological man. Moreover, the memory of preoedipal existence provides women with a model of a cooperative, communal reality that might serve as an alternative to patriarchy.

Such a reality has already been depicted in various forms, both in art and in life. Feminist writers and artists have produced images of equal relationships between women and men, nurturing relationships between women and women, moments of individual and collective transcendence of the isolation and emptiness patriarchy produces, and courageous battles against the cruelest mechanisms by which patriarchy maintains itself.[26] Feminist activists have created egalitarian communities based on the belief that our society can find alternatives to the suicidal course we're presently following, a course that may culminate in a hopelessly poisoned environment, greater and greater inequalities between rich and poor, and ultimately nuclear war.[27]

Psychological man, born in the early part of this century, has aged quickly and no longer seems suited to managing the problems of our culture. The feminist voices that provide alternatives to his character and his world may be muted, but they demand a hearing. We cannot afford to remain deaf to their message.

NOTES

1. W. Aiken and H. LaFollette, "Introduction," in *World Hunger and Moral Obligation,* ed. W. Aiken and H. LaFollette (Englewood Cliffs, NJ: Prentice-Hall, 1977), 1.
2. S. Toton, *World Hunger: The Responsibility of Christian Education* (Maryknoll: Orbis Books, 1982), 58–59.
3. G. Hardin, "Lifeboat Ethics: The Case Against Helping the Poor," in *World Hunger,* ed. Aiken and LaFollette, 11–21.
4. P. Rieff, *The Mind of the Moralist* (Chicago: University of Chicago Press, 1979), 356–57. Why did psychological man emerge in the twentieth century and no earlier? Rieff would reply that conditions for psychological man's existence have occurred only recently. Although Rieff does not examine these explicitly, the frequently mentioned characteristics of modernity play an important role in psychological man's genesis. These characteristics, including structural differentiation and the rise of technology, have combined with the thought of Freud to produce an unprecedented character type. Several other works besides Rieff's have traced this phenomenon. The most prominent include Christopher Lasch, *The Culture of Narcissism* (New York: 1979) and Robert Bellah, et al., *Habits of the Heart* (Berkeley and Los Angeles: University of California Press, 1985).
5. S. Freud, "Recommendations on Analytic Technique," *The Standard Edition of the Complete Psychological Works of Sigmund Freud,* ed. and trans. J. Strachey (London: Hogarth Press, 1961), 12:111–12.
6. Rieff, "Introduction," in *Therapy and Technique,* ed. P. Rieff (New York: Collier Books, 1963), 15.
7. For an extended discussion of psychological man, see Rieff, *The Triumph of the Therapeutic* (New York: Harper Torch Books, 1966). For brief discussions, see Rieff, *Mind,* 329–57, and Rieff, "Introduction," in *Therapy.*
8. Freud, "Inhibitions, Symptoms, and Anxiety," *Standard Edition,* 20:112–18.
9. Freud, *The Future of an Illusion,* in *Standard Edition,* 21:54, 53.
10. Freud, *Civilization and Its Discontents,* in *Standard Edition,* 21:123–24.
11. Freud, "Some Psychical Consequences of the Anatomical Distinction Between the Sexes," *Standard Edition,* 19:257.
12. Freud, *Moses and Monotheism,* in *Standard Edition,* 23:113–15 and passim.
13. Hardin, "Lifeboat Ethics," 14, 15.
14. Hardin, "Lifeboat Ethics," 11–21.
15. Hardin, "Lifeboat Ethics," 12.
16. F. M. Lappé and J. Collins, *Food First: Beyond the Myth of Scarcity* (Boston: Houghton Mifflin Co., 1977), 19–21.
17. Lappé and Collins, *Food First,* 22, 23.
18. S. George, *How the Other Half Dies: The Real Reasons for World Hunger* (Montclair, NJ: Allanheld, Osmun, and Co., 1977), 37.
19. George, *How the Other Half Dies,* 41.
20. Lappé and Collins, *Food First,* 88.
21. Toton, *World Hunger,* 55, 56.
22. Lappé and Collins, *Food First,* 306.

23. Toton, *World Hunger,* 27–37, 38–51.
24. Hardin, "Lifeboat Ethics," 14.
25. You can find examples of this argument in N. Chodorow, *The Reproduction of Mothering* (Berkeley and Los Angeles: University of California Press, 1978) and E. F. Keller, *Gender and Science* (New Haven: Yale University Press, 1985).
26. Examples of these include communal art projects such as *The Dinner Party* by Judy Chicago, novels such as *Fly Away Home* by Marge Piercy, poems such as those in *Chosen Poems* by Audre Lorde, and short stories such as those in *Later the Same Day* by Grace Paley.
27. Greenham Common, the antinuclear women's camp, provides one of the most vivid illustrations of this phenomenon.

Part Three

EMBODIMENT, RELATIONSHIP, AND RELIGIOUS EXPERIENCE

CHAPTER 10

Negotiating Autonomy:
African Women and Christianity

TERRI A. CASTANEDA

By utilizing the dynamics of a broad historical process that provides specific examples of women acting in social contexts, this essay illustrates ways in which some females have made use of the clash of imperialist and indigenous patriarchal cultures to win greater control over their lives. In this instance, we are discussing African women.

In the foreign colonization of Africa, women were subjected to a combination of patriarchal structures both from their own and invading cultures. While undoubtedly victimized because of this, some nevertheless negotiated alternatives to their conventional social roles and status by finding ways of escaping domestic slavery, poverty, and homelessness. A documentation of the lives of individual African women will demonstrate the opportunities that they found through Christian conversion.

In the past, historians have found it difficult to rely solely on the records of colonial governments and mission societies because of their legitimation of colonial rule. They have found anthropological literature equally problematic for its ignoring of colonialism. Now a new scholarship is emerging in African history with such writers as Jean Hay, Kristin Mann, Luise White, and Marcia Wright who seek to interpret the rare instances where individual women emerge from the historical literature as conscious social actors. From the work of these feminist historians, I have brought together this account of African women responding to the presence of Christianity and colonialism.

African women's responses to Christianity have come from a wide range of geographical and sociocultural settings in sub-Saharan Africa: urban to rural, Kikuyu to Yoruba, Protestant to Catholic. Likewise, responses have come from both matrilineal and patrilineal societies and are given equal importance in this essay because, no matter how descent was traced or which postmarital residence patterns predominated, a woman's status in traditional Africa was defined in terms of her relationship to men. Simply stated, in patrilineal societies women were ultimately dependent upon their fathers and husbands and in matrilineal societies, upon the men of their mother's lineage.[1] In presenting evidence from such a broad spectrum, I hope to demonstrate that a number of African women, in varying locations and circumstances, distilled from Christianity and Christian institutions spiritual, physical, psychological, or economic emancipation. I will specifically focus on three institutions from which women derived marriage alternatives and a language for liberation from sexist and colonialist oppression: Christian marriage, Christian missions and convents, and Christian education.

It is ironic that African women could use Christian ideology and institutions to gain leverage in situations over which men typically had control, for the first missionaries to Africa were primarily men—men who were, themselves, products of a Victorian society based upon a male supremacist ideology.[2] Naturally, these male missionaries sought men, not women, as converts. The first converts, young men and boys, possibly selected by the local chief, usually went to the mission grounds to work for wages or to attend school (for which some students were paid). In West Africa young men were attracted to the mission schools because missionaries and the colonial administrations cooperated to educate individuals qualified to become paid civil servants. In East Africa, the sons of landless men, with few or no cattle, eagerly joined mission communities, where they obtained food and clothing in exchange for a nominal amount of daily work. Even more importantly, they obtained training that allowed them to become government clerks. By and large, though, emphasis on the conversion of young men proved to be futile. In the end the missionaries discovered that young men who had gone to the missions, supposedly to read the Scriptures and be prepared for baptism, left as soon as they had acquired the skills they needed for jobs in the civil and commercial sectors.[3]

The missionaries also discovered that older males were just as ambiguous in their commitment to Christianity as their sons. In the case of the adult men, the major deterrent to conversion was not the lure of the colonial service and pay but the conflict between Christian and African marriage. From the start, the missionaries placed emphasis on the institution of Christian marriage, citing it as both the cornerstone of the faith and the key to the Christianization of Africa.[4] They believed that once traditional marriage was replaced with Christian marriage, a new morality would naturally follow in other spheres of African life. Accordingly, they developed tactics intended to promote and facilitate the Christian marriage of their male converts: they refused to sanction specific African marriage customs; they established mission stations to which, or near which, converts were able to move their families; they set up schools to educate an African clergy and laity that, in turn, could aid in the development of native churches and thus ensure the institutionalization of the Christian marriage and family tradition.

While churches may have disagreed along denominational or sectarian lines over such issues as alcohol consumption, the role of women in the church, or the appropriate relationship of the mission societies to the colonial state, they agreed on criteria that qualified a marriage as "Christian": absolute monogamy, absolute indissolubility, and celebration in a form recognized by the Christian churches.[5] In keeping with these criteria, they opposed a number of African marriage and kinship practices, most particularly the payment of the bride-price, which they viewed as a callous, mercantile transaction; levirate marriage, which they often reduced to the superficial inheritance of yet another female body; and polygamy, which they characterized as everything from the legitimization of unbridled lust to the institutionalization of domestic slavery.[6]

Of all these practices, polygamy was by far the most offensive to the missionaries, who had only superficial, if any, knowledge of the local context for the practice. For example, polygamous marriage in Africa joined not only a bride and groom, but lineages, and on occasion, entire villages, which might then become economically and politically allied. Moreover, in many polygamous groups, such as the Yoruba, husbands and wives observe several years of postpartum sexual abstinence, and monogamy, in such cases, not only severely restricts a man's sexual activity, but more importantly, the number of legitimate children he can produce.[7]

Still, polygamy was in direct contradiction to Christian doctrine, not only as practiced in Africa but elsewhere, and it proved to be a tremendous barrier to the campaign to Christianize the "Dark Continent." In the instance of women's lives, however, the fight against polygamy had particular significance because missionaries eventually came to view the wives of polygamous men as victims. Why should they be refused salvation because their husbands refused to accept monogamy?

The missionaries quickly discovered that conversion of the wives of polygamous husbands was not always simple, and their strategy for achieving it was never clear or consistent. Some mission societies concluded that the wives had to be denied baptism, while others accepted these women as potential converts but refused them communion; still others decided that they were entitled to the full privileges of church membership.[8]

Strict insistence upon monogamous marriage, however, produced contradictions that could be just as antithetical to Christian teachings as was polygamy. Missionaries feared that among the potential results of strict opposition to polygamy might be "divorce, fatherless children, destitute women, and prostitution."[9] One missionary succinctly characterized the dilemma: "It is true I have never baptized a polygamist, but I have never ventured to cause a divorce."[10] While in some cases the strong commitment to monogamy did produce some of what missionaries feared, in others it offered a woman opportunity to negotiate a marriage with more security than she would have otherwise experienced without the constraints that Christian ideology imposed.[11] Many women, if they adhered to the mission criteria for marriage, often stood to gain precisely those things that men risked losing: wealth, status, and autonomy.

The special brand of Victorian Christianity, imported in the late nineteenth century to Lagos Colony, Nigeria, and nurtured in mission schools, gave rise to a society of Yoruba-educated elite whose membership relied primarily upon the Christian union as its identifying characteristic. Christian marriages were used by both men and women for social and economic upward mobility in Lagos and other colonies of British West Africa.[12] In addition, when the colonial government passed an ordinance that upheld the mission criteria for marriage in 1884, many Yoruba women entered into Christian marriage for personal reasons: to obtain a permanently monogamous union, to obtain a household separate from that of their affinal kin, and perhaps most importantly to gain the right to inherit property from their husbands. As historian Kristin Mann explains: "The elite expected monogamy would ensure wives' exclusive claims to their husbands' resources [and] free women from emotional and sexual competition with other wives. The new inheritance law gave ordinance wives and their children new rights to men's property in cases of intestacy." Traditional Yoruba marriage afforded none of this.[13]

Emily Cole exemplified the reasons that some Yoruba women entered into Christian marriage. Cole attended schools in England and France for two years and returned to Lagos in 1871 to marry a Saro printer named Richard Beale Blaize. Mann notes that her lifestyle undoubtedly lived up to elite women's expectations of Christian marriage:

Mrs. Blaize assisted her husband in his printing shop as a bride but withdrew from his affairs as he became more successful, devoting her time to raising six children, teaching music and fine arts at home, and organizing ladies' literary and social clubs. The Blaizes lived in one of the grandest homes in Lagos, traveled regularly to England, and gave their children the best upbringing money could buy. . . . R. B. Blaize died in 1904 leaving their children the bulk of an estate valued at "60,000 pounds."[14]

Regardless of the independence, dignity, and security that the Christian concept of marriage may have promised, not all women were in a position to enter such unions, and not all desired marriage. For some, what Christianity offered was an alternative to marriage, an option not always available to women in African society. Among the Kikuyu, for instance, women are theoretically able to exercise choice in the selection of a marriage partner. Anglican missionary records from the early 1900s, however, candidly reveal that those women who first ran to the mission stations in Kenya generally were fleeing from a forced and unwelcome marriage and a reality that, in stressful times, was obviously contrary to the Kikuyu ideal of free choice.[15]

Protestant mission stations were not the only refuge available to African women who sought an alternative to marriage. By the early twentieth century the Roman Catholic church had fully transplanted its structural concept of *civitas dei* to its mission fields. In transferring the same hierarchical categories of the clergy and the laity, the church extended to Africans the same capacity to convert with varying degrees of commitment that its Western membership enjoyed. The ability to offer oneself to the church was particularly beneficial for women like Amartha Sibwi, a young girl from Nzama, Nyasaland. In late 1922 she joined the Order of African Sisters after seeking counsel from the Father Superior on how she might avoid getting married.[16]

By the turn of the century, marriage avoidance had become a goal for many women in and around Nyasaland (now Malawi). For decades colonialism had disrupted traditional life. In countless ways women had become the victims of changing social values and institutions. They were not only subject to being traded and sold as compensation for debts by the men of their own disintegrating societies, but they were also objects to the sexual whims of settlers and colonial personnel. Undoubtedly, their deteriorated status played a part in the popularity of the sisterhood in that region. Historian Ian Linden writes:

It is plain that the Little Servants of the Blessed Virgin Mary gave Catholic girls one of the few channels for female independence in colonial Malawi. Convent life was humanly, materially, and spiritually an improvement on village life; it gave women a dignified and personally fulfilling existence . . . achievement of status, [and] liberation from the constraints of a male-dominated society. . . .[17]

For many African women, membership in a religious order continued to serve as an alternative to marriage despite the pressure of motherhood as the paramount role for the African woman. One African nun from the Sisters of the Child Jesus in Rhodesia, speaking of herself and the other sisters in her group, summed up their decisions to become nuns despite social pressure against it:

When we go to the convent we reject the greatest value of our society to have children of your own. An African woman wants nothing more in life than children. Our whole upbringing is geared toward it. It is our highest ideal. . . . When we enter the convent, we know all this very well.[18]

Clearly, many African women chose a contemplative religious life that liberated them from life patterns dictated by traditional religions and social expectations even though opposed by their families and societies. Whether liberation was a consciously motivating factor, their choices effected independence from conventional social roles and commitments.

As well as serving as an alternative for women who chose not to marry, missions and religious orders were important sanctuaries for women whose marriages had failed or who found themselves in an anomalous position within either their own society or the structure of the church itself. Such was the case for the two founding members of the first religious order for African women in Nyasaland. Both founders were women who were separated from their husbands. One of the founders, Elizabeth Nyambele, had married at the age of fourteen or fifteen but chose not to return with her husband to his village. Soon afterwards she developed sores on her legs and moved close to the Nankhunda Catholic Mission to get treatment and gain employment in the mission orphanage. Her cofounder was Martha Phiri, who suffered from a disease so disfiguring that her husband deserted her. She also found her way to Nankhunda Mission to get treatment and earn her living in the orphanage. In late 1922, the mission sent Elizabeth and Martha to Nguludi where they became the first Sisters of the Little Servants of the Blessed Virgin Mary, the same order that young Amartha Sibwe later joined in order to escape marriage.[19] By working at the mission settlement, Elizabeth and Martha found a way out of the physical hardships of being alone, ill, and without the economic support of a husband, and by joining a religious order they were able to become acceptable and fully participating members of the Catholic church.

Anthropologists and other colonial personnel often criticized the settlement scheme that missionaries had believed was so essential to the maintenance of a Christian life for their early male converts. These critics alleged that the settlements attempted to operate in isolation, thereby promoting the breakup of traditional kinship structures. Missionaries denied the charges, claiming that many African men asked to settle on or near the mission stations. This was true also for many women, for whom the settlements offered a rare and critical opportunity.[20]

For this class of women, Christianity and the missions represented more than a place to seek moral support or economic assistance. Missions often were a last resort, a final hope for protection and refuge from dire circumstances. Marcia Wright has recovered the life histories of four "women in peril" in warlord-torn nineteenth-century East-Central Africa. Known as Chisi, Narwimba, Meli, and Bwanikwa, these women had been repeatedly traded and sold from master to master or husband to husband, often facing homelessness and impoverishment. Village life and economic stability in the area was rapidly dissolving in the second half of the nineteenth century, and all four women were able to gain a sense of security only after taking refuge in Christian communities.

Because Chisi, a widow, even after converting, always maintained her traditional kinship obligations by occasionally leaving the mission (but always returning when her duties were completed), her case particularly demonstrates the manner in which many women successfully negotiated between Christian and traditional life. As Wright explains:

And thus seeing her daughter properly married, Chisi went to Utengule mission station and "cooked for" her son while he undertook his own bride service. This son had various difficulties before settling down, but when he did, his mother set up her own house and gardens within the mission community. She maintained her role as mother and grandmother, going to her daughter when she herself was critically ill and remaining there until she recovered. When a granddaughter contracted an infectious disease, she took her away to an isolated place and kept her there for a year. It is clear that although attracted by the Christian teachings, Chisi did not change her life-style or social expectations when she became converted.[21]

The story of Bwanikwa also exemplifies the vital role the mission played in some women's lives. Bwanikwa was born around 1870 and soon sold into slavery by her father. After having been sold nine times, she agreed to marry Kawimbe, a man traveling with a Christian caravan. At the time, Bwanikwa had just run away from her former husband, Wafwilwa, because she had heard him negotiating her sale to another man. Upon hearing of her new marriage, Wafwilwa (whom Bwanikwa claims to have married out of sheer need for protection and because he had otherwise refused to leave her alone) demanded compensation from Kawimbe. In Bwanikwa's words: "Wafwilwa . . . sent in his account for my keep while I was with him, and Kawimbe paid him a gun. Thus I was enslaved for the tenth and last time."[22] The caravan eventually settled for a time at a mission station in Johnston Falls.

Dugald Campbell, the missionary in charge of the entourage, was amazed at Bwanikwa's obvious ability to provide for herself and also at her insistence upon doing so with total independence:

She did not so much as hint that she would like our help. She set to work. She was a potter, and in her spare time she dug clay, moulded and baked cooking pots and water jars. These she sold or bartered for something else, which she sold again, taking care of the profits. She cultivated and planted and disposed of produce. She kept fowls and sold eggs and chickens. She bought breeding goats and tended them, and traded the surplus.[23]

Some of the drive behind Bwanikwa's energies became apparent to Campbell as she managed to raise enough money, through successful animal husbandry, potting, and trading, to manumit herself from her husband by reimbursing him for the original price he had paid for her plus interest. This was more than a symbolic gesture. Bwanikwa had spent more than two-thirds of her life as a slave or a wife, usually both. Finally, through her own initiative and use of the mission's resources, she was emancipated and able to make her own choices about where and with whom she would live. She remained married to Kawimbe, who treated her, Campbell noted, "with deference and a respect formerly lacking." She continued throughout her life to exercise her autonomy, ministering to the needs of other women as both a doctor and an evangelist.[24]

Although missions attracted women who needed a home, the Christian influence extended beyond the settlement grounds, and many women who remained in their own communities used the physical and spiritual resources of local Christian facilities to improve their quality of life. Historian Jean Hay has demonstrated that the Luo women of Kowe, Kenya, who accepted the new crop technology offered by the local Anglican missionaries during the 1920s, became expert cultivators, thus facilitating their transition into the colonial economy. She also notes that one woman in particular, Loye Elizabeth, the senior wife of a polygamist named Ogumbo, gained such prominence for her agricultural prosperity that she was nicknamed *Wuon Bel,* "owner of the sorghum." Because she so successfully sold her surplus crops, she accumulated her own herd of cattle (a form of wealth typically limited to the male domain), thereby acquiring a significant degree of economic independence from her husband. By becoming the first woman in Kowe to convert to Christianity, she further asserted her independence. Upon conversion, Loye Elizabeth burned the sisal waist tassel that symbolized her married status and began to wear Western clothing, and she was subsequently dispossessed by her husband. When she became widowed Loye Elizabeth set a remarkable precedent by becoming the first woman in Kowe not to "tear off her clothes and wail at the death of her husband, and she refused to be taken in levirate mar-

riage by one of her kinsmen,"[25] choosing to retain the autonomy
and the status normally reserved for men that her agricultural success afforded her.

Anthropologist Sarah LeVine witnessed a contemporary example of a woman using Christian doctrine and the fellowship of the
local church to cope with a disintegrating marriage and the poverty
and precariousness of subsistence on the fringes of a growing cash
economy. In the mid-1970s LeVine worked among Gusii women of
southwestern Kenya to document their personal feelings and experiences relating to pregnancy and childbearing. One informant,
Suzanna Bosibori, was born into a Seventh Day Adventist family
that did not brew or drink beer, that adhered strictly to monogamous marriage, and renounced other Gusii practices.

Suzanna, however, had long left behind her Seventh Day Adventist ideals by the time she married an alcoholic and not terribly
devout Catholic man. His profound ambivalence toward her was
exceeded only by his consistent failure to help her provide for their
children. Because of this, Suzanna brewed beer for income, toiled
in her gardens, and stayed up long nights too worried and exhausted
to sleep. During the course of LeVine's fieldwork, Suzanna suddenly
gave up beer brewing and the precious income it provided her, and
she began keeping the Sabbath by spending her Saturdays in church
with the "morally superior" women of the community, praying,
singing hymns, and reviewing the doctrine of the Calvinist work
ethic. This was a source of grievous aggravation to her husband and
her mother-in-law because it resulted in a loss of time and income
from gardening and beer brewing. When LeVine questioned her
about her sudden return to Seventh Day Adventist practices,
Suzanna revealed that she was following the advice of her mother
who had suggested that even though Suzanna could not keep her
husband from getting drunk, she, at least, could stay sober and
thereby escape becoming embroiled in fights that inevitably ended
with her being beaten.

For Suzanna, invoking the SDA church was a coping mechanism
that relieved the pressure and drudgery of her married life. The
church offered her both mental and physical solace. As she told
LeVine, "Why shouldn't I have one day's rest in the week? Even if
I dig every day, we never have enough to eat. So let me dig six days
and go on the seventh to church and hear what they have to tell me
there." The doctrine and the women's group helped her gain a sense

of being in charge of her own life, despite her poverty, exhaustion, and irresponsible husband.[26]

These examples illustrate clearly how convents, missions, and local churches fostered autonomy for women who sought them out. They provided a community—either the settlement to which Elizabeth Nyambele and Martha Phiri turned or the fellowship like that of the Seventh Day Adventist group that Suzanna Bosibori joined. They were places in which women like Bwanikwa and Loye Elizabeth found access to resources that enabled them to take control of their lives, communities where, as women living in a rapidly changing and male-dominated world, they could find ways to prevail over normally uncontrollable circumstances.

Neither the enforcement of Christian criteria for marriage nor the establishment of missions and local churches, however, offered women the greatest latitude for gaining autonomy. Rather, the missionaries' extension of education to the African woman created an opportunity whereby women could manipulate Christian doctrine for their own purposes and for the greater social and political causes of African women in general. Nevertheless, even this opportunity became available only indirectly, out of the missionary concern for African men.

As the first few classes of mission-educated young men approached marriageable age, the missionaries realized that there were no suitable marriage partners among the still "pagan" population of young women. This was considered a serious problem, "for the 'backwardness' of women compared with men was widely regarded as a serious danger for the embryonic African church." A missionary to South Africa stated that he viewed "the improvement of the females as a most urgent necessity," for each day he saw "male converts being dragged backwards and downwards by their heathen wives."[27] The solution adopted by the missionaries was to ensure Christian steadfastness in the young men by providing them with Christian wives. Thus they extended to women the male privilege of education.

Fairly early in the mission experience, schools for the express purpose of graduating marriageable Christian women sprang up all over sub-Saharan Africa. In the British colony of Natal in Southeast Africa, American missionaries sought to train wives for African pastors "in an institution 'modeled after the Mount Holyoke Seminary.'" In Kenya, boarding schools were established in 1923 at

Kahuhia and Kabete by the Anglican Church Missionary Society. In Lagos Colony, Nigeria, during this same period, the Christian education of women became so important for one group of Yoruba elite that men often financed the education of their fiancees, and some fathers sent daughters, rather than sons, abroad to gain the schooling necessary to make an elite match in marriage. The Ecoles de fiancées in Cameroon and similar institutions, such as the Ecole Normale de Jeunes Filles in Senegal, were equally important for the training of wives and mothers in French West Africa.[28]

In these mission schools, the ideology of domesticity so fundamental to the Victorian ideal of Christian marriage dominated the curriculum. South African feminist scholars Gaitskell and Cock have each documented the determination of the churches and the South African administrations to train women in the art of domesticity.[29] What was conceived as a sexist strategy for the provision of "suitable" wives and, in South Africa, as a racist tactic to train servants for the European settlers was turned by socially and politically conscious women into a skillful manipulation of Christian ideology. Especially in South Africa, where the use of migrant labor produced incredible poverty, forcing men to desert their families at an appallingly rapid rate, the education of women turned out to be a true double-edged sword.

The ideology of domesticity perpetuated in Christian mission education became a rationale and political tool for South African women trying to maintain independence from the control of the state.[30] In 1913, Blomfontein, the Orange Free State capital, became the scene of anti–pass law demonstrations. These demonstrations were led by African women who preferred going to jail to being subjected to legislation requiring them to prove they were employed in a white household. The president and another active member of the Methodist women's church group, or *manyano,* were front-runners in the campaign to assert the right of black women not to enter the labor market. By invoking the very ideology that had educated them to become model Victorian wives for African men and domestic servants for Europeans and that asserted the moral and social responsibility of women to become devoted full-time wives and mothers, they protested the racism underlying the labor policies.

The *Rukwadzano rweWadzimai* is a women's church organization within the United Methodist Church. It was first chartered in 1929 in Southern Rhodesia at Old Umtali Methodist Mission, and its rules still reflect the classic blending of Christianity with the domestic ideal so characteristic of colonial mission education. In the early 1930s, the group primarily promoted greater choice and dignity in marriage by emphasizing a Christian ideal between husband and wife. A Methodist minister explains: "They sought an alternative to women's inferior status in the patrilineal and often polygamous marriages [and] opposed the traditional custom of pledging a baby girl to her later husband before she becomes of age to choose for herself."[31]

Today, though still embracing an ideology of education and domesticity, the *Rukwadzano* works not only for intramarital harmony, but for social and political equality as well. By the mid-1970s, when it boasted a membership just under 9,000, the *Rukwadzano*, in addition to financing high schools for girls, developing scholarship programs for gifted young women and men, and encouraging women to become financially self reliant, had become a strong political voice against the segregationist policy of Ian Smith's regime and government persecution of religious leaders. As one member described its mission: "We need morally tough mothers to bring up a morally tough new generation fit and prepared to overcome the dire problems raised by the sheer necessity to survive."[32]

Crossroads Squatter Camp at Cape Town, South Africa, provides yet another example of the same move to fuse social activism with an ideology of domesticity. In the late 1970s, rather than face the loneliness, poverty, and indignity of the reserves while their husbands were away in migrant labor barracks, the women of Crossroads chose to break the law and live in town with their husbands as nuclear units. Gaitskell discusses their case: "The women there appear to exhibit a striking attachment to the domestic ideology. They assert the value of wifehood and shared family life." In the words of one of the Crossroads women:

When you are married you are meant to stay with your husband. It's God's law. My belief is this: that when you are married to your husband, whether he is in Cape Town or whatever . . . you should stay together where he is working. Because you are depending on this husband for food, for clothing, for shelter, and in the case of illness. . . . To have squatter camp, Crossroads, is to keep our life. . . . We suffer too much. Because we won't get moved away from our husbands.[33]

As stated earlier, these glimpses into the lives of women in varied African settings offer insight into the dynamics of a broad historical process and provide specific examples of women as social actors. The introduction of Christianity to sub-Saharan Africa created a situation in which women could negotiate between two institutional and belief systems for the purpose of gaining autonomy. At the point where the two ideological and patriarchal systems of Christianity and traditional African society conflicted, women strove to obtain new freedom for action.

These individual African women emerge as more than the passive pawns of men and of the colonial machinery. We see them as real persons making choices in the ways they approach the exigencies of day-to-day life. We see them as women converting to Christianity despite familial and societal pressure against it. We see them using Christian doctrine and institutions to ameliorate their own situations or to obtain sanctuary from the daily chaos that encompassed their lives. Most importantly, we see African women consciously manipulating the doctrine of domesticity to challenge the various ideologies and institutions of the colonial system. In spite of the patriarchal interpretations and strategies that missionaries carried to Africa, many women used Christian doctrine and institutions to negotiate their own well-being, not only in a traditionally male-dominated world, but also in a world in which social control was rapidly slipping out of the hands of the African and into the hands of the colonial state.

NOTES

1. See C. Meillassoux, *Maidens, Meal, and Money: Capitalism and the Domestic Community* (Cambridge: Cambridge University Press, 1981).

2. J. F. Ade Ajayi, *Christian Missions in Nigeria, 1841–1891: The Making of a New Elite* (Evanston: Northwestern University Press, 1965), 15; and K. Mann, "The Dangers of Dependence," *Journal of African History* 24 (1984): 37–56.

3. K. Mann, "Marriage Choices Among the Educated African Elite in Lagos Colony, 1880–1915," *International Journal of African Historical Studies* 14 (1981): 204; G. Muriuki, *A History of the Kikuyu 1500–1900* (Oxford: Oxford University Press, 1974), 178–79; J. Murray, "The Kikuyu Female Circumcision Controversy," (Ph.D. diss., UCLA, 1974), 60.

4. A. Hastings, *Christian Marriage in Africa* (London: Holy Trinity Church, 1973), 5.
5. Hastings, *Christian Marriage*, 5.
6. Bride-price is defined as "money or goods given to the bride's kin by the groom or his kin before or upon marriage (also called bride wealth)," C. R. Ember and M. Ember, *Cultural Anthropology* (Englewood Cliffs: Prentice-Hall, 1973), 384. Levirate marriage is a "custom whereby a man marries his brother's widow." Ember and Ember, *Cultural Anthropology*, 386. On polygamy, see J. L. Kellersberger, *Congo Crosses: A Study of Congo Womanhood* (Boston: 1936), and R. W. Strayer, *The Making of Mission Communities in East Africa: Anglicans and Africans in Colonial Kenya, 1875–1935* (Albany: State University of New York Press, 1978), 79.
7. The distorted image of polygamy that many missionaries carried into the field undoubtedly played a large part in the failure to convert a significant number of African men to monogamy. A Presbyterian missionary writing in the 1930s stated that polygamy was the Congo's greatest curse and source of peril. And in reference to the offending husbands, the missionary noted, "They cling to the belief that many wives bring prestige, oblivious to the fact that the King of the Belgians has more power than all of their chiefs put together, and yet he, and all others like him, have entered monogamous marriages." Kellerberger, *Congo Crosses*, 76. No doubt, such ethnocentric interpretations of polygamy did little to aid the African in understanding why polygamous marriages were unacceptable to the missionaries. Indeed, in 1909 a recently converted Lunda evangelist in Northern Rhodesia was overheard explaining to a chief, "The bread and wine at the Lord's table is very little, and if you and one wife come you will get a little, but if you bring a lot of wives there will not be enough." R. Rotberg, *Christian Missionaries and the Creation of Northern Rhodesia, 1880–1924* (Princeton: Princeton University Press, 1965), 130. For further discussions of this subject see Ember and Ember, *Cultural Anthropology*, and Serena Nanda, *Cultural Anthropology* (New York: Van Nostrand Reinhold, 1980).
8. See discussions in Hastings, *Christian Marriage*, 11–26; and Strayer, *Mission Communities*, 79–80.
9. J. B. Webster, "Attitudes and Policies of the Yoruba African Churches Towards Polygamy," in *Christianity in Tropical Africa*, ed. C. G. Baeta (Oxford: Oxford University Press, 1968), 224.
10. Quoted in Webster, "Attitudes and Policies," 224.
11. For instance, in the British colony of Lagos, Nigeria, the colonial government passed the Marriage Ordinance of 1884, giving state support to the missionary fight against polygamy. One result of this was that well-educated, elite Yoruba men were often forced into illegal polygamy. The inheritance rights of children produced from illegal unions and the rights of the women themselves were never secure. The situation was made even more difficult when men decided to ignore their first wife in favor of another. Under colonial law, if a man died intestate, his ordinance wife and her children inherited his estate. However, some men legally disinherited their ordinance wives by simply drawing up a will in which they were purposefully excluded. While missionaries had welcomed state support

for their stand against polygamy, they certainly had not intended to create a class of destitute and disinherited women and children. See K. Mann, "Dangers of Dependence" and "Marriage Choices."

12. K. Mann, "Marriage Choices."
13. K. Mann, "Dangers of Dependence," 50. Unfortunately, not all women who converted were completely successful in achieving the conditions of marriage which Christianity and the 1884 ordinance promised. A number of the Yoruba men who first entered monogamous Christian marriages subsequently decided to engage in illegal polygamy, sometimes abandoning their ordinance wives and children. Enforcement of the ordinance was haphazard, and what had appeared to many women converts to be the promise of newfound security was no security at all. See K. Mann, "Dangers of Dependence," and "Marriage Choices."
14. K. Mann, "Dangers of Dependence," 50.
15. Strayer, *Mission Communities*, 3.
16. I. Linden, *Catholics, Peasants, and Chewa Resistance in Nyasaland* (Berkeley and Los Angeles: University of California Press, 1974), 166, 173.
17. Linden, *Catholics*, 176.
18. M. A. Weinrich, "An Aspect of the Development of Religious Life in Rhodesia," in *Themes in the Christian History of Central Africa*, ed. T. O. Ranger and J. Weller (Berkeley and Los Angeles: University of California Press, 1975), 218–37.
19. Linden, *Catholics*, 173.
20. E. Grau, "Missionary Policies as Seen in the Work of Missions with the Evangelical Presbyterian Church, Ghana," in *Christianity in Tropical Africa*, ed. Baeta, 66–67.
21. M. Wright, "Women in Peril: A Commentary on the Life Stories of Captives in Nineteenth-Century East-Central Africa," *African Social Research* (December 1975), 811.
22. Wright, "Bwanikwa: Consciousness and Protest Among Slave Women in Central Africa, 1886–1911," in *Women and Slavery in Africa*, ed. C. C. Robertson and M. A. Kalein (Madison: University of Wisconsin Press, 1983), 258.
23. Wright, "Bwanikwa," 260.
24. Wright, "Bwanikwa," 260. See p. 261 for a brief discussion of her activities as a doctor and an evangelist.
25. M. J. Hay, "Luo Women and Economic Change," in *Women in Africa*, ed. N. J. Hafkin and E. G. Bay (Stanford: Stanford University Press, 1976), 101.
26. Sarah LeVine, *Mothers and Wives: Gusii Women of East Africa* (Chicago: University of Chicago Press, 1979), 58. For an example of women converting to Christianity to escape the drudgery of beer brewing, see Walter H. Sangree, "The Bantu Tiriki of Western Kenya," in *Peoples of Africa*, ed. James L. Gibbs, Jr. (New York: Holt, Rinehart & Winston, Inc., 1965), 43–79.
27. Strayer, *Mission Communities*, 81; J. Cock, *Maids and Madams* (Johannesburg: 1981), 286.
28. On schooling in Natal, see N. Etherington, *Preachers, Peasants, and Politics in Southeast Africa, 1835–1880* (London: Royal Historical Society, 1978), 28. On Kenya, see Strayer, *Mission Communities*, 81. On Lagos Colony, Nigeria,

see Mann, "Dangers of Dependence." On Cameroon, see M. R. Bureau, "Influence de la Christianisation sur les Institutions Traditionelles des Ethnies Coteires du Cameroun," in *Christianity in Tropical Africa,* ed. Baeta, 179. On Senegal, see P. R. Sabatier, "Educating Teachers, Wives, and Mothers in Colonial French West Africa: Rufisque, the Ecole Normale de Jeunes Filles" (Paper presented at the conference, African Women: Historical Dimensions, The University of Santa Clara, California, 16 May 1981).

29. See D. Gaitskell, "Housewives, Maids, or Mothers: Some Contradictions of Domesticity for Christian Women in Johannesburg, 1903–1939," *Journal of African History* 24 (1983), 241–256 and Cock, *Maids and Madams.*

30. Gaitskell, "Housewives," 255.

31. D. Muzorewa, "Through Prayer to Action: the Rukwadzano Women of Rhodesia," in *Christian History of Central Africa,* ed. Ranger and Weller, 257.

32. Muzorewa, "Prayer to Action," 268.

33. Gaitskell, "Housewives," 255, 256.

CHAPTER 11

Piety, Persuasion, and Friendship: Female Jewish Leadership in Modern Times

ELLEN M. UMANSKY

During the late nineteenth and early twentieth centuries, a handful of Jewish women emerged as religious leaders in England and the United States. Though unordained, they assumed a wide variety of modern rabbinic functions. They led worship services, regularly preached from the pulpit, taught religious school classes, conducted weddings and funerals, and prepared proselytes for conversion. Although they did not identify themselves as rabbis, each was heralded as such by congregants, the Jewish community, and/or the press. Unlike traditional rabbis, these women were not scholars. Instead, their religious authority rested solely on what Max Weber, in his study of religious leadership and charisma, has identified as the personal gifts of revelation and friendship.[1]

By examining the sermons and addresses of two of these women, this essay attempts to ascertain both the nature of their religious visions and the significance of gender in their creation. Without ignoring the importance of individual factors, the ways in which these visions differed from those of male contemporaries are also explored. It offers two suggestions as to why male and female visions differed, the first, relating to the question of authority, the second, to the historical context in which Jewish women's spirituality needs to be viewed.

This essay focuses on the religious visions of Lily Montagu, founder of the Liberal Jewish movement in England and lay minister of the West Central Liberal Jewish Congregation; and those of Tehilla Lichtenstein, cofounder and leader of the New York–based Society of Jewish Science. Unlike other women who occupied similar, but brief, positions of religious leadership during the late nineteenth and early twentieth centuries,[2] Montagu and Lichtenstein maintained their positions for well over thirty years. Consequently, they left hundreds of sermons and addresses upon which to draw. Both women, moreover, saw themselves as disciples of men (Lily Montagu of Claude Montefiore, Tehilla Lichtenstein of her husband, Morris) with whom they claimed to share similar, if not identical religious visions. Thus, in attempting to discern whether the voices and visions of nineteenth- and twentieth-century Jewish female religious leaders significantly differed from those of their male contemporaries, a comparison of the sermons of Lily Montagu and Tehilla Lichtenstein with those of Claude Montefiore and Morris Lichtenstein proves particularly instructive.

In exploring female religious leadership within Judaism, one needs to bear in mind that positions of religious leadership were traditionally held by men. While *halachah,* Jewish law as formulated by several generations of rabbis during the first centuries of the common era, does not explicitly prohibit women from assuming such positions, rabbinic Judaism's understanding that women's roles as wives and mother are "natural" and therefore preferred helped create an environment in which only exceptional women could aspire to, much less achieve, prominence as religious leaders.[3]

According to the Talmud (the compilation of Jewish law completed ca. 500 C.E.), just as the private sphere of religious life, as maintained within the home, was the natural domain of women, so the public sphere was that of men. As a consequence, women's participation in synagogue life, as set forth in the Talmud and later rabbinic codes, was clearly limited. Only men could help form a *minyan,* the quorum of ten necessary for public worship, only men could be called up to the Torah, and only they could lead the congregation in prayer. Though women's private devotions may well have been encouraged, women, unlike their male counterparts, were not required to participate in daily public worship.

Moreover, those who attended the morning, afternoon, and evening services of necessity occupied a separate women's gallery where they remained unseen and unheard. Justification for this custom was that both women's presence and voices distract men.

Since only men "counted" as congregants, only their spiritual lives received serious attention. That women, hidden from view behind a curtain, could barely see the goings-on below, much less hear the words of prayer, was deemed unimportant.

While a woman able to read the Hebrew text might lead the women through the service, most had, at best, a minimal knowledge of Hebrew and frequently read the prayers aloud from translations of the prayer book into the vernacular. Popular among medieval and early modern Eastern European women were such Yiddish texts as the *Ts'eno Ur'eno* (Go Out and See) and the *Lev Tov* (Good Heart). Women also read special *techinot,* devotional prayers written in Yiddish by and for women. In America, by the middle of the nineteenth century, prayer translations for women appeared in English as well.[4]

For the most part, these translated texts were not read in the synagogue but in the home. The *Ts'eno Ur'eno,* a popular Yiddish version of the Pentateuch divided into weekly sections, enabled women to follow at home the portion of the Torah which was being read in *shul* (synagogue). Books of devotional prayers did not literally translate the prayer book but contained prayers corresponding to women's home-centered religious obligations as well as to life experiences of the pious woman. For example, Rabbi Abraham Hirschowitz's *Religious Duties of the Daughters of Israel,* a thin volume published in English in 1902, contains prayers and elaborate explanations for women's three special *mitzvot* (commandments): *challah* (the preparation of dough for the Sabbath), *hadlakah* (the kindling of the Sabbath lights), and *niddah* (laws pertaining to menstruation). It discusses laws concerning *kashrut,* the dietary regulations for which women assumed greatest responsibility and expertise, and religious duties incumbent on every parent in the raising of a child. In it are a number of meditations, translated from the prayer book or from other "authoritative sources," including prayers said in the morning and the evening and after lighting the Sabbath candles; prayers for each of the major holy days and festivals; a short form of the grace after meals; a prayer for the bride on her wedding day and for a parent on the occasion of her son's or daughter's wedding; a prayer for the recovery of a sick child; a prayer for thanksgiving after recovering from childbirth (to be recited in the synagogue); a brief confession to be recited on one's deathbed; and a brief memorial prayer for the dead. Also included are morning and evening prayers to be taught by mothers to their children.[5]

As Hirschowitz's book reveals, women's religious lives were home-centered and private in nature. Though women might attend synagogue, they were not obligated to do so. Moreover, their relegation to the women's gallery, the recitation of prayers in a language they barely knew, and their own religious duties as wives and mothers, which made synagogue attendance difficult if not impossible, helped foster a sense of religiosity that was personal rather than communal. This sense of religiosity focused upon one's own experiences rather than on the experiences of the Jewish people as a whole. As Mark Zborowski and Elizabeth Herzog maintain in *Life Is with People,* traditional Eastern European Jewish women wept as they read from such texts as the *Ts'eno Ur'eno,* for they identified their troubles with the troubles of Israel. Such passages were viewed as expressions of their *own* joys and sorrows.[6]

Admittedly, *Life Is with People* often romanticizes the religious life of medieval Jewry. Yet the fact remains that women's reading of the Torah in Yiddish (a language of great emotion and of everyday life) rather than in Hebrew, the traditional language of prayer, and the accompanying of this reading with legends and homilies rather than with detailed grammatical, philosophical, or legal explications of the text, helped to encourage the equation of religiosity with personal piety. While historians often emphasize study as an essential component of Jewish religious life, study was a privilege reserved almost exclusively for men. If, then, the term *rabbi* traditionally referred to one who was a scholar, it is not surprising that, given the cultural and social milieu in which they were raised, no woman prior to the second quarter of the twentieth century received rabbinic ordination. Moreover, the traditional form of ordination empowering the rabbi to act not only as an interpreter of Jewish law but also as a judge created legal obstacles as well.[7] In short, while most of man's religious life was focused on the dual obligations of study and private and communal prayer, women's religious life was rooted primarily in private devotions that reflected the realities of daily existence.

The advent of modernity in the eighteenth and nineteenth centuries helped create new social and educational opportunities for Jewish women. While secular learning threatened men's total absorption in Torah study, many families encouraged daughters "to learn the language of their neighbors [and] to acquire a familiarity with foreign language and literature,"[8] providing an important visible symbol of Jewish adaptability within the non-Jewish world.

The new opportunities available to secular Jewish women contrasted with the more limited opportunities of traditional Judaism. As a result, by the nineteenth century, German religious reformers such as Abraham Geiger denounced women's subordinate position, declaring that the spirit of the age demanded that this status be overthrown. In an essay entitled "The Position of the Female Sex in the Judaism of our Time," he suggested that whenever possible, men and women should assume the same religious obligations. He argued for women's ability to grasp the depths of religious belief and insisted that no worship service either in form or content exclude women from participation.[9] During the 1840s, Geiger helped organize a series of conferences in which "like-thinking, progressive rabbis" examined a number of Judaism's traditions and beliefs in light of the outlook and spirit of the modern age. Though in many ways the declarations of equality that emerged from these conferences were more theoretical than real, a number of steps were taken to create a greater role for women within the Jewish community, such as to count women in the quorum necessary for public worship, to introduce religious instruction for girls, and, in the Berlin Reform Temple, to seat women and men on the same floor.[10]

The rise of Jewish religious liberalism, if not the Reform movement itself, created a climate in which women could emerge as leaders during the nineteenth and early twentieth centuries.[11] Indeed, by 1928, when Lily Montagu became lay minister of the newly organized West Central Liberal Jewish Congregation and even more so, by 1938, when Tehilla Lichtenstein became spiritual leader of the Society of Jewish Science—a group with strong historical and theological ties to Reform Judaism—women had already begun, in Lily Montagu's words, to "come down from [their] synagogue galleries to enter into the life of the synagogue" and share their religious visions with others.[12]

Lily Montagu: Judaism as Personal Religion

Lily Montagu, born in 1873 in London, first began leading worship services at age seventeen at the Orthodox West End Synagogue, the congregation to which she and her family belonged.

These services were special Sabbath services for children, instigated by Montagu with the encouragement of the synagogue's spiritual leader, Simeon Singer. The services contained elements of the traditional Sabbath service and were conducted primarily in English, and the order of worship varied from week to week. At each, Montagu gave informal talks rather than sermons. She led these services through 1909, the year in which the organization that she founded in 1902—the Jewish Religious Union—declared its commitment to the teachings of Liberal Judaism.

Beginning in 1893, she also led worship services at the West Central Jewish Girls' Club, a social and educational organization that she (with the assistance of her sister, Marian, and their cousin, Beatrice Franklin) had formed for Jewish girls of the working classes. Though most of the club members were religiously apathetic, Montagu created and led evening, Sabbath afternoon, and holiday services at the club for well over thirty years. In 1913, these services gained recognition as the "West Central Section" of the newly expanded Jewish Religious Union for the Advancement of Liberal Judaism. This group later formed the nucleus of the West Central Liberal Jewish Congregation, established in 1928 with Montagu as its lay minister, a position to which she was formally inducted in 1944.

While most of Montagu's own congregants were girls, and later women, of the working classes, her eventual emergence as a religious leader within the Liberal Jewish movement put her in touch with thousands of men and women of different nationalities, social classes, and religious backgrounds. By 1918 she began to preach at the Liberal Jewish Synagogue (the Liberal Jewish movement's largest congregation) and soon after, at Liberal synagogues throughout England, many of which she helped establish and for which she served as president or chair. By the 1920s she began to preach in Reform synagogues in Europe and America and by the 1930s in Reform synagogues throughout the world.

In her sermons, she emphasized Judaism as personal religion, that which is capable of creating and sustaining a personally meaningful religious faith. Equating religiosity with inner piety, she maintained that faith in God, which she identified as the "first principle of Judaism," depended not on intellectual knowledge but rather on opening oneself up to the eternal Divine Presence. The emotional rather than the intellectual component of Judaism, she

believed, brought one closer to God. Though recognizing that traditional symbols and observances could serve as important religious
stimuli, that which she and other classical Reformers identified as
"vehicles towards holiness," she insisted that communion with God
could be achieved simply by "letting our minds, for a short time at
least [once] each day, be permeated by God's spirit."[13] She talked
of *feeling* the divine presence, of knowing in one's heart, as well as
in one's mind, that God is the creator of the world and of humanity—a loving, merciful, and just God. If there is evil in the world,
it is not God who is responsible but we who have closed our ears
to God's teachings.

For Lily Montagu, as for Claude Montefiore and other early
twentieth-century Reformers, Jews had been chosen to bear witness
to the reality of God and to bring others to an awareness of this
reality by spreading God's ethical teachings. Unlike Montefiore and
other male religious Reformers, who frequently offered rationalistic
explanations for their convictions, Montagu asserted that spiritual
beliefs were "derived from intuition, unexplained and inexplica-
ble." She viewed them as responses to a universal spiritual need, a
"longing by God's children" to commune with their "Father." Quot-
ing her favorite poet, Robert Browning, she spoke of the "infinite
pain of finite hearts which yearn," a yearning conditioned by faith
in one's kinship with the Divine. Though this faith "is supported
by the testimony of the past and the character of our ancient worship," it is primarily based on intuition, "assisted by the actual
experience of everyday life."[14]

To Montagu, then, one did not need to become a scholar to find
a religious purpose and to become "aflame with God." We have
only ourselves, she insisted, "the small, weak, imperfect Jews and
Jewesses . . . alone with the Alone," but with the power within
ourselves to lead to a "complete at-one-ment with God."[15] Montagu frequently spoke of using one's mind as well as heart in the
service of religion. Yet in describing the importance of the intellect,
she warned her listeners that far more dangerous than "want of
study" was "want of thinking." She thus decried those who "accept
what their fathers give them in the way of religion and do not
assimilate their possessions through the power of thought. Even the
belief in God cannot influence our lives unless we think about it.
It is not a matter of lip service. We have to turn this thought over
and over in our minds every day of our lives."[16]

Speaking of self-fulfillment in terms of belief in God, she described her own belief as that which "I have inherited from my Jewish ancestors and *made my own.*"[17] To do so, she continually reexamined Judaism's traditional teachings in light of both modern-day realities and her own experience. The realities to which she referred most often included Jewish political emancipation, social interaction between Jews and non-Jews, the participation of Jews within European and American cultural life, and secular economic, educational, and political opportunities available to women. The experiences to which she referred included books that she had read, plays, movies, and works of art that she had seen, friendships that she had made, and walks that she had taken.

Montagu insisted that by reflecting contemporary reality, the teachings of Liberal Judaism, as articulated by Claude Montefiore in his theological writings, were relevant to the modern Jew. These teachings included the rejection of Jewish nationality, replaced by the concept of Jews as members of a religious brotherhood, the rejection of traditional ceremonies and observances that made social interaction between Jews and Christians difficult, the universalistic belief that beauty and truth could be articulated by non-Jewish as well as Jewish authors, and Liberal Judaism's commitment to the religious equality of women. In reiterating these teachings, albeit through her own words and images, Montagu identified herself as Montefiore's disciple. Yet despite her indebtedness to him, the focus of Lily Montagu's sermons differed sharply from those of her mentor.

In preaching at Liberal Jewish services, Claude Montefiore spoke on such topics as "The Place of Judaism in the Religions of the World," "Jewish Conceptions of Immortality," "Judaism, Unitarianism, and Theism," "The Justification of Liberal Judaism," and "Judaism and Democracy." Lily Montagu, however, talked of "Immortality in Literature," "The Sun as Preacher," that which she had "Seen at the Tate Gallery," and differences between "Acting and Real Life." Montefiore's major concern was to articulate the principles of Liberal Judaism. Montagu's was to show the ways in which those principles might be discovered. She sought to impress upon her listeners that the teachings of Liberal Judaism could be found within the ordinary and the everyday. To her, it was this discovery that made Liberal Judaism a personally meaningful, *living* form of religion.

Like Montefiore, Montagu firmly believed that Liberal Judaism served "the cause of truth."[18] Yet, unlike Montefiore, she used specific examples to underscore the ways in which this truth was revealed. Most frequently, she used examples from her own life. She spoke of people who had come to her in distress and advice that she had given, as well as books, poems, and plays that had influenced her own spiritual growth. Sometimes, as in "If Winter Comes," a sermon on the reality of evil and the possibility of hope, she simply used the title of a play she had seen to express a religious truth that she believed important. She frequently made up examples to illustrate her point more clearly. For instance, in writing about what she believed to be the difference between the ways in which men and women approach religion, she asked her listeners to use their imaginations:

Father takes his child to Synagogue while no service is in progress and carries him round and shows him the various features, including his special seat, and the Ark, and explains that the books of the Bible are contained in the Scroll which is in the Ark. He is informative and interests his child. The Sabbath comes and the boy or girl is dressed in his best clothes and accompanies his Daddy to the Synagogue and carries his prayer book. The child sits between him and Mummy. Daddy occasionally shows him the place in the book, and he stops fidgeting for a moment. He is happy and prepared to repeat the experiment on subsequent Sabbaths. . . .

In contrast Montagu describes the mother's method.

The element of thanksgiving is a good preparation for prayer. She remembers a beautiful fungus which she and Johnny admired together while on their walk. . . . "Johnny," she says, "do you remember our walk today and that fungus we saw, and the lovely streaks of colour, the red and yellow bits, and the little bits of green and brown, and how we wished we could have found a mushroom, but then we said it would not have been half as pretty? Shall we thank God for making that fungus?" "Yes, lets, Mummy." . . . Another night Mummy and Johnny make a list of the people they both love and ask God to bless them. They make their prayers together and they are their own special prayers.[19]

Lily Montagu used such examples to show that, while men constantly analyzed and sifted their ideas, women took greater risks and were more creative. She believed that it was no coincidence that in discussions on the source of authority in Progressive Judaism men seemed more interested in external authority than women. Men, she said, often thought it necessary for scholars to decide whether specific observances should be followed. Women, on the other hand, believed that what the "big people" thought was less important than what they themselves had observed. Thus, in response to the question of whether more Hebrew should be added to the liturgy, a woman might declare that Hebrew "is no use for those who do not understand it," and to the question of whether it was essential to have a cantor singing during the worship service, she might respond, "If I want the best singing, I go to the Opera. When I am at a service, I want to sing and join in, and I know my children do [too]."[20]

Her reliance on personal experience rather than on theological principles led Montagu to write sermons that not only sounded less scholarly, or as she observed, less "objective" than those of Montefiore, but also served as a bridge between her audience and herself. Although both supporters and detractors often alluded to her spiritual greatness, Lily Montagu consciously sought to identify with her listeners. Claiming that she and they were not spiritual giants as was Isaiah, but ordinary people, she suggested that each "in his small way feel the contact with God and His cleansing power operating over our human weaknesses and clearing them away."[21] Her intent was not to preach *to* her listeners, but to *share* her faith with them. She hoped that her faith, rooted in experiences that perhaps were like theirs, would serve to encourage, inspire, and lead her listeners to recognize, as she had, that the core of true religion would be found neither in outward observance nor formally written creeds but in the soul of the individual.

Tehilla Lichtenstein: Visions of an Applied Judaism

Tehilla Lichtenstein merits the distinction of having been the first Jewish woman to occupy a pulpit in America. Her attainment, however, came about by circumstance rather than by design. Her husband, Morris Lichtenstein, a Reform rabbi and leader of the Society of Jewish Science, died in 1938. In his will, he requested that his wife succeed him as the society's spiritual leader. Jewish Science was founded for two major reasons: to stem the tide of Jews, mostly women, who were joining Christian Science churches,[22] and to bring religiously apathetic and/or uncommitted Jews into the Jewish community. First conceived in 1916 by Alfred Geiger Moses, a Reform rabbi in Mobile, Alabama, and elaborated upon by Morris Lichtenstein in a number of publications, it offered a vision of science and health set within a Jewish context. While acknowledging the reality of matter (and therefore of physical suffering) as well as the benefits of modern medicine, Jewish Science maintained that God alone is the true source and restorer of health. One might make use of physicians and/or practitioners as instruments of God's beneficence, but only faith made one "receptive to divine healing ... actually set[ting] into motion the expression of the healing forces within us."[23]

Like Lily Montagu, Tehilla Lichtenstein was not trained to become a religious leader. Born in 1893 in Palestine, she, again like Montagu, was raised as an Orthodox Jew. Her father, Chaim Hirschensohn, was a prominent rabbi and Talmudic scholar. He encouraged all of his daughters to pursue a good secular education, but he provided minimal religious education. Thus, as did Montagu, Lichtenstein could, and frequently did, quote from such authors as Browning, Shakespeare, Emerson, and Eliot, but she rarely quoted from Jewish sources other than the Bible. Indeed, the contrast between Lichtenstein's knowledge of non-Jewish and Jewish texts is even more striking than in the case of Montagu, who left school at the age of fifteen. Lichtenstein received a B.A. in classics from Hunter College and an M.A. in literature from Columbia University. She was pursuing her doctorate in English literature when she left school to marry Morris Lichtenstein in 1920.

Although it is unclear whether Morris Lichtenstein deserves sole credit as the founder of the Society of Jewish Science or whether he and Tehilla founded the society together, we do know that from its inception, Tehilla helped disseminate its ideas by serving as principal of its Sunday school and editor of the monthly *Jewish Science Interpreter*. During her thirty-five years as the society's leader, she edited the *Interpreter*, delivered weekly sermons, gave classes in Jewish Science and occasionally on the Bible, counseled those in need, and trained a number of her congregants as practitioners, or spiritual healers. She lectured widely and, during the 1940s, had weekly radio broadcasts about her movement.

Her vision of Jewish Science as that which "reveals to the Jew the great treasures that are contained within Judaism,"[24] owed a great deal to the writings of Morris Lichtenstein. Indeed, Lichtenstein maintained that her own spiritual vision was both inspired by his writings and in strict accordance with his entire philosophy of life and religion. Identifying herself as his disciple and clearly revering him, she denied that she ever consciously modified his teachings.[25] Yet a comparison of their sermons reveals that the spiritual visions of Morris and Tehilla Lichtenstein were not identical. While most of his sermons focused on that which the human mind could know, hers explored the feelings that led one to such knowledge. Like Claude Montefiore, Morris Lichtenstein emphasized the principles or "fundamentals" of Judaism. Like Lily Montagu, Tehilla Lichtenstein emphasized the daily experiences through which these fundamentals might be revealed.

Given Jewish Science's claim to be nothing more than "applied Judaism," Morris Lichtenstein attempted, far more than Montefiore, to show how Jewish teachings might be applied to the realities of life. Yet Lichtenstein primarily spoke in generalities. He spoke about sickness and suffering, "man" and his character, and nature and its observable changes. Tehilla Lichtenstein, on the other hand, used concrete examples, drawn from her experiences or from her imagination. Having spent much of her life as a wife and mother, most of her personal examples related to motherhood, marriage, and the home.[26] Thus she described human progress as going forward "like vacuum machines, picking up the bad with the good," and she wrote of a young boy's wishing he could relive his party so as to choose strawberry over vanilla ice cream and to sit nearer to the cookies. In giving advice "About Ruling Others and Yielding to Others," she reminded her congregants that just as "there is not much joy in . . . anxious and intense motherhood," so it is important to know when to leave one's friends alone.[27]

On the joys of motherhood, she maintained that one could learn a great deal from children about the promise of life, the reality of truth, and the beauty of nature. The child "is still unworldly, untainted, uncontaminated by worldly standards and worldly desires and worldly ambitions" and thus "in nearness to God and his distance from worldliness [is wrapped] in the mantle of holiness." It is this quality in the child "which most charms us, which most captivates us, which leaves us breathless, [and] which makes the whole world fall prostrate and worship."[28]

About the importance of self-control, Morris Lichtenstein emphasized self-direction, self-assertion, and self-expression. Tehilla Lichtenstein also preached on this subject, but her sermon, entitled "Controlling the Tongue and the Temper," consciously sought to ask her listeners to think of the importance of self-control in terms of their own experience.

If you had a sharp-bladed instrument in your hands that could cut and slash and wound and mar and even kill, would you hurl it violently at those that you loved? Would you throw it at your children, at your life-companion, at your dearest friends? Your answer to this question is, of course, a horrified "No!" You may even think the question is absurd. But the fact remains that you have such an instrument in your possession, and that [in impatiently or angrily reproaching others] you are hitting out with it every day, hurting and destroying with it those whom you love best in all the world.[29]

In "Cures for Minds in Distress," Tehilla Lichtenstein described the causes of stress. Her husband described these causes as "rapidly multiplying needs [that] have intensified man's struggle for existence to an unlimited degree, and, in consequence . . . [have] drained his nervous strength . . . to the point of exhaustion."[30] Unlike Morris, Tehilla said,

We are all subject to disappointments and sorrows; they are part of the woof and warp, part of the indicated pattern of life. Who has not known the loss of a loved one? Who has not suffered setbacks in his business? Who has not been shocked by the disloyalty of friends or the suffering of dear ones or a thousand and one ill fortunes that are part of the heritage and destiny of man?[31]

Lichtenstein emphasized the joys of spirituality and the practical application of religion. She defined her aim as to "revive the religious consciousness of the Jew [and] to resuscitate for him the neglected values of Judaism."[32]

Her focus on daily experience led Tehilla Lichtenstein to emphasize, far more than her husband, relationships between human beings: between husband and wife, parent and child, Jew and non-Jew, young person and old person, individuals of different nations, and of nations themselves, between friends as well as between brothers and sisters. The significance of these relationships, as she saw them, was twofold. First, they underscored the conviction that as God's children we have a responsibility towards one another, and second, they awakened feelings of love that served as a model of the relationship between the individual and God. Though she some-times described God as Father: "kind, benevolent, loving and accessible,"[33] she more frequently spoke of the Divine in terms of the love between parent and child and particularly between child and mother.

Without actually identifying God as a female divinity, she (unlike her husband) often made an analogy between running to one's mother and entering into the divine presence. We run to God, she maintained, as we do to our mothers, saying, "I need you and want your strength." Further, as our mothers are there for us, so, she added, is God. "God has given each one of us, whether blessed by the stimulus of poverty or blessed by the ease of affluence, the same equalizing gift—our mother's love, which is, on this earth, the nearest thing, the closest thing, to the love that God bears for mankind. Mother's love is of the same substance, it is of the same divine fabric, and expresses itself in the same boundless way." In describing God not only as a parent but also as a brother, Lichtenstein emphasized the nonhierarchical nature of the human-divine relationship. Using the model of friendship, she enjoined her congregants to help God. Once you do so, she concluded, you will "count with God as much as God counts with you."[34]

Jewish Female Visions: Some Conclusions

In comparing the spiritual visions of nineteenth- and early twentieth-century Jewish female leaders like Lily Montagu and Tehilla Lichtenstein, one is struck by the extent to which both relied on daily experience as a source of religious knowledge and truth. Neither claimed, as did Claude Montefiore and other male Reformers, that one's conscience was the supreme authority in separating truth from falsehood.[35] Similarly, neither emphasized, as Morris Lichtenstein did, the importance of the mind in obtaining spiritual knowledge. Indeed, both believed that religious truth could only be grasped intuitively, for to them religion was primarily emotional in nature. As a consequence, their spiritual visions, grounded in their own lives and reflecting their own feelings and perceptions, were intensely personal. Had Montagu and Lichtenstein possessed a greater knowledge of Jewish texts, they might have turned to them more frequently. Lacking this knowledge, they were forced to turn inward and replaced religious scholarship with religious feeling.

To a large extent, one can attribute their not becoming scholars to the fact that the history and culture of their communities neither prepared nor encouraged them to do so. Montagu was convinced that she was intellectually incapable of becoming a scholar; Lichtenstein was too intellectually dependent on her husband to see herself as anything other than his disciple. Consciously or unconsciously, their Orthodox upbringing may have led them to think of Jewish scholarship as an exclusively male privilege. Nevertheless, even women who came from Reform backgrounds, such as Paula Ackerman, did not become scholars. Although Ray Frank attended classes at Hebrew Union College in Cincinnati, she received insufficient encouragement to remain longer than one semester. In brief, not only the religious but also the social and cultural (non-Jewish) milieu in which they lived led them to think of marriage and motherhood, rather than scholarship, as woman's true vocation.[36]

Although recent scholarship has identified the equation of true religion with inner piety as a Protestantized notion of religion, one which many Jews, including those women who became religious leaders, gleaned through a familiarity with non-Jewish texts (or with liberal Jewish texts that had been influenced by them), it may well be that Jewish women *traditionally* associated religiosity with inner piety. Largely ignorant of Jewish texts and excluded from participation in public worship, their religious consciousness thus came through private devotions and popularly written stories and legends that generated great emotion. One finds this sense of religiosity, rooted in popular literature rather than in traditional texts, in the writings of Lily Montagu, Tehilla Lichtenstein, and other nineteenth- and early twentieth-century Jewish women who attained religious leadership positions. Though these women, unlike their female ancestors, successfully moved beyond the private religious spheres of family and home, they continued to articulate traditional domestic and female values. While far more work needs to be done in uncovering the religious lives of premodern Jewish women, what we do know suggests that the visions of these women echoed the visions of earlier generations of women who could not articulate or record their own.

NOTES

1. M. Weber, *The Sociology of Religion,* intro. T. Parsons, trans. E. Fischoff (Boston: Beacon Press, 1963), 47.
2. For example, Ray Frank, popular lecturer and journalist of the 1890s, and Paula Ackerman, the spiritual leader of Temple Beth Israel in Meridian, Mississippi, from 1951–1953.
3. Such exceptional women include Beruriah, the wife of Rabbi Meir, who is recognized in the Talmud as a scholar; the daughter of the twelfth-century Gaon of Baghdad, Samuel ben Ali; and, in the nineteenth and early twentieth century, Hannah Rachel Werbermacher, known as the "maid of Ludomir," who earned the reputation of being a Hasidic *rebbe.*
4. C. Baum, P. Hyman, and S. Michel, *The Jewish Woman in America* (New York: The New American Library, 1977), 58. Among the earliest prayer books in English for women was M. J. Raphall, *Devotional Exercises for the Daughters of Israel, Intended for Public and Private Worship, on the Various Occasions of Woman's Life* (New York: L. Joachimssen, 1852).
5. Rabbi Abraham E. Hirschowitz, ed., *Religious Duties of the Daughters of Israel* (New York: A. E. Hirschowitz, 1902).
6. Mark Zborowski and Elizabeth Herzog, *Life Is with People* (New York: International Universities Press, 1952), 126.
7. The first woman ordained as rabbi was Regina Jonas, privately granted her rabbinical diploma by Rabbi Max Dienemann of Offenbach, Germany. Although Jonas functioned briefly as a rabbi, she was imprisoned at the Theresienstadt concentration camp in 1940 and died soon after. It was not until 1972, with the ordination of Sally Priesand from the Reform movement's Hebrew Union College-Jewish Institute of Religion in Cincinnati, that a woman was ordained from a rabbinical seminary. For a fuller discussion of the evolution of the rabbinate and changes made in the traditional form of ordination, see the article on "Semikha," *Encyclopedia Judaica* XIV (Jerusalem: 1971), 1140ff.
8. Jacob Katz, *Out of the Ghetto* (Cambridge: Harvard University Press, 1973), 84.
9. Abraham Geiger, "Die Stellung des weiblichen Geschlechtes in dem Judenthume Unserer Zeit," *Wissenschaft Zeitschrift fur judische Theologie,* Dritter Band (Stuttgart, 1837), 13, 14.
10. In 1851 Rabbi Isaac Meyer Wise, a German Jew who became a leader of American Reform, introduced family pews in his congregation in Albany, a move that followed his earlier innovation in 1846 of admitting women into the synagogue choir. By the end of the century, progressive European and American congregations practiced confirmation as a ceremony formally recognizing the entrance of both boys and girls into Jewish communal life.
11. Although apparently Ray Frank, an American journalist and popular preacher during the 1890s, once led High Holy Day services in an Orthodox synagogue in Victoria, British Columbia (see Simon Litman, *Ray Frank Litman: A Memoir* [New York: New York Historical Society, 1957]), she

primarily preached from the pulpits of Reform congregations. Others, like Lily Montagu and Paula Ackerman, had Reform pulpits of their own. These women also went on extensive lecture tours, speaking most frequently to Reform congregations. Ackerman, after resigning in September 1953 as spiritual leader of Temple Beth Israel in Meridian, Mississippi, spoke to Liberal Jews throughout the South; Frank, to many along the Pacific Coast; and Montagu, to Reform congregations and lay organizations throughout the world.

A number of women prominent in other fields occasionally preached from Reform pulpits as well. In 1897, Hannah Greenbaume Solomon, cofounder and national president of the National Council of Jewish Women, preached at Sinai Temple in Chicago, invited by its rabbi, Dr. Emil Hirsch. In that same year, Maud Nathan, president of the Consumers' League of the City of New York, preached at Temple Beth-El in New York on "The Heart of Judaism" (Maud Nathan, *Once Upon a Time and Today* [reprint, New York: Arno Press, 1974), 122. While Montagu is noted as having been the first Jewish women to preach in a Liberal synagogue in both England (1918) and Germany (1928), others, including her educator sister Henrietta, soon followed her example.

12. Lily H. Montagu, "Address," Germany, 1930, in *Lily Montagu: Sermons, Addresses, Letters, and Prayers* (hereafter *LMS*), ed. Ellen M. Umansky (Lewiston, N.Y: Edwin Mellon Press, 1985), 168.

13. Montagu, "A New Life Begins Today," sermon, October 1959, *LMS,* 85.

14. Montagu, "Kinship with God," sermon, 15 June 1918, *LMS,* 113.

15. Montagu, "Faith in God," sermon, 1 May 1943, *LMS,* 100.

16. Montagu, "Belief in Spiritual Progress," Club Letter No. 35, March 1942, *LMS,* 70–71.

17. Montagu, Club Letter No. 6, June 1939, *LMS,* 74.

18. C. G. Montefiore, "Great is Truth and Strong Above All Things" (Address delivered at the service of the Jewish Religious Union, 4 March 1905, Edinburgh, 14.

19. Montagu, "The Spiritual Contribution of Women as Women," sermon, 26 November 1948, *LMS,* 171–72.

20. Montagu, "The Spiritual Contribution of Women," 173.

21. Montagu, "Here Am I: Send Me," sermon, 17 June 1944, *LMS,* 128–29.

22. Perhaps because they found in Christian Science a greater religious role than that afforded to them in Judaism, and/or because, like other American women of the period they found mind-cure faiths, like Christian Science, particularly attractive. See Donald Meyer, *The Positive Thinkers* (New York: Pantheon, 1980), chap. 3.

23. Tehilla Lichtenstein, "Combining Religion with Medicine," MSS Coll. #22, Box 1, Folder 5, American Jewish Archives (AJA), Cincinnati, Ohio.

24. T. Lichtenstein, *What to Tell Your Friends About Jewish Science* (New York: Society of Jewish Science, 1951), 3.

25. J. Appel, "Christian Science and the Jews," *Jewish Social Studies* (April 1969), 2:114.

26. In looking at these examples, one should note that they are not just gender-bound but class-bound (i.e., middle class) as well.

27. T. Lichtenstein, "The Changing Relationships Between Man and Women," MSS Coll. #22, Box 1, Folder 4, AJA; "Have You Straightened Your Accounts?" MSS Coll. #22, Box 2, Folder 8, AJA; "About Ruling Others and Yielding to Others," MSS Coll. #22, Box 1, Folder 1, AJA.
28. T. Lichtenstein, "What Our Children Can Teach Us," *Jewish Science Interpreter* (November-December 1938), 2–3.
29. T. Lichtenstein, "Controlling the Tongue and the Temper," *Jewish Science Interpreter* (February 1938), 8.
30. Morris Lichtenstein, "Civilization and Stress," *Jewish Science Interpreter* (October 1932), 5–6.
31. T. Lichtenstein, "Cures for Minds in Distress," *Jewish Science Interpreter* (October 1932), 5–6.
32. T. Lichtenstein, "What Does Jewish Science Offer to the Jew?" *Jewish Science Interpreter* (December 1939) 11:2.
33. T. Lichtenstein, "The God of Nature and the God of Israel," MSS Coll. #22, Box 2, Folder 7, AJA.
34. T. Lichtenstein, "Don't Be Afraid," MSS. Coll. #22, Box 1, Folder 6, AJA; "A Corsage for Mother," MSS Coll. #22, Box 1, Folder 6, AJA; "How Much Do You Count?" MSS Coll. #22, Box 3, Folder 3, AJA.
35. See, for example, Claude Montefiore's essay on "Liberal Judaism and the Old Testament," in *Liberal Judaism and Hellenism and Other Essays,* (London: Macmillan and Co., 1918), 4ff.
36. The various justifications for assuming or relinquishing religious leadership are significant. Tehilla Lichtenstein and Paula Ackerman became religious leaders only after their husbands' deaths (having received their prior approval). Ray Frank, who predeceased her husband, abandoned her career as a preacher for the "true priesthood" of marriage and motherhood (although, ironically, she was never able to have children). Lily Montagu, who never married, was unprepared even to think of becoming a scholar, for she convinced herself that her life as a single woman, however useful, was "second best" to a life of motherhood and marriage.

CHAPTER 12

Madonnas for a New World: Harriet Beecher Stowe's Iconography of Faith

PATRICIA R. HILL

Harriet Beecher Stowe's New England novels have been widely held to embody her struggles with the harsh doctrines of Calvinism, her purported rebellion against Puritanism and her father's God.[1] Stowe's historical fictions dissect Puritan culture, exposing its narrowness and celebrating its glories, but to focus as critics have done on her portrayal of Puritanism is to miss her point. Religion was the Beecher family business, and novels were Stowe's pulpits. It is when one reads the novels as sermons addressed to contemporary readers that Stowe's "message" emerges. In offering such a reading of *The Minister's Wooing*, the first of four New England novels, I hope to show that Puritan culture or rather, more accurately, post-Revolutionary Newport caught up in the conflict between Old Calvinists and New Divinity men, served as the backdrop on which Stowe painted her vision of a more perfect Christianity, a religion peculiarly consonant with the experiences of women as lovers, wives, and mothers.

In her quest for a satisfying religious vision, Stowe ranged, like a surprising number of evangelical Protestants in the mid-nineteenth century, with apparent ease through Christian history and across doctrinal boundaries; she selected those elements of disparate traditions that suited her as a Romantic and a Victorian. Perhaps the most striking instance of this is the extent to which, in *The Minister's*

Wooing, Stowe appropriated Catholic doctrine and iconography for her sermon on suffering and salvation.

The shift in subject from the evils of slavery, which had occupied center stage in her two previous novels, had its immediate cause in Stowe's own need for consolation in the face of a family tragedy, the death of her oldest son and favorite child in the summer of 1857. Henry Stowe's drowning, in a possibly unconverted state, had forced Stowe to confront not only a devastating loss but also her own unresolved views on redemption and damnation. In her experience of grief and in her resolution of the religious questions it raised, Stowe felt she had explored the central mysteries of Christian faith and learned a lesson that she was anxious to share with fellow sufferers. Nearly a year after Henry's death she wrote to her dear friend Lady Byron a letter sketching the outlines of what became her settled convictions in the wake of tragedy. Composed just as she began writing *The Minister's Wooing,* this letter suggests the emotional dynamic that impelled Stowe to offer a meditation on suffering to her public and provides a guide for determining what in the novel represents her personal faith.

The letter opens with an intimation that Lady Byron had failed her in a time of crisis: "I did long to hear from you at a time when few knew how to speak, because I knew that you knew everything that sorrow can teach,—you whose whole life has been a crucifixion, a long ordeal."[2] Now Stowe, too, has learned the lessons sorrow teaches, and she obviously does not intend to nurse her knowledge in silence. She asserts her belief that Lady Byron is not a solitary sufferer, but of the company of those followers of the " 'Lamb' . . . who are sent into the world, as he was, to suffer for the redemption of others." For finite humans to be suffering for the redemption of others is a most un-Puritan and, indeed, un-Protestant conception in that it is Christ alone who atones for human sin; having diverged this far from orthodoxy, Stowe offers an even more startling notion. She suggests that the salvific effect of Lady Byron's "crucifixion" will reach beyond the grave, that her suffering will save Lord Byron's soul. She asserts that Lady Byron's reward in heaven "will be to see the angel, once chained and defiled within him, set free from sin and glorified, and so know that to you it has been given, by your life of love and faith to accomplish this glorious change." The characterization of Byron as a fallen angel reveals

Stowe's thoroughly Romantic sensibility, but the passage is particularly striking in the hope it holds out for those who die unconverted.

The religious views expressed in this letter are not anomalous in Stowe's thought; the letter represents a personal and private articulation of the same faith that she embodied in fictional form and offered publicly in *The Minister's Wooing*. One finds in the novel the same emphasis on redemptive suffering. And as Lady Byron is portrayed in the letter as a type of Christ, called to a ministry of suffering, so, too, in the novel do women emerge as especially prone to suffer and thereby to become agents of salvation. And just as Stowe appears in the letter to have borrowed freely from certain Catholic doctrinal traditions, the novel also reveals how profoundly her encounter with Catholic Europe earlier in the decade had affected her religious vision. Stowe's integration of some elements of Catholic doctrine into her faith and her evident appreciation of Catholic art does not indicate a sort of crypto-Catholicism. Rather it suggests a Protestant individualism, verging on the Antinomian, that allowed her great freedom in shaping a woman's religion peculiarly suited to her own circumstances.

While Stowe could discuss matters of faith and theology openly and directly with Lady Byron, she realized (and occasionally regretted) that the American public—especially the female portion of it—was increasingly impatient with sermons not cast in fictional form. How then could she clothe her message, how address serious religious questions in a novel? She found the solution in turning to historical fiction. Stowe conceived of early New England culture as obsessed by theological discussion and doctrinal debate; to recreate it in novelistic form meant that religious issues would inevitably and naturally arise. They had inescapably to be faced in this novel where the minister of the title is Jonathan Edwards's disciple, Samuel Hopkins, and the Byronic hero of the subplot is Edwards's wayward grandson, Aaron Burr.

A sketch of the novel's rather melodramatic plot should make it abundantly clear that the plot is not the point. Stowe's choice of Hopkins, best known for his elaboration of the concept of entire disinterested benevolence—succinctly summed up by Stowe as "the duty of being so wholly absorbed in the general good of the universe as even to acquiesce in [one's] own final and eternal destruction, if the greater good might thereby be accomplished"—allowed her to explore the full range of her ambivalence on the subject of New England theology. For while Stowe labeled "entire disinterested benevolence" a hard doctrine, she found a certain moral sublimity in it. And if Hopkins's personality lacked the aesthetic sensibility that, she suggests, might have been developed had he had the good fortune to live in Michelangelo's Florence, the good doctor is nevertheless an admirable and sympathetic figure in his role as a staunch opponent of the slave trade on which Newport's economy subsisted.

The good doctor, however, serves Stowe's purposes primarily as a foil for the more perfect model of Christianity embodied in the heroine, Mary Scudder. Mary, the only daughter of the doctor's landlady, is Hopkins's pupil and protegé. The widow Scudder hopes to marry her daughter to the minister, but Mary loves her irreligious sailor cousin, James Marvyn. It is only after James is reported lost at sea that Mrs. Scudder maneuvers Mary and the doctor into an engagement. With the wedding less than a week away, James turns up alive and well, converted and wealthy. Mary, however, refuses to break her pledge to the minister and conceals from him her love for James. At this juncture, Miss Prissy, spinster dressmaker to the community, interferes; urged on by black Candace, she tells the doctor the truth. He renounces his claim and officiates at Mary's wedding to James.

This main plot is mirrored in another love triangle, which features Aaron Burr's attempted seduction of Virginie de Frontignac, the beautiful young wife of one of Lafayette's colonels. It is Mary who interferes in this instance, confronting Burr with the "truth" of his immoral conduct and its inevitable consequences for his vulnerable victim.

But if the critics are all agreed that the plot is not the point, there is far less agreement about what precisely is Stowe's point. One group of critics focuses on Stowe's delineation of Puritan theology and reads the novel either as "an expose of the pernicious effects of Calvinism" or, conversely, as her accommodation to the fundamental truths of Calvinism, her "final yes" to her Puritan heritage. Even for those critics who recognize that Stowe had detached herself from her Puritan heritage long before Henry Stowe's death, who realize that Stowe was a Romantic evangelical, and who mention that this novel shows evidence of Stowe's encounter with Catholic Europe, Puritan and biographical issues continue to loom large. The assumption is made that escaping the remorseless logic of Calvinism is the dynamic at the heart of Stowe's intellectual and religious life. Some have seen in this "retreat" from Calvinism a lamentable sentimentalization and feminization of religion. Feminist critics, in a variation on this theme, have argued that Stowe replaced an oppressive patriarchal religion with a matriarchal one that offered women liberation from male theologies.[3]

There is an element of truth about the novel in all these perspectives. Feminist critics have been particularly helpful in shifting the focus to the content of the religion that Stowe substituted for Hopkinsianism, but they have failed to appreciate the cultural divide between Stowe's era and our own. Until we understand Stowe as a Romantic and a Victorian, we will not understand how she arrived at the convictions expressed in her letter to Lady Byron, nor will we be able to delimit the very special place women occupy in Stowe's religious vision.

Stowe's message to her readers was grounded in Romantic aesthetic theory, which she coupled with a characteristic Victorian veneration of womanhood. Stowe linked these Romantic and Victorian notions in a religious epistemology that reveals just how far she distanced herself from her Puritan heritage. As a Romantic evangelical, she believed that one gains knowledge of the Divine through feeling. She conceptualized this through metaphor, in what is perhaps the most famous passage from *The Minister's Wooing:*

There is a ladder to heaven, whose base God has placed in human affections, tender instincts, symbolic feelings, sacraments of love, through which the soul rises higher and higher, refining as she goes, till she outgrows the human, and changes, as she rises, into the image of the divine. At the very top of this ladder, at the threshold of Paradise, blazes dazzling and crystalline that celestial grade where the soul knows self no more, having learned, through a long experience of devotion, how blest it is to lose herself in that eternal Love and Beauty of which all earthly fairness and grandeur are but the dim type, the distant shadow.[4]

While earthly fairness and grandeur were, to Stowe, but a dim type of eternal beauty, she nevertheless granted to art the power to excite the human affections, tender instincts, and symbolic feelings that were rungs on the ladder to heaven. Stowe appreciated the labors of those who had reasoned their way to the sublimity of disinterested benevolence through systematic theologies; she believed, however, that only a few choice souls were capable, either intellectually or temperamentally, of reaching heaven by this method. She herself preferred the emotional path that she celebrated in her heroine.

Mary was by nature of the class who never reason abstractly, whose intellections all begin in the heart. . . . In all the system which had been explained to her, her mind selected points on which it seized with intense sympathy. . . . The sublimity of disinterested benevolence, the harmony and order of a system tending in its final results to infinite happiness, the goodness of God, the love of a self-sacrificing Redeemer, were all so many glorious pictures, which she revolved in her mind with small care for their logical relations (MW, 249).

Like her heroine, Stowe thought in pictures; although she owned a love for music, art was, for her, primarily visual. And, as an American, she considered herself aesthetically deprived. Living in the culturally raw world of Cincinnati in the 1830s and 1840s, Stowe pored over the volumes of the English critic Anna Jameson, "whose works on arts and artists were," she reported, "for years almost my only food for a certain class of longings."[5]

The unparalleled success of *Uncle Tom's Cabin* provided Stowe with the means of satisfying her longings. The letters she wrote during her triumphal first tour of Europe indicate that she missed no opportunity to explore her personal emotional responses to the glories of Catholic art. Admittedly an idealist, Stowe "expected a divine baptism, a celestial mesmerism"; she was frequently disappointed, "left quite in possession of [her] sense." With characteristic fairmindedness, she confided that it was "too much to ask of any earthly artist . . . to gratify the aspirations and cravings of those who have dreamed of them for years unsatisfied" (SM, 1:323).

If she was not enraptured, Stowe nevertheless felt strongly that Protestants, especially American Protestants, could learn much from Catholic art. Her remarks along these lines focus particularly on paintings of the Madonna. She had often thought, she wrote, "that, in the reaction from the idolatry of Romanism, we Protestants were in danger of forgetting the treasures of religious sweetness, which the Bible has given us in [Mary's] brief history" (SM, 2:351). But while paintings of the Madonna served to remind Protestants of Mary's significance, they failed, in Stowe's opinion, to represent adequately "the *scriptural* ideal" (SM, 2:350). The great exception was Raphael's Sistine Madonna which, Stowe said (in words that echo biblical accounts of Mary and suggest Stowe's own identification with the Madonna), "excited my ponderings" (SM, 2:342). She was disappointed in the coloring, conception, and arrangement of the painting, but she felt that "the deep-feeling soul which conceived this picture has spread over the whole divine group a tender and transparent shadow of sorrow. It is this idea of sorrow in heaven—sorrow, for the lost, in the heart of God himself—which forms the most sacred mystery of Christianity; and into this innermost temple of sorrow had Raphael penetrated." Stowe reported that "this picture . . . has formed a deeper part of my inner consciousness than any I have yet seen. I can recall it with perfect distinctness, and often return to ponder it in my heart" (SM, 2:343).

Stowe admitted this particular painting to the canon of revelation that in true Protestant fashion she ordinarily limited to the scriptural record. For, despite the stimulus to religious reflection that a handful of paintings offered, Stowe concluded that "there is more pathos and beauty in those few words of the Scripture, 'Now there stood by the cross of Jesus his mother,' than in all these galleries put together" (SM, 2:350).

And yet, Stowe was not satisfied to know Mary from the Bible alone. She called for a "new school of art, based upon Protestant principles," for, she argued, "whatever vigor and originality there might once be in art, based on Romanism, it has certainly been worn threadbare by repetition" (SM, 2:351). The new art would, she hoped, be American as well as Protestant. In common with other American *literati* of the antebellum period, she longed for the "full advent of our American day of art, already dawning auspiciously" (SM, 1:325). And she wanted American artists to work with American materials. She sighed, in language echoing Emerson and Thoreau, "When we shall see a New England artist, with his easel, in the fields, seeking hour after hour, to reproduce on the canvas the magnificent glories of an elm, with its firmament of boughs and branches, . . . then the morning star of art will have risen on our hills" (SM, 2:347).

In *The Minister's Wooing,* Stowe tried to become that New England artist. In Mary Scudder she painted her New World Madonna. There is no doubt from Mary's first appearance in the novel that she is chosen among women. The initial description echoes the Frederick Goodall painting of Mary offering doves at the temple that

Stowe selected for the frontispiece of her 1873 gift book, *Women in Sacred History*. Mary, characterized as an "only daughter, the gentle Mary," is pictured standing "in the doorway with the afternoon sun streaming in spots of flickering sunlight on her smooth pale hair." Moreover, "she stands reaching up one hand and cooing to something among the apple blossoms; and now a Java dove comes whirring down and settles on her finger, and we, that have seen pictures, think . . . of some old pictures of the girlhood of the Virgin" (MW, 14). Mary's bedroom is described, significantly, as having "the quiet hush of some little side chapel in a cathedral"; its dimensions are "small enough for a nun's apartment" and "the bed and low window are draped in spotless white" (MW, 22).

Mary's identity with the Madonna—and her complex and ambiguous relationship to her Puritan world—are reinforced in a description of her garret retreat that invests Mary with Stowe's own fondness for icons. (Stowe's Hartford neighbors were scandalized by the Madonna hanging on her bedroom wall.) Mary's garret has two icons: the "dusky picture, in an old tarnished frame" of a Puritan ancestor, "one of the sufferers in the time when witches were unceremoniously helped out of the world, instead of being, as nowadays, helped to make their fortune in it by table-turning"; and "an old engraved head of one of the Madonnas of Leonardo da Vinci, a picture which to Mary had a mysterious interest, from the fact of its having been cast on shore after a furious storm." But though her Puritan ancestress has a place of honor on Mary's wall, it is to the da Vinci engraving that Mary turns most often: "[She] felt the seaworn picture as a constant vague inspiration" (MW, 181, 183).

In her association with the seaworn engraving, Mary remains a dim type of the ideal. Similarly, Stowe tentatively associates her with a New World Puritan model for saintly virginity by claiming that Mary's demeanor evoked in Aaron Burr "a shadowy recollection" of the lyrical account, found among his grandfather's papers, describing Sarah Pierrepont, Edwards's future wife. Stowe pictures Burr as so struck with this passage "beautifully expressing an ideal womanhood" that he copied it into his notebook. For the edification of her readers, Stowe includes almost in its entirety Edwards's famous sketch of Sarah Pierrepoint, the "young lady who is beloved of that Great Being who made and rules the world" and who possesses "a strange sweetness in her mind, and singular purity in her affections" (MW, 193–94).

Midway through the novel, when the heroines of the plot and subplot are brought together in the same room, Stowe explicitly compares them to painted Madonnas that were in her opinion only partial and inadequate representations of the biblical model. Virginie calls to mind a Madonna by Rubens: "A superb Oriental sultana, with lustrous dark eyes, redundant form, jeweled turban, standing leaning on the balustrade of a princely terrace, and bearing on her hand, not the silver dove, but a gorgeous paroquet." In contrast, Mary is compared with "the faded, cold ideals of the Middle Ages, from which [Rubens] revolted" and with "a sketch of Overbeck's." The effect on Mary of her encounter with the sensuous Catholic beauty is emblematic of the relationship between the two women in the novel. In "the tropical atmosphere of this regal beauty . . . all the slumbering poetry within [Mary] seemed to awaken . . . as when one for the first time stands before the great revelation of Art." Like the snowy Alps that reflect the rose tints of sunset in so many Romantic travelers' accounts, Mary's delicate face and figure reflect the glowing loveliness of her visitor (MW, 217).

Catholic Virginie and Puritan Mary represent two aspects of the Madonna, but it is Mary who takes on the lovely attributes of Virginie, adding them to her own sterling qualities. Mary's transformation in this scene into a type more nearly approximating Stowe's ideal prefigures her transformation, in climbing the ladder to heaven, into the image of the Madonna in the one painting that realized Stowe's ideal.

The rungs of the ladder that Mary climbs to reach this pinnacle are those human emotions connected to the most common experiences of women. Women, Stowe believed, were bound by nature to fall in love. "If women have one weakness more marked than another, it is towards veneration. They are born worshippers,—makers of silver shrines for some divinity or other which, of course, they always think fell straight down from heaven." According to Stowe, when a woman falls in love with a man, she invariably invests him with the qualities of her ideal, and "having made him up, . . . worship[s] him." But if there is a tinge of cynical humor in this description of woman's weakness for man, there is none in Stowe's belief that God made women capable of such love for men in order to stimulate a power of self-sacrifice that made them worthy to be priestesses in their domestic temples. In her iconographic imagination, woman's self-sacrificing nature was embodied in Domenichino's "Last Communion of St. Jerome" with its depiction of "the faithful Paula, with her beautiful face, prostrate in reverence before poor, old, lean, haggard, dying St. Jerome, . . . an emblem and sign of woman's eternal power of self-sacrifice to what she deems noblest in man" (MW, 133–34).

Few men are saints, however, and Stowe expected that most women would inevitably be disappointed in the failure of the object of their love to measure up to their ideal. They would suffer through such disappointment and thereby begin to understand God's sorrow for the lost. Such suffering would occur even in the context of a love that culminated in marriage, but disappointment in a husband might be mitigated by the higher consolations of motherhood. Motherhood, in turn, would bring its own sorrows as children were inevitably lost. Such sorrow, Stowe says, "the bleeding heart of the Mother of God alone can understand" (MW, 278). Consolation for a mother's grief could be found only in the love of a God whose sorrow for the lost resembles the mother's own sorrow.

Certainly experiences of love and sorrow are rungs on the ladders to heaven of the women in *The Minister's Wooing.* The first rung on Mary's ladder is a love for James that brings her to a state of willingness to sacrifice her own eternal salvation for his redemption. The sorrow that James's reported loss at sea brings to Mary and to his mother provides Stowe with the occasion for offering the sermon on sorrow that lies at the heart of *The Minister's Wooing.*

In the portrait of Mrs. Marvyn, driven to the edge of insanity by her anguish, Stowe exposes the psychological damage inflicted on a sensitive soul by the unrelenting Puritan doctrine of eternal damnation. Mrs. Marvyn's sanity is saved when she listens to the spiritual advice of the exslave Candace who rocks her in her arms and tells her "de Lord ain't like what ye tink—He *loves* ye, honey!" Candace urges her to forget all "dese yer great and mighty tings [the doctor's] got to say" and "come right down to whar poor ole black Candace has to stay allers . . . [and] look right at Jesus." Candace reminds Mrs. Marvyn of "how He looked on his mother, when she stood faintin' an' tremblin' under de cross, jes' like you." She assures Mrs. Marvyn that Jesus "knows all about mothers' hearts; He won't break yours." Candace croons over and over that Mrs. Marvyn must just look at Jesus and have faith (MW, 253–54).

But if Mrs. Marvyn's sorrow is a mother's sorrow that teaches her something of the nature of God overlooked in Hopkinsian precepts, Mary's sorrow produces a more miraculous transformation. Mary, as Stowe made apparent from the novel's beginning, is not an ordinary woman; in her sorrow she does not look at and identify with Jesus' mother standing at the foot of the cross. Instead, she becomes something more than the Madonna; she becomes a type of Christ. News of James's death functions as Mary's crucifixion. Its immediate effect is to cause her collapse. She is laid lifeless on her mother's bed and is prayed over by the good doctor. She rises in the morning and goes about her mother's business, fixing breakfast for the hired men. In the succeeding weeks and months, Mary moves through infinite sorrow to infinite peace. This process culminates in her transfiguration, which Stowe describes in terms of a face illuminated with a radiance akin to the celestial radiance that illuminated the resurrected Christ in "an hour when the fishermen of Galilee saw their Master transfigured, his raiment white and glistening, and his face like light" (MW, 264, 228).

Stowe's doctrine of sorrow, her belief in its sanctifying power, is more Catholic than Protestant in tone. She elaborates this doctrine in the chapter titled "Mysteries" that is the sermonic core of her fiction. Sorrow she calls "the great birth-agony of immortal powers," and says it is "godlike." Stowe perceived in the natural order "an ascending scale, marked by increasing power to suffer." This placed women with their greater capacity for suffering higher on the scale than men, nearer to the divine with which one could ultimately merge through sorrow, since "sorrow is divine" (MW, 261–63).

At the heart of the Christian faith from Stowe's perspective is the mysterious transmutation of sorrow into joy. This, as she describes it, is the central message of the Bible which distinguishes the Christian faith from all other religions and philosophies. The hope of joy that Stowe holds out is not confined to reigning with God in heaven. She also argues that one can experience it in this world, that nature itself produces a force to counter suffering. Stowe says, "After great mental conflicts and agonies must come a reaction, and the Divine Spirit, co-working with our spirit, seizes the favorable moment, and interpenetrating natural laws with a celestial vitality, carries up the soul to joys beyond the ordinary possibilities of mortality." When Mary Scudder's soul had risen to this state of joy, she "moved in a world transfigured by a celestial radiance," and "her face . . . wore . . . the victorious sweetness of that great multitude who have come out of great tribulation." Stowe does not hesitate to claim that here she has painted a heroine in whose eyes "there was that nameless depth that one sees with awe in the Sistine Madonna,—eyes that have measured infinite sorrow and looked through it to an infinite peace" (MW, 263–64).

After this transfiguration, in the phase of her life before James's unexpected return, Mary takes on a role within the community that reveals another dimension to Stowe's affinity for Catholicism. Mary serves as priest and intercessor for those whose souls are troubled. Stowe compares Mary's bosom to a confessional and sanctuary and writes that as "a sanctified priestess of the great worship of sorrow . . . so many sought her prayers, that her hours of intercession were full" (MW, 277). In the novel Stowe does not put the efficacy of Mary's intercession to the test of redeeming a soul that has passed beyond the vale; James, after all, turns up alive. Yet his conversion is attributed to the agency of Mary's self-sacrificing example working on his heart; and so, like other women in Stowe's fiction—and like Lady Byron—Mary is credited with being the savior of her husband.

That Stowe's New World Madonna has Christlike powers transcending those granted the Virgin in Catholic Mariology is evident in the final glimpse we are given of Mary after she has entered the sanctified state of marriage and motherhood. Stowe paints this last portrait in a domestic frame, albeit one where earthly home nearly merges into heavenly mansion:

On a beautiful elevation, a little out of the town of Newport, rose a fair and stately mansion, whose windows overlooked the harbor, and whose wide, cool rooms were adorned by the constant presence of the sweet face and form which has been the guiding star of our story. The fair poetic maiden, the seeress, the saint, has passed into that appointed shrine for woman, more holy than cloister, more saintly and pure than church or altar, a Christian home. Priestess, wife, and mother, there she ministers daily in holy works of household peace, and by faith and prayer and love redeems from grossness and earthliness the common toils and wants of life. (MW, 410)

In this passage Mary has become a Madonna in the house, a priestess in the shrine of the home. She is the real presence in the communion of the family, a living icon adorning the rooms of her husband's mansion.

One can chart similar rungs on the ladder of the other Madonna in the novel. Virginie's alternating experience of love and sorrow are the rungs on which she climbs to heaven. Even her adulterous love for Aaron Burr teaches her the power and grandeur of love. She tells Mary that she "loved him with a religion" and "would have died for him." She was "astonished [she] could feel so," and, until her confessor warned her that she was in danger of falling into mortal sin, "did not dream that this could be wrong." How could she have imagined this love was sinful "when it made [her] feel more religious than anything in [her] whole life?" (MW, 283).

That adulterous passions could lead one into mortal sin seems a natural enough warning from a confessor. The spiritual advice Stowe has the Abbé Lefon offer Virginie bears the stamp of Stowe's own special concern with redemptive suffering. The abbé points out that as a heretic Burr is headed for hell; he tells Virginie that she "must offer [herself] a sacrifice." If she will give up her love for Burr, the abbé suggests that "God would perhaps accept it as a satisfaction, and bring him into the True Church at last" (MW, 283–84). Virginie struggles unsuccessfully to relinquish her love, until— confronted with evidence of Burr's falseness—she runs away from the social whirl of Philadelphia to take refuge in Mary's humble cottage.

The chastened Virginie searches for a new object for the power of loving that has been awakened in her. She tries to give herself wholly to Christ, as Mary and the abbé advise, but is at first unable to do so. Instead, she turns to Mary whom she compares with Saint Catherine and "our dear Lady" (MW, 287). She is somewhat troubled by the knowledge that Mary is a heretic, as Mary is by Virginie's Catholicism, but the two women defy their mentors on this point, and "the Catholic and the Puritan, each strong in her respective faith, yet melting together in that embrace of love and sorrow, joined the great communion of suffering" (MW, 288). Virginie remains at the cottage, with Mary as her spiritual guide (and shield when Burr comes to tempt Virginie), until Mary's wedding. She then returns to her own husband and country, finding in her marriage and in motherhood a new and deeper joy. Yet Burr remains in her prayers, the prayers that Mary Scudder suggested to him in their final interview were his only hope of salvation.

Yes, Mr. Burr, if ever your popularity and prosperity should leave you, and those who now flatter should despise and curse you, she will always be interceding with her own heart and with God for you, and making a thousand excuses where she cannot deny; and if you die, as I fear you have lived, unreconciled to the God of your fathers, it will be in her heart to offer up her very soul for you, and to pray that God will impute all your sins to her, and give you heaven (MW, 346–47).

In contrast to the women, the men in *The Minister's Wooing* are saved not through lessons taught by emotions that come naturally in the course of their lives but through the agency of women. For Doctor Hopkins, it is the face of a woman that brings the experience of love, and it is the loss of Mary that brings suffering, but his is the only case where there is any correspondence to the experience of the women. And, as his is one of the few souls that reason took straight to the top of the ladder, the experience of earthly emotions is simply humanizing for him, not salvific. Mary's self-sacrificial love demonstrates to James the inadequacy of his own love. He learns the nature of divine love, therefore, not by analogy from his love for Mary, but from hers for him. Aaron Burr only pretends to love Virginie, and her loss occasions him no redeeming sorrow. He is Stowe's Byronic hero, however, and the monument that Virginie's son places over his unmarked grave in the novel's last scene hints that Virginie's unceasing intercession has proved salvific—as Stowe believed Lady Byron's would prove for Lord Byron.

What Stowe has shaped in *The Minister's Wooing* is then a gospel for women. The good news she preaches to women is that their life experiences are teaching them by analogy the deepest truths of Christianity. This places them in a position to save those they love, either by exerting a salvific influence as objects of veneration or, more actively, by ministering to humanity as priestesses and intercessors. Women have in their nature the capacity to become types both of the Mother of God and of her Son. They are saviors of men.

For Stowe to posit women as agents of salvation and to take seriously their power of intercession represented a radical departure from Protestant doctrine. Stowe accepted the portrayal in Catholic tradition of Mary as an intercessor in heaven, but this was not all she accepted from Catholicism. She also allowed herself to contemplate the possibility that the unconverted inhabit a purgatory-like place of future probation, and that prayers for the dead might therefore prove efficacious. In *The Minister's Wooing* she attributes to Abbé Lefon the warning of her favorite Catholic mystic Fenelon (the similarity between the names is surely not accidental) against the application of reason to the mysteries of faith. To this she adds—and rejoices in—her own belief that since it is "the blessed gift of womanhood . . . which resists the chills of analysis" (MW, 211), women can more easily than men avoid the temptation to destroy faith with reason. But Catholic teachings only supplied a richer palette for Stowe to use in painting her own picture of faith.

Ultimately, Stowe's iconographic imagination was not dogmatic. Her religion was grounded not in doctrinal traditions, but in intuitive judgments of religious truth that derived from personal experience of human emotions. She measured doctrines as she judged art, against the "glorious pictures, which she revolved in her mind." Those doctrines, like those paintings, that matched her ideals formed a part of her inner consciousness. As a Victorian she quite naturally glorified motherhood; the love of mothers, she claimed, transcended the merely human and participated in the divine. And while Stowe did not suggest that God was literally both male and female in nature, in her description "the All-Father treats us as the mother does 'her infant crying in the dark;' He does not reason with our fears, or demonstrate their fallacy, but draws us silently to His bosom, and we are at peace" (MW, 309). If mother love provided the closest human analogue to the love of God, it does not follow that Stowe's religion was, as has been said, a religion of love. For Stowe's personal experience taught her that a mother's love would inevitably be tinged with sadness and anguish as well as joy. Her religion therefore can more aptly be characterized as a religion of the interpenetration of love and sorrow, which she believed could be found in its most exalted form in the heart of God and in a mother's love. It is not surprising then that Stowe's imagination revolved so often around the images of Mary in the scriptures and in Catholic art and that she should choose to construct her religious vision around a New World Madonna. In Mary Scudder she painted herself and her readers an icon on which suffering Victorian womanhood could focus its meditations and derive hope of transcendence through a faith peculiarly suited to woman as the Victorians conceived her.

Stowe's particular faith is both time- and culture-bound. If her sermon has any prophetic quality, it resides in the picture of Mary and Virginie reaching out to each other across boundaries of language, class, nationality, and doctrine. Stowe's method of theological construction supplies a model for appropriating from various traditions those aspects of belief and doctrine that affirm the value of women's lives, but her particular views can hardly be transformed into a retrievable source for contemporary feminist theology. Within her own historical context, Stowe's vision, in moving women to center stage as moral and spiritual forces, had certain feminist tendencies. By adding new dimensions to the claims of women within the evangelical nexus, she did define an empowering spirituality for a sizable segment of the female population. Her historical fiction supplied women with a usable "past," an ancestral portrait suggesting a less ambiguous lineage than the dusky icon on Mary Scudder's wall and a model for saintliness more fully realized than Jonathan Edwards's lyrical but all too brief sketch of Sarah Pierrepont.

NOTES

1. This is a view advanced by C. Rourke in *Trumpets of Jubilee* (New York: Harcourt Brace, 1927) and E. Wilson in *Patriotic Gore* (New York: Oxford University Press, 1962), as well as HBS's grandson L. B. Stowe in *Saints, Sinners, and Beechers* (Indianapolis: Bobbs-Merrill, 1934). Other critics from C. Foster and A. Crozier to A. Douglas have improvised variations on this theme.

2. The text of Stowe's letter to Lady Byron appears in C. E. Stowe's *Life of Harriet E. Beecher* (Boston: Houghton Mifflin Press, 1889), 339–40.

3. The phrase "an exposé of the pernicious effects . . ." is Wilson's in *Patriotic Gore,* 49; C. Foster argues in *The Rungless Ladder* (Durham: Duke University Press, 1954), 127, that the denouement of *The Minister's Wooing* allowed Stowe to say "a final yes" to Calvinism. L. Buell in an influential article, "Calvinism Romanticized: Harriet Beecher Stowe, Samuel Hopkins, and *The Minister's Wooing,*" *ESQ: A Journal of the American Renaissance* 24 (1978): 119–32, demonstrates the appropriateness of placing Stowe in the context

of conservative Calvinist circles rather than the liberal Unitarian-Trans-cendentalist axis. P. Williams's unpublished dissertation, "A Mirror For Unitarians: Catholicism and Culture in Nineteenth Century New England Literature" (Yale University, 1970), includes a most perceptive discussion of Stowe's relationship to Catholicism; yet his inclusion of this discussion in a study of Unitarian fascination with Catholicism demonstrates the need for the corrective that Buell's article offers. A. Crozier's fine study, *The Novels of Harriet Beecher Stowe* (New York: Oxford University Press, 1969), places Stowe's work in the literary context of Scott and Byron, emphasizing her romanticism, yet argues that although Stowe dismissed Puritan theology she remained a literary Puritan. A. Douglas, in *The Feminization of American Culture* (New York: Knopf Press, 1977), places Stowe among the feminizers of American Protestantism whom she seems almost to despise. Feminist critics like G. Kimball, in *The Religious Ideas of Harriet Beecher Stowe: Her Gospel of Womanhood* (New York: E. Mellen, 1982), and D. Berkson, in "Millennial Politics and the Feminine Fiction of Harriet Beecher Stowe," in *Critical Essays on Harriet Beecher Stowe,* ed. E. Ammons (Boston: G. K. Hale, 1980), have celebrated and, I think, overdrawn the feminist and radical implications of Stowe's New England novels; this leaves them disappointed and straining for an explanation of what they read as antifeminist sentiments in Stowe's postwar society novels.

4. H. B. Stowe, *The Minister's Wooing* (1859; reprint, Boston: Houghton Mifflin, 1896), 66. All further references to this work (MW) appear in the text.

5. H. B. Stowe, *Sunny Memories of Foreign Lands* (Boston: Phillips Samson, 1854), 2:107. All further references to this work (SM) appear in the text.

CHAPTER 13

Aesthetic Vision, Prophetic Voice: Intimacy and Social Justice in Kaethe Kollwitz and Dorothea Lange

GREGOR GOETHALS

Dorothea Lange and Kaethe Kollwitz, artists active in the early twentieth century, came from two distinct cultural traditions and worked in different media; yet, their formal visual language and symbols were similar. A comparison of the work of these women can highlight their contributions to modern sensibilities. In their images these artists transcended narrow aesthetic concerns as they became more deeply drawn into the moral and social issues of their cultures. At a time when women found it difficult to break out of stereotypical roles, these women artists created visual metaphors that anticipated an understanding of human experience that would be emphasized late in the century by liberation and feminist theologians.

In the following interpretation I emphasize two contributions in the work of these women to our ethical and theological reflections. First, in their concern for social issues, they give visual expressions to the prophetic dimensions of biblical theology. Second, their preoccupation with visual metaphors of human relationships parallels current themes in liberation and feminist theology.

Kollwitz and Lange continued in the twentieth century the tradition of literary and visual artists who were passionately committed to social justice. Like Ben Shahn and John Heartfield, who were among their contemporaries, they extended the concerns of Goya and Daumier, who in earlier European societies used their art to disclose human compassion, violence, and folly. Other contemporaries of these women shared their interest in social problems and reform, but their work took different directions. Painters Mondrian and Kandinsky, for example, led artists of the twentieth century into abstract art partly in search of reform of a materialistic society. In their revolt against materialism they replaced recognizable subject matter with nonrepresentational forms which, they believed, held the promise of universal communication and represented a new religious consciousness.

Kollwitz and Lange, in focusing on the human predicament, and especially on the victims of society, belong by contrast in the biblical prophetic tradition. Their works echo, perhaps unconsciously, the words of Amos when he lashed out at the powerful who sell the poor for silver. The anguish over war and death in Kollwitz's work takes us back to the yearnings for peace expressed in Micah's admonition to beat swords into plowshares and spears into pruning hooks. Pictorial themes of love and justice remind us of the songs of the psalmist. Today, their works might harmonize with the call of liberation theologians for churches to face their tacit involvement in authoritarian structures and their passivity in accepting the oppression of the poor and landless throughout the world. Kollwitz and Lange could, in fact, serve as models for artists today who do not want to retreat into aestheticism. Beyond that, however, they are models for all individuals who resist a reductionist dichotomy that insists upon a simplification of political ideology into dichotomies such as "communism" versus "free enterprise." Both women understood that human desperation and the drive to escape hunger, poverty, and powerlessness cannot be labeled simply as "ideology" and dismissed. At a time when genuine prophetic iconoclasm is rare, the work of these women reminds us of the artist's responsibility to the community.

Taking a more speculative approach in interpreting their work, we may ask: what philosophical or theological insights do their images suggest? Sketching tentative responses to this question requires attention to two characteristics in the work of these artists: the concentration on human relationships and the blurring of boundaries with the result of re-forming individual figures into powerful symbolic compositions. When we place these qualities alongside certain theological themes, we discover important congruities.

In her book *Metaphorical Theology*, Sallie McFague explores the various metaphors we use as we attempt to develop a language about God. She concludes with Simon Weil that "when we try to speak of God there is nothing which resembles what we can conceive when we say that word." The strength of her book lies, nevertheless, in her careful analysis of the metaphors we use. In particular, she stresses the importance of relationships in developing models of God. We use, she says, the relationships nearest and dearest to us as metaphors for that which finally cannot be named. Her own feminine model for divine-human relationships is not only appropriate but required if both men and women are to experience fully the sense of God's gracious love for all people. Feminine models, she says, suggest "re-birth, nurture, unmerited love, security in God alone, compassion, forgiveness, service."[1]

Commensurate with these concepts, images created by Lange and Kollwitz offer insights that words cannot express. Kollwitz and Lange created rich and profound visual resources for reflecting upon human relationships—persons to persons, persons to nature, and persons to death. In their images graciousness and compassion are linked to power through simplified, clear, forceful compositions. Parental love—encompassing, bewildering, grieving, and joyous—radiates from both male and female figures. While these images embody the very qualities characteristic of McFague's model for divine-human relationships, the artists' use of both male and female figures to communicate these qualities challenges easy stereotyping of masculinity and femininity. Precisely for these reasons, both artists merit our full attention.

The atmosphere in which Kaethe Kollwitz grew up contributed significantly to both her prophetic vision and her aesthetic expression. She was introduced to religious and social concerns at an early age by her maternal grandfather, a pastor whose concepts of Christian community led him to be expelled from the state Lutheran church in Germany. Her artistic inclinations were nurtured by her parents who found artists with whom she could study, for at that time no academies or colleges were open to women. Eventually she was able to do advanced work in Berlin at an art school for women. There she met a sympathetic teacher through whom she became aware of the work and ideas of Max Klinger, a sculptor and etcher who believed that the more tragic dimensions of life could be best expressed in drawing and the graphic arts. In 1891 she married Dr. Karl Kollwitz, a doctor committed to the practice of medicine among the poor in Berlin. In this environment her two sons were born, and here she continued her work as an artist.

Her work at this time reflected a preoccupation with social justice. A series of prints was inspired by a dramatic production of Gerhart Hauptman's drama, *The Weavers,* and they were entitled *Poverty, Death, Conspiracy, March of the Weavers, Riot,* and *The End.* While related to the Hauptman drama about the plight of Silesian weavers, the cycle of prints became an opportunity for Kollwitz to give concrete shape to her own profound engagement with human hope and despair. A second cycle of seven etchings was entitled *Peasant War.* Its symbols were taken in part from the tales of violence and heroism associated with the German Peasant War when in the early years of the Reformation the rural poor revolted against the power of the nobility and the church.

Later in her life Kollwitz's involvement with suffering became more direct and intense, without the mediation of drama or history. The loss of her own son in World War I and her husband's work in the slums of Berlin in the aftermath of Germany's defeat provided her intimate experiences of grief that came to characterize her work. She continued her activity as an artist in Berlin even though Hitler's regime forbade galleries to exhibit her prints and sculpture. She left her Berlin home only when Allied planes began to bomb the city.

From Kollwitz's world came images of the human pathos that was an immediate and inescapable aspect of life around her; her drawings, woodcuts, etchings, and lithographs portray mothers, children, the hungry, grief-stricken parents, sickness, and death. The persistence of these images and the strength with which they were developed transcend particular national situations. They have a compelling power to exceed particular boundaries by drawing the viewer into the realm of universal human experience. This forceful, unflinching encounter with her environment links Kollwitz's work with that of Dorothea Lange.

Born in Hoboken, New Jersey, Dorothea Lange was brought up in an environment quite unlike that of Kollwitz. Her father left the family, and she was raised by her mother and grandmother in a setting that provided little stimulus for an intellectual or artistic career. Years later, in reflecting on her early experiences, she remarked that the most formative element of her life which "guided me, instructed me, helped me, and humiliated me" was a crippled right leg, the result of polio.[2] The humiliation became a force that sensitized and equipped her with an unusual capacity to relate to all kinds of people and situations.

Not interested in college, Lange decided to seek a career in photography upon graduation from high school. To please her mother and grandmother who could not understand her decision, she attended the New York Training School for Teachers for a brief time. Meanwhile, she purchased a camera and spent the next few years working with photographers, performing a variety of tasks from typing and selling to printing and camera work. Along with this on-the-job training she studied for a short while at Columbia with the photographer-teacher Clarence White. She became familiar with the work being exhibited at Alfred Stieglitz's Photo-Secession Gallery in New York as well.

In 1918 Lange cut her ties to New York and set out with a friend for a trip around the world, in hopes of later setting up her own studio. After being robbed, however, they were stranded in San Francisco. There Lange found temporary work, and in time she opened a portrait studio. She wanted to relate to persons and could draw out of her sitters the expressions and gestures that sparked their individuality. While she didn't aspire to be a "great photographer," she genuinely wished to be useful, to fill a need. Her personal interpretation, she said, was secondary to that of the individual she sought to portray.[3] Eventually, that sense of responsivity would lead her to different subjects—not the well-to-do but the poor and powerless, disenfranchised by the social and economic conditions of America's Great Depression.

Many events contributed to Dorothea Lange's decision to move toward the portrayal of those who had lost their places in the scheme of things. Now married and the mother of two sons, she and her husband, painter Maynard Dixon, decided to give up their house, move into their studios, and enroll their two boys in boarding school. Lange commented later that the pain of separation from her children drove her into an intense period of work. As the Depression worsened, she saw its effects all around her and began to photograph some of its unemployed victims in the streets of San

Francisco. Soon her work caught the attention of Paul Taylor, a sociologist who had been working with California's migrant workers. She eventually divorced Dixon and married Taylor. Together they pursued a lifelong collaboration on documentary studies involving text and pictures.

Dorothea Lange, like Kaethe Kollwitz, became concerned with the social and economic crisis in which she lived. As a photographer, she produced images that differed in format and medium from those of Kollwitz. Yet her images performed similar functions; they were symbolic records of the darker side of the human condition, which communicated on a larger, public scale the plight of individuals who otherwise had no voice. At a time when the concept of "art for art's sake" was widely held by many distinguished artists, these women concentrated upon the human predicament. Rather than isolating the aesthetic realm from life or dehumanizing it, they used its full power to express and probe the depths of individual and social suffering. Kollwitz's subjects were the urban poor in Berlin slums, while Lange's were displaced migrant workers, disoriented by the disasters of America's Depression and drought of the 1930s. Both made powerful use of the mother-and-child motif to dramatize human compassion and the plight of the innocent. A comparison of certain images will highlight common elements and distinguish the particular skills of the artists.

Among Kollwitz's many variations on the mother-child motif is a charcoal drawing of 1932 entitled *Mother with Children*. Broad, simple strokes depict a woman holding two children. The artist has drawn the figures from an intimate perspective, emphasizing the faces and the inclusive arms of the woman who gathers the children close to her. No face is shown in full detail. Instead they are so bound together that the shapes seem to recombine into an integrated, forceful, organic form. Lange used a similar approach in the composition of *Migrant Mother, Nipomo, California* (1936), which became one of the most frequently reproduced photographs of that era. After making a number of prints of the woman and her three children, she chose a close, private view that reveals the expressive face of the mother. Like Kollwitz's drawing, her photographic composition fuses the separate entities into a symbolic whole, dissolving sharp boundaries. The face and body of the mother provide the pictorial and emotional structure, while the forms of the children, seen only partially, revolve around this central figure. Turned away from the viewer, their faces buried, the two older children cling to the mother; only a portion of her infant's face is visible. As the children cluster around the woman, they appear to be drawn to her body by a gravitational force. In these two representations Kollwitz and Lange have blurred the boundaries of individuals, bonding and fashioning them into powerful symbols of parental nurture and compassion.

Contrasting environments and fateful circumstances in the lives of these two women artists led them, of course, in different directions and to different themes. For Kollwitz there was a greater, more direct engagement with sickness and death, especially after the death of her son and the defeat of Germany in World War I. Many of her drawings and prints concentrate on death. In one moving drawing, *Mother with Sick Child,* apparently made in preparation for a woodcut, a woman beside the bed of her sick child looks down upon the infant. Anticipating the woodcut, the artist has made alterations in the drawing, originally executed in black ink on a toned paper. Correcting the drawing with a white gouache paint, she has covered the features of the child's face. A viewer studying the drawing is struck by the dramatic effect. Contrasting with the warm tones of the paper, the bleak, ghostly white on the face of the child and the intent gaze of the woman suggest that even as her vigil takes place, death is touching the child.

The theme of death in Kollwitz's work achieved one of its most forceful expressions in an etching, *Mother with Dead Child.* In this print a solitary figure gathers into her arms the body of a dead child. The form of the woman, bent and arched over her child, is so intertwined with the child's form that they seem as one. A viewer must look carefully to distinguish the separate figures. Closer study discloses the interlocked simplified human volumes: the massive arms and legs of the mother and the head and shoulders of the child, all bound together in a convoluted but cohesive shape. In a pathetic yet powerful visual climax, the heads of the two figures almost converge. Bowed in grief, the nearly grotesque face of the woman presses down upon the form of the child, whose uptilted peaceful head and lifeless body are folded in her arms. These closely interwoven forms are locked together so forcibly that the unity of this composite, organic shape seems to defy even the separation of death.

Like Kollwitz, Lange's compassionate eye led her to look at her own land and its people. Collaborating first with Paul Taylor to produce a sociological photograph, she was asked in 1935 by Roy Stryker to become a member of a team of documentary photographers that he headed to work for the Farm Security Administration. Their task was to record the people who had been victimized by the drought and the Depression. These photographers were also committed to documenting the reform programs that had been initiated by the Roosevelt administration.

Lange's contribution to the documentary tradition emerged from her own empathetic spirit and her skill in transforming transitory experiences and emotions into concrete photographic expression. As we have seen in *Migrant Mother,* Lange had an unusual ability to use the camera to frame and interpret relationships. In assignments for the Farm Security Administration her images relate people to the land. *Sharecroppers, Eutah, Alabama* illustrates her capacity to symbolize the relationship between the figures and their environment. In this rectangular photograph the division of land and sky falls just below the horizontal axis of the composition. From an unusually low angle, Lange pictures three toiling figures against this broad background of earth and space. A male figure, the tallest of the group, occupies the center of the composition, initiating a symmetry in the total image. Two smaller figures, one on the right and one on the left, complete a triangular composition. Wearing hats to shield them from the sun, the three look downward upon the land they till. While these individuals are separated by the furrows, they are drawn together by the angular lines of their hoes, which suggest smaller triangular units within the composition. Their simple tools visually and symbolically connect each figure to the other and each to the earth itself.

A similar relationship of people to the earth is found in Lange's photograph *Stoop Labor.* Again, the camera angle is almost at ground level. The horizon in this case is just slightly above center. As in *Sharecroppers,* the artist has used only a few figures to symbolize the relationship. The four forms, silhouetted against the sky, are not standing straight and tall; nor are they dignified by tools. Their bodies are stooped and bent double; their arms, legs, and heads seem rooted in the earth. These human shapes begin to resemble the organic forms they harvest and, like a part of the crop itself, grow out of the earth.

Of course, Kollwitz and Lange were not the only prophetic

voices among artists at this time. Others in America and Europe were equally committed to social justice and peace. A brief look at some likeminded contemporaries helps to highlight qualities that, nevertheless, distinguish the work of these two women. In Germany, photographer John Heartfield attacked the rising militarism of that country. Heartfield, one of the most heroic critics of the Third Reich, was still producing vitriolic images in the mid-1930s. Some of the boldest were directly aimed at Hitler and his Nazi regime. Narrowly escaping arrest, he had to flee to England for his life.

Kollwitz shared with Heartfield a view of the artist as an iconoclast whose images attack an unjust social system. Her images, however, were more general and universal, while Heartfield's satire ridiculed specific programs and policies of the German military-industrial establishment. Combining unusual skills in photography with a biting humor, he achieved absurd and ironic impact through photo-montages and distorted images. In 1934, for example, Heartfield produced a photo-montage that vividly captured the complicated relationships among industrial, military, and religious authorities. Heartfield recomposed photographs of bombs into a clustered, upright mass, their architectonic shapes rising like a giant cathedral. Upon this massive "religious" edifice, he imposed a gabled doorway reminiscent of the great Gothic entryway; people are shown moving into its sacred space. Crowning the great "towers," however, there are no crosses. Instead, the bomb-shaped structures are adorned with the signs of the dollar, the British pound, and the Nazi swastika. At the bottom right, far removed from the public crowd entering the "cathedral," is a group of well-dressed men who have taken off their elegant top hats in gestures of respect. The caption reads: "Hymn to the forces of yesterday; we pray to the power of the bomb."

In America a number of artists in the 1930s shared Dorothea Lange's social concerns and desire to use art to call attention to the plight of the poor and dispossessed. Her work is comparable to that of others on the team of Farm Security Administration photographers with whom she collaborated. In particular, her attitudes and commitments resemble most closely those of the painter-photographer Ben Shahn, who portrayed those whom society condemned. Long before he worked for the FSA Shahn was expressing concern for social justice. He was one of the first to protest through his paintings the treatment of Sacco and Vanzetti, left-wing labor agitators who were unjustly executed in 1927 in spite of worldwide protests. Throughout his life he remained sensitive to the responsibilities of the artist in public life. Like Lange, Shahn photographed for the FSA in sections of the country beset with unusual poverty, landless people, and poor housing. For example, in *Arkansas, 1936* Shahn photographed cotton pickers at work in the fields. As they work through the furrows, the field hands drag behind them huge, extended bags, gradually filling them with cotton balls. Shahn's men and women appear to be strange appendages of the earth, bound to it by trailing, swelling umbilical cords.

Nevertheless, while Kollwitz and Lange were not alone in expressing social concerns, their own visions were empowered in their own distinctive ways. First, the work of both women has unusual intensity and intimacy. Second, their dominant interest was in human relationships, a theme that recurs throughout their work. Finally, they show an extraordinary talent for simplified, powerful compositions. The architectonic forms and pristine order in their designs purge their images of any sentimentality.

In Lange's case, from her earliest days as a portraitist, she demonstrated a capacity to put people at ease by relating to them in ways that allowed her to capture on film familiar expressions and gestures, unguarded moments of human warmth or anxiety. Those who worked with her later as a documentary photographer in the 1930s observed that this gift allowed her to mingle and talk with migrant workers and rural poor and to photograph unobtrusively among them. Accompanying her sensitivity to people was her intuition of the right human moment to record, the existential situation that *ought* to be represented. When asked many years later about one of her earliest scenes of the depression, *The White Angel Breadline* (1933), Lange replied that there are moments when time stands still and you hold your breath, hoping it will wait for you. She continued,

And you just hope you will have enough time to get it organized in a fraction of a second on that tiny piece of sensitive film. Sometimes you have an inner sense that you have encompassed the thing generally. You know then that you are not taking anything away from anyone, their privacy, their dignity, their wholeness.[4]

Though a genius at capturing spontaneity, Lange did not hesitate to crop her photographs to intensify poignant, dramatic moments. In a famous photograph *Ditched, Stalled, and Stranded, San Joaquin Valley, California* (1935), the worn, tense face of a migrant laborer seems to engage photographer and viewer with an expression of helplessness and exhortation. The confrontational, emotional impact of this print was enhanced when the photograph was cropped to exclude the image of the man's wife sitting beside him. By narrowing the focus and concentrating only upon the figure and face of the distressed laborer, Lange heightened, intensified, and memorialized this moment of bewilderment.

For Kaethe Kollwitz, intensity meant a narrowing of her vision to delve deeper into the themes of poverty, death, and war. In one print, *Parents,* from a series of woodcuts entitled *War,* two kneeling figures are embracing. Bent over and clasping each other, the man and woman have coalesced into one massive shape. This woodcut also underscores the persistent motif of human relationships in an array of groupings—workers, parents, women with children—throughout her work. Even the encounter with death is portrayed as a relationship in a series of lithographs entitled *Death.* In one, death is shown seizing a woman as an abductor might rush in and startle a victim. Yet another portrays a dark but gentler relationship with death. Although the title is *Death Holds a Girl on His Lap,* an enveloping maternal figure is shown holding a child in an almost comforting attitude. Doubtless her preoccupation with death, demonstrated in her images of grieving men and women, was accelerated by the death of her son Peter. Yet she spoke of the difficulty in balancing the objectivity of the artist and the grief of a mother: "For work, one must be hard and thrust outside of oneself what one has lived through. As soon as I begin to do that, I again feel myself a mother who will not give up her sorrow. Sometimes it all becomes too terribly difficult."[5] Whether they objectify her own sorrow or that of others, Kollwitz's drawings and prints depicting human loss and sadness have endured because of their universal quality through which viewers recognize themselves.

The visual power of Lange's photographs and Kollwitz's graphic art is strengthened by the intensity and intimacy with which they represented human pathos. Both focused on human relationships to communicate depths of love and grief where boundaries are vague and diffuse. The strongest link between the two women artists, however, is their common tendency to organize the picture plane into simple, severe volumes. Both artists modified, combined, and transformed human shapes. Sometimes these volumes present metaphors of organic structures, while in others the ordering principles seem more geometric.

Lange's *Woman of the High Plains, Texas Panhandle* (1938), shows a lone, gaunt, weathered woman looking over the land. Attired in the simplest kind of garment, she could be identified with any rural culture. The horizon is very low and the lean, heroic form of the woman is silhouetted against the sky. One is reminded of sparse, rugged trees on lands that have been tilled for generations, withstanding storms and drought; the human form, bound to the earth, endures.

Kollwitz's work reveals a similar tendency to simplify human figures and organize them into both a formal and symbolic order. In a print, a lithograph of 1925 entitled *Woman and Child,* a woman holds an infant close to her face. The tiny child, nestled in an almost fetal position, partially obscures the woman's face. This lithograph is one of the clearest illustrations of the way this artist has dissolved the boundaries of individual entities and forged them into a strong, cohesive volume. Indeed, the line that defines the woman's forehead easily glides over to shape the head of the infant, continuing downward as the contour of her arm, which is gently bracing the child's back. With minimal lines and deep shadows Kollwitz has created a metaphor of nurture that transforms the initial subject of mother and child. The organic void containing both figures might well be the shape of pregnancy, symbolizing the protective, embryonic process humans share with other creatures. The emphasis upon ordering and recombining volumes seen here and elsewhere indicates the natural connection between Kollwitz's graphic art and her sculpture.

Last but by no means least, a shared focus on parental love, reflected by both male and female figures in ways that challenge stereotypes along gender lines unites Lange and Kollwitz while distinguishing them from many of their contemporaries. Dorothea Lange, for example, has used two portraits of a young father to express the human experience of nurturing. In *First Born, Berkeley* (1952), a young man is holding his first child. The frontal view emphasizes the man's face and his sense of awe as he holds the infant. His arms, extended awkwardly like a carefully constructed platform, support the small, blanketed figure. Later, in *Second Born, Berkeley* (1955), the photographer gives another frontal view of the same figure, a more mature, self-confident father whose arms are now accustomed to the body of a child. As he cradles the infant against his body, the figures are closely integrated.

Kaethe Kollwitz's images of human bonding, especially the parental ones, are presented with such intensity that theological analogies become complex and difficult. The density of her images, the fusion and integration of one form with another are more pronounced than they are in Lange. The differences in media obviously play a part. Since Kollwitz's work includes drawings, prints, and sculpture, her designs are naturally more generalized than the particular portraits of people and places in Lange's photographs. Beyond differences in media, however, there is a marked tendency for Kollwitz to discover and represent a comprehensive order drawn from a diversity of parts, blending and fusing disparate elements into a whole. The observer is left with the impression of an inextricable interconnectedness and diffusion of boundaries in a family grouping—perhaps in all of life.

Certainly a measure of greatness of these artists was their capacity to take familiar experiences and render them visible in new ways. To the degree that we are affected by their reordered symbols, some of our own concepts may be changed. Their images reflect no traditional religious subjects; nevertheless, precisely because they depict those human relationships nearest and dearest to us their visions of human experience have ethical and philosophical implications. They express and shape universal human experiences of both suffering and nurture with such power that their works help us to refine, even reform, our own symbolic structures, both theological and anthropological. In this sense Kollwitz and Lange transcend their times and cultures and enable later generations to learn from them.

Were we to draw inferences from their works, they would suggest the inescapable bonding of human beings exemplified through touching bodies. As anthropological or theological models they make love and justice primary. Both women envisioned the connections in human relationships that extend our responsibilities to one another. Lange and Kollwitz might well be uncomfortable if we were to speculate further. On the other hand, they might be gratified if their images deepen our understanding of the relationships which shape our metaphors for divine and human love. These two artists remind us of the full range of passions and sensibilities that are revealed when the aesthetic vision is united with a prophetic voice.

NOTES

1. S. McFague, *Metaphorical Theology: Models of God in Religious Language* (Philadelphia: Fortress, 1982), 194, 177.
2. D. Lange, "The Making of a Documentary Photographer," interview with Suzanne Riess, Berkeley, CA, 1968, transcript, Regional Oral History Office, The Bancroft Library, University of California, Berkeley and Los Angeles: University of California Press,
3. Lange, "Photographer," 90–91.
4. M. Meltzer, *Dorothea Lange: A Photographer's Life* (New York: Farrar, Straus & Giroux, Inc., 1978), 71.
5. Kollwitz, *The Diary and Letters of Kaethe Kollwitz* (Chicago: Henry Regnery Co., 1955), 72.

About the Authors

LINELL E. CADY, who received her M.T.S. and her doctorate from Harvard, is Assistant Professor in the Religious Studies Department at Arizona State University. She has written articles on such topics as Kierkegaard and Royce, the foundations of ethics, and hermeneutics and tradition. She is currently working on the issue of a public theology.

CLAUDIA V. CAMP is Assistant Professor of Religion at Texas Christian University where she has taught since 1980. She received her Ph.D. from Duke University in Hebrew Scripture, with a secondary emphasis in hermeneutics. Her most recent publication is *Wisdom and the Feminine in the Book of Proverbs*, a literary, sociological, and theological study of the female imagery for personified Wisdom.

TERRI A. CASTANEDA is a Ph.D. candidate of Anthropology at Rice University. She currently works as Curator in Anthropology at the Houston Museum of Natural Science and as Editorial Assistant for *Cultural Anthropology*, journal of the Society for Cultural Anthropology. Her primary interests relate to the historical ties between museums, anthropology, and colonialism.

CAROL CHRIST, who received her Ph.D. from Yale, teaches Religious Studies at San Jose State University in California and was recently awarded a fellowship as a Research/Resource Associate in Women's Studies at Harvard Divinity School. Her published works include *Womanspirit Rising*, which she edited with Judith Plaskow, and *Diving Deep and Surfacing*. She is currently working on a study of symbols of God and Goddess in feminist thealogy.

PAULA M. COOEY is Associate Professor in Modern and Contemporary Religious Thought at Trinity University in San Antonio, Texas. She received her M.T.S. from Harvard Divinity School where she was also a Research/Resource Associate in Women's Studies, and her Ph.D. from Harvard University. Author of *Jonathan Edwards on Nature and Destiny: A Systematic Analysis* and several articles in women's studies and religion, she is currently working on the relation between touch and woman's identity as woman. Funding for "The Word Become Flesh: Woman's Body, Language, and Value" was provided by the Gretchen C. Northrup Junior Faculty Fellowship of Trinity University.

SHEILA GREEVE DAVANEY is Associate Professor of Theology at the Illiff School of Theology. Her master's and doctoral degrees are from Harvard where she was also a Research/Resource Associate in Women Studies. She is the author of *Divine Power* and the editor of *Feminism and Process Thought.* Her current research is focused on the relation between feminist theology and social theories of knowledge, in particular the relation between power and knowledge.

SHARON A. FARMER, Assistant Professor in the History Department at the University of California, Santa Barbara, is currently completing a book on the interaction between social change, ritual life, and the uses of history in shaping medieval communities. Her publications include "Persuasive Voices: Clerical Images of Medieval Wives," *Speculum: A Journal of Medieval Studies* (July, 1986). She received her Ph.D. from Harvard in 1983 and held, between 1984 and 1986, a Mellon Postdoctoral Fellowship at Rice University. Her general research interests include medieval monastic culture, women's roles in medieval religious life, and cultural definitions of gender. Funding for "Softening the Hearts of Men: Women, Embodiment, and Persuasion in the Thirteenth Century" was provided by the Mellon Foundation.

ELISABETH SCHÜSSLER FIORENZA holds degrees in theology from the Universities of Würzburg and Munster and is currently the Talbot Professor of New Testament Studies at the Episcopal Divinity School in Cambridge, Massachusetts. She has been active in the women's movement for some time, and her previous feminist works include *In Memory of Her* and *Bread Not Stone,* as well as numerous articles in New Testament and women's studies.

GREGOR GOETHALS, Associate Professor of Art History at the Rhode Island School of Design, is a graphic designer and illustrator of children's books. Many of her wall hangings and murals decorate buildings throughout the country, particularly the South. Head of the graduate program at Rhode Island School of Design, she received her M.A. and B.D. from Yale University and her Ph.D. in Sociology of Religion from Harvard University. Author of *The TV Ritual: Worship at the Video Altar* and creator of a traveling exhibit of TV images entitled *America's Super Symbols,* she is currently working on a study of the religious right's use of electronic media.

PATRICIA R. HILL is Assistant Professor of History at Wesleyan University. She holds an M.T.S. from Harvard Divinity School and a doctorate in the History of American Civilization from Harvard University. In addition to articles and reviews in encyclopedias and professional journals, she is the author of *The World Their Household: The American Woman's Foreign Mission Movement and Cultural Transformation, 1870–1920.* As a Radcliffe Research Scholar in 1984–85, she began research for the biography of Harriet Beecher Stowe that she is currently engaged in writing. Funding for "Madonnas for a New World: Harriet Beecher Stowe's Iconography of Faith" was provided by the Radcliffe Research Scholars Award.

MARY ELLEN ROSS received her M.Div. from Harvard Divinity School and her Ph.D. in Religion from the University of Chicago and teaches religious ethics at Trinity University in San Antonio, Texas. She is currently working on the issue of pornography as a problem in sexual ethics.

ROSEMARY RADFORD RUETHER, who received her doctorate from the Claremont School of Theology, is Georgia Harkness Professor of Applied Theology at the Garrett-Evangelical Theological Seminary in Evanston, Illinois. Her contributions to feminist studies include *Mary: The Feminine Face of the Church, New Woman/New Earth,* and *Sexism and God-Talk,* as well as many articles in journals and anthologies.

ELLEN M. UMANSKY is Associate Professor of Religion at Emory University. She is author of *Lily Montagu and the Advancement of Liberal Judaism: From Vision to Vocation* and editor of *Lily Montagu: Sermons, Addresses, Letters, and Prayers* and is currently working on a book tracing the formulation and growth of Jewish Science and the roles played by Morris and Tehilla Lichtenstein in its development.